david a. kolb

Case Western Reserve University

EXPERIENTIAL LEARNING

Experience as The Source of Learning and Development

Prentice-Hall, Inc., Englewood Cliffs, New Jersey 07632

Library of Congress Cataloging in Publication Data

KOLB, DAVID A.
    Experiential learning.

    Bibliography: p.
    Includes index.
    1. Learning by discovery. I. Title.
LB1067.K63 1984   370.15′2   83-9638
ISBN 0-13-295261-0

Editorial/production supervision and interior design: Pamela Wilder
Cover design: Ben Santora
Manufacturing buyer: Ed O'Dougherty

Printed in the United States of America

10 9 8 7 6 5 4 3 2 1

ISBN 0-13-295261-0

Prentice-Hall International, Inc., *London*
Prentice-Hall of Australia Pty. Limited, *Sydney*
Editora Prentice-Hall do Brasil, Ltda., *Rio de Janeiro*
Prentice-Hall Canada Inc., *Toronto*
Prentice-Hall of India Private Limited, *New Delhi*
Prentice-Hall of Japan, Inc., *Tokyo*
Prentice-Hall of Southeast Asia Pte. Ltd., *Singapore*
Whitehall Books Limited, *Wellington, New Zealand*

For *Jonathan*

Contents

v

part II   THE STRUCTURE OF LEARNING
          AND KNOWLEDGE

part III   LEARNING AND DEVELOPMENT

The significance for educators is profound because, among other things, Kolb leads us (again, so gently) away from the traditional concerns of credit hours and calendar time toward competence, working knowledge, and information truly pertinent to jobs, families, and communities.

The book is no "piece of cake." Despite its graceful aesthetic and illuminating diagrams, from mandalas to tight-lipped 2 × 2 tables that management professors love to show on the overhead screen, the author takes us on a fascinating but densely written journey in and around some of the most seminal thinkers who laid the foundations of "experience-based learning"— great minds such as Dewey, Lewin, and Piaget. Nor does he neglect other auxiliary players like Maslow, Rogers, and Erikson. Aside from creating a framework that removes whatever residual guilt those of us have felt or feel when using experience-based learning within the formal classroom boundaries, Kolb provides a thick texture of understanding by building his framework on the wonderful armatures of that trinity: Dewey, Lewin and Piaget.

As I say, this is an important book, one the field has been waiting for, worth every ounce of energy it takes to read. But, because of its revolutionary undertones, read it at your own risk. For each reader must take the risk of creating a life of his or her own. When you think about it, you are the thread that holds the events of your life together. That's what Kolb gets us to understand.

Warren Bennis
Joseph DeBell Chair of Management and Organization
School of Business Administration
University of Southern California

Foreword

This is a very special and important book. I say that at the outset because the book is written with such grace and gentleness, with such clarity and directness, that you will know that David Kolb has written an excellent treatise on learning theory, certainly for educators and quite possibly for Educated Persons, whatever that means. But as you read on—as *I* read on, I had to catch my breath every once in a while, wondering if the velocity of my excitement would *ever* cease.

Kolb has written a wonderful book, one I've been waiting for—without quite realizing it—for a long time. It's a book (I'm only guessing here) that he took a very, *very* long time to write, since it is crafted so carefully and is so deeply nuanced that you are certain that it's been filtered and re-set and re-drafted many times, like a precious stone, turned and polished into a lapidary's gem.

Why this excitement? Well, the hyper-ventilation I alluded to above is based on Kolb's achievement in providing the missing link between theory and practice, between the abstract generalization and the concrete instance, between the affective and cognitive domains. By this BIG achievement he demonstrates conclusively—and is the first to do so—that learning is a social process based on carefully cultivated experience which challenges every precept and concept of what nowadays passes for "teaching." And with this major achievement he knowingly shifts the ecology of learning away from the exclusivity of the classroom (and its companion, the Lecture) to the workplace, the family, the carpool, the community, or wherever we gather to work or play or love.

Preface

It has been seventeen years since I first began exploring the implications of experiential learning theory and experimenting with techniques of learning from experience. This involvement with experiential learning has been one of the most stimulating and rewarding associations of my adult life. The rewards of this long involvement have been multifaceted, ranging from the discovery of an intellectual perspective on human learning and development that is at once pragmatic and humanistic, to techniques of experience-based education that have added vitality to my teaching and to a personally enriching network of colleagues interested in experiential learning—researchers, educators, and practitioners.

My purpose in writing this book is to share these rewards through a systematic statement of the theory of experiential learning and its applications to education, work, and adult development. Drawing from the intellectual origins of experiential learning in the works of John Dewey, Kurt Lewin, and Jean Piaget, this book describes the process of experiential learning and proposes a model of the underlying structure of the learning process based on research in psychology, philosophy, and physiology. This structural model leads to a typology of individual learning styles and corresponding structures of knowledge in the different academic disciplines, professions, and careers. The developmental focus of the book is based on the thesis, first articulated by the great Russian cognitive theorist L.S. Vygotsky, that learning from experience is the process whereby human development occurs. This developmental perspective forms the basis for applications of experiential learning to education, work, and adult development.

Part I "Experience and Learning" begins in Chapter One with a review of the history of experiential learning as it emerged in the works of Dewey, Lewin, and Piaget and an analysis of the contemporary applications of experiential learning theory in education, organization development, management development, and adult development. Chapter Two compares the learning models of Dewey, Lewin, and Piaget and identifies the common themes that characterize the experiential learning process.

Part II "The Structure of Learning and Knowledge" begins in Chapter Three with a structured model of the learning process depicting two basic dimensions—a prehension or "grasping" dimension and a transformation dimension. Philosophical, physiological, and psychological evidence for this model are reviewed. Chapter Four focuses on individuality in learning with the development of a typology of learning styles based on the structural model of learning presented in Chapter Three. Assessment of individual learning styles, using the Learning Style Inventory is described. Data are presented relating individual learning styles to personality type, educational specialization, professional career, current job, and adaptive competencies. Chapter Five presents a typology of social knowledge structures—formism, contextualism, mechanism, and organicism—and relates these knowledge structures to academic fields of study and career paths.

Part III "Learning and Development" begins in Chapter Six with a statement of the experiential learning theory of development wherein adult development is portrayed in three stages—acquisition, specialization, and integration. The chapter describes how conscious experience changes through these developmental stages via higher levels of learning. Chapter Seven documents specialization as the major developmental process in higher education, describing the consequences of matches and mismatches between student learning styles and the knowledge structures of different fields of study. Relationships between professional education and later career adaptation are also examined. This section called "managing the learning process" describes applications of experiential learning theory to teaching and administration. Chapter Eight describes the challenges of integrative development in adulthood by examining the life structures of integrated and adaptively flexible individuals as measured by the Adaptive Style Inventory. Integrity is posed as the pinnacle of development, conceived as the highest form of learning.

I want to acknowledge those colleagues who have been instrumental in the creation of this work. First are those close co-workers who have struggled with me on innumerable theoretical and methodological issues—Ronald Fry, Mark Plovnick, Donald Wolfe, Marcia Mentkowski, and Sister Austin Doherty at Alverno College, and our CWRU research team, especially Ronald Sims, Walter Griggs, Jan Gypen, and the late Glen Gish. I also wish to thank my colleagues at the Council for Advancement of Experiential Learning (CAEL), notably Morris Keeton and Arthur Chickering, for encouraging me in the application of experiential learning theory to higher education and adult learning. I have enjoyed a similar creative collaboration with Richard Baker in the applications of experiential learning theory to management, whereas Bernice McCarthy has been a major collaborator in the world of elementary and secondary education. I am particularly grateful to Suresh Srivastva, Richard Boyatzis, and Richard Boland for their careful review and helpful feedback on an earlier draft of the manuscript. I am indebted to the Spencer Foundation and the National Institute of Education for their support of some of the research reported in this work. Finally I wish to acknowledge the able and dedicated assistance of Marian Hogue in the preparation of the manuscript. The quality of this book has been enhanced by all these contributions.

David A. Kolb
Cleveland, Ohio

one

The Foundations of Contemporary Approaches to Experiential Learning

The modern discovery of inner experience, of a realm of purely personal events that are always at the individual's command and that are his exclusively as well as inexpensively for refuge, consolidation and thrill, is also a great and liberating discovery. It implies a new worth and sense of dignity in human individuality, a sense that an individual is not merely a property of nature, set in place according to a scheme independent of him . . . but that he adds something, that he makes a contribution. It is the counterpart of what distinguishes modern science, experimental hypothetical, a logic of discovery having therefore opportunity for individual temperament, ingenuity, invention. It is the counterpart of modern politics, art, religion and industry where individuality is given room and movement, in contrast to the ancient scheme of experience, which held individuals tightly within a given order subordinate to its structure and patterns.

John Dewey, Experience and Nature

Human beings are unique among all living organisms in that their primary adaptive specialization lies not in some particular physical form or skill or fits in an ecological niche, but rather in identification with the process of adaptation itself—in the process of learning. We are thus the learning species, and our survival depends on our ability to adapt not only in the reactive sense of fitting into the physical and social worlds, but in the proactive sense of creating and shaping those worlds.

Our species long ago left the harmony of a nonreflective union with the "natural" order to embark on an adaptive journey of its own choosing. With this choosing has come responsibility for a world that is increasingly of our own creation—a world paved in concrete, girded in steel, wrapped in plastic, and positively awash in symbolic communications. From those first few shards of clay recording inventories of ancient commerce has sprung a symbol store that is exploding at exponential rates, and that has been growing thus for hundreds of years. On paper, through wires and glass, on cables into our homes—even the invisible air around us is filled with songs and stories, news and commerce interlaced on precisely encoded radio waves and microwaves.

The risks and rewards of mankind's fateful choice have become increasingly apparent to us all as our transforming and creative capacities shower us with the bounty of technology and haunt us with the nightmare of a world that ends with the final countdown, ". . . three, two, one, *zero.*" This is civilization on the high wire, where one misstep can send us cascading into oblivion. We cannot go back, for the processes we have initiated now have their own momentum. Machines have begun talking to machines, and we grow accustomed to obeying their conclusions. We cannot step off—"drop out"—for the safety net of the natural order has been torn and weakened by our aggressive creativity. We can only go forward on this path—nature's "human" experiment in survival.

We have cast our lot with learning, and learning will pull us through. But this learning process must be reimbued with the texture and feeling of human experiences shared and interpreted through dialogue with one another. In the overeager embrace of the rational, scientific, and technological, our concept of the learning process itself was distorted first by rationalism and later by behaviorism. We lost touch with our own experience as the source of personal learning and development and, in the process, lost that experiential centeredness necessary to counterbalance the loss of "scientific" centeredness that has been progressively slipping away since Copernicus.

That learning is an increasing preoccupation for everyone is not surprising. The emerging "global village," where events in places we have barely heard of quickly disrupt our daily lives, the dizzying rate of change, and the exponential growth of knowledge all generate nearly overwhelming needs to learn just to survive. Indeed, it might well be said that learning is an increasing *occupation* for us all; for in every aspect of our life and work, to stay abreast of events and to keep our skills up to the "state of the art" requires more and more of our time and energy. For individuals and organizations alike, learning to adapt to new "rules of the game" is becoming as critical as performing well under the old rules. In moving toward what some are optimistically heralding as "the future learning society," some monumental problems and challenges are before us. According to some observers, we are on the brink of a revolution in the educational system—sparked by wrenching economic and demographic forces and fueled by rapid social and technological changes that render a "front-loaded" educational strategy obsolete. New challenges for social justice and equal opportunity are arising, based on Supreme Court decisions affirming the individual's right of access to education and work based on proven ability to perform; these decisions challenge the validity of traditional diplomas and tests as measures of that ability. Organizations need new ways to renew and revitalize themselves and to forestall obsolescence for the organization and the people in it. But perhaps most of all, the future learning society represents a personal challenge for millions of adults who find learning is no longer "for kids" but a central lifelong task essential for personal development and career success.

Some specifics help to underscore dimensions of this personal challenge:

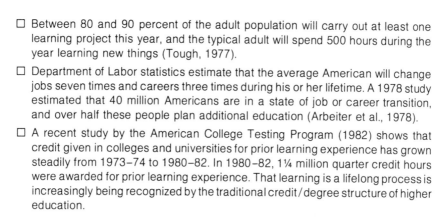

☐ Between 80 and 90 percent of the adult population will carry out at least one learning project this year, and the typical adult will spend 500 hours during the year learning new things (Tough, 1977).

☐ Department of Labor statistics estimate that the average American will change jobs seven times and careers three times during his or her lifetime. A 1978 study estimated that 40 million Americans are in a state of job or career transition, and over half these people plan additional education (Arbeiter et al., 1978).

☐ A recent study by the American College Testing Program (1982) shows that credit given in colleges and universities for prior learning experience has grown steadily from 1973–74 to 1980–82. In 1980–82, 1¼ million quarter credit hours were awarded for prior learning experience. That learning is a lifelong process is increasingly being recognized by the traditional credit/degree structure of higher education.

People do learn from their experience, and the results of that learning can be reliably assessed and certified for college credit. At the same time, programs of sponsored experiential learning are on the increase in higher education. Internships, field placements, work/study assignments, structured exercises and role plays, gaming simulations, and other forms of experience-based education are playing a larger role in the curricula of undergraduate and professional programs. For many so-called nontraditional students—minorities, the poor, and mature adults—experiential learning has become the method of choice for learning and personal development. Experience-based education has become widely accepted as a method of instruction in colleges and universities across the nation.

Yet in spite of its increasingly widespread use and acceptance, experiential learning has its critics and skeptics. Some see it as gimmicky and faddish, more concerned with technique and process than content and substance. It often appears too thoroughly pragmatic for the academic mind, dangerously associated with the disturbing antiintellectual and vocationalist trends in American society. This book is in one sense addressed to the concerns of these critics and skeptics, for without guiding theory and principles, experiential learning can well become another educational fad—just new techniques for the educator's bag of tricks. Experiential learning theory offers something more substantial and enduring. It offers the foundation for an approach to education and learning as a lifelong process that is soundly based in intellectual traditions of social psychology, philosophy, and cognitive psychology. The experiential learning model pursues a framework for examining and strengthening the critical linkages among education, work, and personal development (Figure 1.1). It offers a system of competencies for describing job demands and corresponding educational objectives and emphasizes the critical linkages that can be developed between the classroom and the "real world" with experiential learning methods. It pictures the workplace as a learning environment that can enhance and supplement formal education and can foster personal development through meaningful work and career-development opportunities. And it stresses the role of formal education in lifelong learning and the development of individuals to their full potential as citizens, family members, and human beings.

In this chapter, we will examine the major traditions of experiential learning, exploring the dimensions of current practice and their intellectual origins. By understanding and articulating the themes of these traditions, we will be far more capable of shaping and guiding the development of the exciting new educational programs based on experiential learning. As Kurt Lewin, one of the founders of experiential learning, said in his most famous remark, "There is nothing so practical as a good theory."

EXPERIENTIAL LEARNING IN HIGHER EDUCATION: THE LEGACY OF JOHN DEWEY

In the field of higher education, there is a growing group of educators—faculty, administrators, and interested outsiders—who see experiential education as a way to revitalize the university curriculum and to cope with many of the changes facing higher education today. Although this movement is attributed to the educational philosophy of John Dewey, its source is in reality a diverse group spanning several generations. At one recent conference of the National Society for Internships and Experiential Education (NSIEE), a speaker remarked that

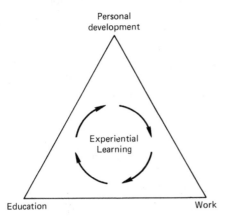

Figure 1.1 Experiential Learning as the Process that Links Education, Work, and Personal Development

there were three identifiable generations in the room: the older generation of Deweyite progressive educators, the now middle-aged children of the 1960s' Peace Corps and civil-rights movement, and Vietnam political activists of the 1970s. Yet it is the work of Dewey, without doubt the most influential educational theorist of the twentieth century, that best articulates the guiding principles for programs of experiential learning in higher education. In 1938, Dewey wrote *Experience and Education* in an attempt to bring some understanding to the growing conflict between "traditional" education and his "progressive" approach. In it he outlined the directions for change implied in his approach:

> If one attempts to formulate the philosophy of education implicit in the practices of the new education, we may, I think, discover certain common principles. . . . To imposition from above is opposed expression and cultivation of individuality; to external discipline is opposed free activity; to learning from texts and teachers, learning through experience; to acquisition of isolated skills and techniques by drill is opposed acquisition of them as means of attaining ends which make direct vital appeal; to preparation for a more or less remote future is opposed making the most of the opportunities of present life; to static aims and materials is opposed acquaintance with a changing world. . . .
>
> I take it that the fundamental unity of the newer philosophy is found in the idea that there is an intimate and necessary relation between the processes of actual experience and education. [Dewey, 1938, pp. 19, 20]

In the last 40 years, many of Dewey's ideas have found their way into "traditional" educational programs, but the challenges his approaches were developed to meet, those of coping with change and lifelong learning, have increased even more dramatically. It is to meeting these challenges that experiential educators in higher education have addressed themselves—not in the polarized spirit of what Arthur Chickering (1977) calls "either/orneriness," but in a spirit of cooperative innovation that integrates the best of the traditional and the experiential. The tools for this work involve many traditional methods that are as old as, or in some cases older than, the formal education system itself. These methods include apprenticeships, internships, work/study programs, cooperative education, studio arts, laboratory studies, and field projects. In all these methods, learning is experiential, in the sense that:

> . . . the learner is directly in touch with the realities being studied. . . . It involves direct encounter with the phenomenon being studied rather than merely thinking about the encounter or only considering the possibility of doing something with it. [Keeton and Tate, 1978, p.2]

In higher education today, these "traditional" experiential learning methods are receiving renewed interest and attention, owing in large measure to the changing educational environment in this country. As universities have moved through open-enrollment programs and so on, to expand educational opportunities for the poor and minorities, there has been a corresponding need for educational methods that can translate the abstract ideas of academia into the concrete practical realities of these people's lives. Many of these new students have not been rigorously socialized into the classroom/textbook way of learning but have developed their own distinctive approach to learning, sometimes characterized as "survival skills" or "street wisdom." For these, the field placement or work/study program is an empowering experience that allows them to capitalize on their practical strengths while testing the application of ideas discussed in the classroom.

Similarly, as the population in general grows older and the frequency of adult career change continues to increase, the "action" in higher education will be centered around adult learners who demand that the relevance and application of ideas be demonstrated and tested against their own accumulated experience and wisdom. Many now approach education and midlife with a sense of fear ("I've forgotten how to study") and resentment based on unpleasant memories of their childhood schooling. As Rita Weathersby has pointed out, "adults' learning interests are embedded in their personal histories, in their visions of who they are in the world and in what they can do and want to do" (1978, p. 19). For these adults, learning methods that combine work and study, theory and practice provide a more familiar and therefore more productive arena for learning.

Finally, there is a marked trend toward vocationalism in higher education, spurred on by a group of often angry and hostile critics—students who feel cheated because the career expectations created in college have not been met, and employers who feel that the graduates they recruit into their organizations are woefully unprepared. Something has clearly gone awry in the supposed link between education and work, resulting in strong demands that higher education "shape up" and make itself relevant. There are in my view dangerous currents of antiintellectualism in this movement, based on reactionary and counterproductive views of learning and development; but a real problem has been identified here. Experiential learning offers some avenues for solving it constructively.

For another group of educators, experiential learning is not a set of educational methods; it is a statement of fact: People *do learn* from their experiences. The emphasis of this group is on assessment of prior experience-based learning in order to grant academic credit for degree programs or certification for licensing in trades and professions. The granting of credit for prior experience is viewed by some as a movement of great promise:

> *The great significance of systematic recognition of prior learning is the linkage it provides between formal education and adult life; that is, a mechanism for integrating education and work, for recognizing the validity of all learning that is relevant to a college degree and for actively fostering recurrent education. [Willingham et al., 1977, p. 60]*

Yet it has also raised great concern, primarily about the maintenance of quality, since such assessment procedures might easily be abused by "degree mills" or mail-order diploma operations. To respond to both these opportunities and these concerns, in 1973 the Cooperative Assessment of Experiential Learning (CAEL) project was established in cooperation with the Educational Testing Service to create and implement practical and valid methodologies for assessing what people have learned from their prior work and life experience.[1]

As might be expected, researchers and practitioners in this area are more concerned with *what* people learn—the identifiable knowledge and skill outcomes of learning from accumulated experience—than they are with *how* learning takes place, the process of experiential learning. This emphasis on the outcomes of learning and their reliable assessment is critical to the establishment of effective links between education and work, since this linkage depends on the accurate identification and matching of personal skills with job demands. Since the Supreme Court's *Griggs v. Duke Power* decision, establishing an equitable and valid matching process has become a top priority in our nation's efforts toward equal employment opportunity. In that case, Griggs, an applicant for a janitorial job, sued to challenge a requirement that applicants have a high school diploma. In supporting Griggs, the court ruled that no test, certificate, or other procedure can be used to limit access to a job unless it is shown to be a valid predictor of performance on that job. This ruling, which has since been extended and supported by other high-court rulings, has set forth a great challenge to educators, behavioral scientists, and employers— to develop competence-based methods of instruction and assessment that are meaningfully related to the world of work.

Taken together, the renewed emphasis on "traditional" experiential learning methods and the emphasis on competence-based methods of education, assessment, and certification signal significant changes in the structure of higher education. Arthur Chickering sees it this way:

> . . . there is no question that issues raised by experiential learning go to the heart of the academic enterprise. Experiential learning leads us to question the assumptions and conventions underlying many of our practices. It turns us away from credit hours and calendar time toward competence, working knowledge, and information pertinent to jobs, family relationships, community responsibilities, and broad social concerns. It reminds us that higher education can do more than develop verbal skills and deposit information in those storage banks between the ears. It can contribute to more complex kinds of intellectual development and to more pervasive dimensions of human development required for effective citizenship. It can help students cope with shifting developmental tasks imposed by the life cycle and rapid social change.

[1] CAEL has since changed its name to the Council for the Advancement of Experiential Learning to reflect its broader interests in experiential learning methods as well as assessment.

If these potentials are to be realized, major changes in the current structures, processes, and content of higher education will be required. The campus will no longer be the sole location for learning, the professor no longer the sole source of wisdom. Instead, campus facilities and professional expertise will be resources linked to a wide range of educational settings, to practitioners, field supervisors, and adjunct faculty. This linking together will be achieved through systematic relationships with cultural organizations, businesses, social agencies, museums, and political and governmental operations. We no longer will bind ourselves completely to the procrustean beds of fixed time units set by semester, trimester, or quarter systems, which stretch some learning to the point of transparency and lop off other learning at the head or foot. Instead, such systems will be supplemented by flexible scheduling options that tailor time to the requirements for learning and to the working realities of various experiential opportunities. Educational standards and credentials will increasingly rest on demonstrated levels of knowledge and competence as well as on actual gains made by students and the value added by college programs. We will recognize the key significance of differences among students, not only in verbal skills and academic preparation but also in learning styles, capacity for independent work, self-understanding, social awareness and human values. Batch processing of large groups will be supplemented by personalized instruction and contract learning.

The academy and the professoriat will continue to carry major responsibility for research activities, for generating new knowledge, and for supplying the perspectives necessary to cope with the major social problems rushing toward us. That work will be enriched and strengthened by more broad-based faculty and student participation and by its wide-ranging links to ongoing experiential settings. [Chickering, 1977, pp. 86-87]

EXPERIENTIAL LEARNING IN TRAINING AND ORGANIZATION DEVELOPMENT: THE CONTRIBUTIONS OF KURT LEWIN

Another tradition of experiential learning, larger in numbers of participants and perhaps wider in its scope of influence, stems from the research on group dynamics by the founder of American social psychology, Kurt Lewin. Lewin's work has had a profound influence on the discipline of social psychology and on its practical counterpart, the field of organizational behavior. His innovative research methods and theories, coupled with the personal charisma of his intellectual leadership, have been felt through three generations of scholars and practitioners in both fields. Although the scope of his work has been vast, ranging from leadership and management style to mathematical contributions to social-science field theory, it is his work on group dynamics and the methodology of action research that have had the most far-reaching practical significance. From these studies came the laboratory-training method and T-groups (T = training), one of the most potent educational innovations in this century. The action-research method has proved a useful approach to planned-change interventions in small groups and large complex organizations and community systems. Today this methodology forms the cornerstone of most organization development efforts. The consistent theme in all Lewin's work was his concern for the integration of theory and practice, stimulated if not created by his experience as a refugee to the United States from Nazi Germany. His classic studies on authoritarian, democratic, and *laissez faire* leadership styles were his attempt to understand in a practical way the psychological dynamics of dictatorship and democracy. His best-known quotation, "There is nothing so practical as a good theory," symbolizes his commitment to the integration of scientific inquiry and social problem solving. His approach is illustrated no better than in the actual historical event that spawned the "discovery" of the T-group (see Marrow, 1969). In the summer of 1946, Lewin and his colleagues, most notably Ronnald Lippitt, Leland Bradford, and Kenneth Benne, set out to design a new approach to leadership and group-dynamics training for the Connecticut State Interracial Commission. The two-week training program began with an experimental emphasis encouraging group discussion and decision making in an atmosphere where staff and participants treated one another as peers. In addition, the research and training staff collected extensive observations and recordings of the groups' activities. When the participants went home at night, the research staff gathered together to report and analyze the data collected during the day. Most of the staff felt that trainees should not be involved in these analytical sessions where their experiences and behavior were being discussed, for fear that the discussions might be harmful to them. Lewin was receptive, however, when a small group of participants asked to join in these discussions. One of the men who was there, Ronald Lippitt, describes what happened in the discussion meeting that three trainees attended:

> Sometime during the evening, an observer made some remarks about the behavior of one of the three persons who were sitting in—a woman trainee. She broke in to disagree with the observation and described it from her point of view. For a while there was quite an active dialogue between the research observer, the trainer, and the trainee about the interpretation of the event, with Kurt an active prober, obviously enjoying this different source of data that had to be coped with and integrated.
>
> At the end of the evening the trainees asked if they could come back for the next meeting at which their behavior would be evaluated. Kurt feeling that it had been a valuable contribution rather than an intrusion, enthusiastically agreed to their return. The next night at least half of the 50 or 60 participants were there as a result of the grapevine reporting of the activity by the three delegates.
>
> The evening session from then on became the significant learning experience of the day, with the focus on actual behavioral events and with active dialogue about differences of interpretation and observation of the events by those who had participated in them. [Lippitt, 1949]

Thus the discovery was made that learning is best facilitated in an environment where there is dialectic tension and conflict between immediate, concrete experience and analytic detachment. By bringing together the immediate experiences of the trainees and the conceptual models of the staff in an open atmosphere where inputs from each perspective could challenge and stimulate the other, a learning environment occurred with remarkable vitality and creativity.

Although Lewin was to die in 1947, the power of the educational process he had discovered was not lost on the other staff who were there. In the summer of 1947, they continued development of the insights they had gained in a three-week program for change agents, this time in Bethel, Maine. It was here that the basic outlines of T-group theory and the laboratory method began to take shape. It is important to note that even in these early beginnings, the struggle between the "here-and-now" experiential orientation and the "there-and-then" theoretical orientation that has continued to plague the movement was in evidence:

> *There resulted a competition between discussing here-and-now happenings, which of necessity focused on the personal, interpersonal and group levels; and discussing outside case materials. This sometimes resulted in the rejection of any serious consideration of the observer's report of behavioral data. More often it led eventually to rejection of outside problems as less involving and fascinating.* [Benne, 1964, p. 86]

Later, in the early years of the National Training Laboratories,[2] this conflict expressed itself in intense debates among staff as to how conceptual material should be integrated into the "basic encounter" process of the T-group. And still later, in the 1960s, on the waves of youth culture, acid rock, and Eastern mysticism, the movement was to be virtually split apart into "West Coast" existential factions and "East Coast" traditionalists (Argyris, 1970). As we shall see later in our inquiry, this conflict between experience and theory is not unique to the laboratory-training process but is, in fact, a central dynamic in the process of experiential learning itself.

In its continuing struggle, debate, and innovation around this and other issues, the laboratory-training movement has had a profound influence on the practice of adult education, training, and organization development. In particular, it was the spawning ground for two streams of development that are of central importance to experiential learning, one of values and one of technology. T-groups and the so-called laboratory method on which they were based gave central focus to the value of subjective personal experience in learning, an emphasis that at the time stood in sharp contrast to the "empty-organism" behaviorist theories of learning and classical physical-science definitions of knowledge acquisition as an impersonal, totally logical process based on detached, objective observation. This emphasis on subjective experience has developed into a strong commitment in the practice of experiential learning to existential values of personal involvement, and

[2]Now known as the NTL Institute for Applied Behavioral Sciences.

responsibility and humanistic values emphasizing that feelings as well as thoughts are facts.

To the leaders of the movement, these values, coupled with the basic values of a humanistic scientific process—a spirit of inquiry, expanded consciousness and choice, and authenticity in relationships—offered new hope-filled ideals for the conduct of human relationships and the management of organizations (Schein and Bennis, 1965). More than any other single source, it was this set of core values that stimulated the modern participative-management philosophies (variously called Theory Y management, 9.9 management, System 4 management, Theory Z, and so on) so widely practiced in this country and increasingly around the world. In addition, these values have formed the guiding principles for the field of organization development and the practice of planned change in organizations, groups, and communities. The most recent and comprehensive statement of the relationship between laboratory-training values and experiential learning is the work of Argyris and Schon (1974, 1978). They maintain that learning from experience is essential for individual and organizational effectiveness and that this learning can occur only in situations where personal values and organizational norms support action based on valid information, free and informed choice, and internal commitment.

Equally important, there has emerged from the early work in sensitivity training a rapidly expanding applied technology for experiential learning. Beginning with small tasks (such as a decision-making problem) that were used in T-groups to focus the group's experience on a particular issue (for example, processes of group decision making), there has developed an immense variety of tasks, structured exercises, simulations, cases, games, observation tools, role plays, skill-practice routines, and so on. The common core of these technologies is a simulated situation designed to create personal experiences for learners that serve to initiate their own process of inquiry and understanding. These technologies have had a profound effect on education, particularly for adult learners. The training and development field has experienced a virtual revolution in its methodology, moving from a "dog and pony show" approach that was only a fancy imitation of the traditional lecture method to a complex educational technology that relies heavily on experience-based simulations and self-directed learning designs (Knowles, 1970). Indeed, there are many who share the view of Harold Hodskinson, a former director of the National Institute for Education and the current president of the NTL Institute, that these private-sector innovations in educational technology are challenging the ability of the formal educational establishment to compete in an open market. Along with the American Society for Training and Development (ASTD), specialized associations of academics and training and development practitioners have been formed to extend experiential approaches that were initially focused on the human-relationship issues emphasized in T-groups to other content areas, such as finance, marketing, and planning through the use of computer-aided instruction, video recording, structured role-play cases, and other software and hardware techniques. In addition, there are countless small and relatively large organizations specializing in the various educational technologies that have grown to support the $50 billion training and development industry in the United States. Although the laboratory-training movement has not been responsible for all these developments, it has had an undeniable influence on many of them.

JEAN PIAGET AND THE COGNITIVE-DEVELOPMENT TRADITION OF EXPERIENTIAL LEARNING

The Dewey and Lewin traditions of experiential learning represent external challenges to the idealist or, as James (1907) terms them, rationalist philosophies that have dominated thinking about learning and education since the Middle Ages; Dewey from the philosophical perspective of pragmatism, and Lewin from the phenomenological perspective of Gestalt psychology. The third tradition of experiential learning represents more of a challenge from within the rationalist perspective, stemming as it does from the work of the French developmental psychologist and genetic epistemologist Jean Piaget. His work on child development must stand on a par with that of Freud; but whereas Freud placed his emphasis on the socioemotional processes of development, Piaget's focus is on cognitive-development processes—on the nature of intelligence and how it develops. Throughout his work, Piaget is as much an epistemological philosopher as he is a psychologist. In fact, he sees in his studies of the development of cognitive processes in childhood the key to understanding the nature of human knowledge itself.

It was in Piaget's first psychological studies that he came across the insight that was to make him world-famous. He began to work as a student of Alfred Binet, the creator of the first intelligence test, standardizing test items for use in IQ and aptitude tests. During this work, Piaget's interests began to diverge sharply from the traditional testing approach. He found himself much less interested in whether the answers that children gave to test problems were correct or not than he was in the process of reasoning that children used to arrive at the answers. He began to discover age-related regularities in these reasoning processes. Children at certain ages not only gave wrong answers but also showed qualitatively different ways of arriving at them. Younger children were not "dumber" than older children; they merely thought about things in an entirely different way. In the 50 years that followed this discovery, these ideas were to be developed and explored in thousands of studies by Piaget and his co-workers.

Stated most simply, Piaget's theory describes how intelligence is shaped by experience. Intelligence is not an innate internal characteristic of the individual but arises as a product of the interaction between the person and his or her environment. And for Piaget, action is the key. He has shown, in careful descriptive studies of children from infants to teenagers, that abstract reasoning and the power to manipulate symbols arise from the infant's actions in exploring and coping with the immediate concrete environment. The growing child's system of knowing changes qualitatively in successively identifiable stages, moving from an enactive stage, where knowledge is represented in concrete actions and is not separable from the experiences that spawn it, to an ikonic stage, where knowledge is represented in images that have an increasingly autonomous status from the experiences they represent, to stages of concrete and formal operations, where knowledge is represented in symbolic terms, symbols capable of being manipulated internally with complete independence from experiential reality.

In spite of its scope and the initial flurry of interest in his work in the late 1920s, Piaget's research did not receive wide recognition in this country until the 1960s. Stemming as it did from the French rationalist tradition, Piaget's work was not readily acceptable to the empirical tradition of American psychology, particularly since his clinical methods did not seem to meet the rigorous experimental standards that characterized the behaviorist research programs that dominated American psychology from 1920 to 1960. In addition, Piaget's interests were more descriptive than practical. He viewed with some disdain the pragmatic orientation of American researchers and educators who sought to speed up or facilitate the development of the cognitive stages he had identified, referring to these interests in planned change and development as the "American question."

Piaget's ultimate recognition in America was due in no small part to the parallel work of the most prominent American cognitive psychologist, Jerome Bruner. Bruner saw in the growing knowledge of cognitive developmental processes the scientific foundations for a theory of instruction. Knowledge of cognitive developmental stages would make it possible to design curricula in any field in such a way that subject matter could be taught respectably to learners at any age or stage of cognitive development. This idea became at once a guiding objective and a great challenge to educators. A new movement in curriculum development and teaching emerged around this idea, a movement focused on the design of experience-based educational programs using the principles of cognitive-development theory. Most of these curriculum-development efforts were addressed to the subject matters of science and mathematics for elementary and secondary students, although related efforts have been made in other subject areas, such as social studies, and such experience-based curricula can be found in some freshman and sophomore college-level courses. The major task addressed by these programs was the translation of the abstract symbolic principles of science and mathematics into modes of representation that could be grasped by people at more concrete stages of cognitive development. Typically, this representation takes the form of concrete objects that can be manipulated and experimented with by the learner to discover the scientific principle involved. Many of these were modifications of Piaget's original experiments—for example, allowing children to pour water back and forth from tall, thin beakers to short, fat ones to discover the principle of conservation.

When introduced in the proper climate, these experience-based curricula had the same exhilarating effect on the learning process as Lewin's discovery of the T-group. Children were freed from the lockstep pace of memorizing (or ignoring) watered-down presentations of scientific and mathematical principles that in some cases actually made learning more advanced principles more difficult; for example, to spend years learning to count only in base 10 makes learning base 2, 3, and so on, much more difficult. Learning became individualized, concrete, and self-directed. Moreover, the child was learning about the process of discovering knowledge, not just the content. Children became "little scientists," exploring, experimenting, and drawing their own conclusions. These classrooms buzzed with the excitement and energy of intrinsically motivated learning activity. These experience-based learning programs changed the educational process in two ways. First, they altered the *content* of curriculum, providing new ways of teaching subjects that were formerly thought to be too advanced and sophisticated for youngsters; and second, they altered the learning *process*, the way that students went about learning these subjects.

Even though in many quarters these innovations met an enthusiastic reception and eventual successful implementation, they also provoked strong reaction and criticism. Some of these criticisms were justified. This new way of learning required a new approach to teaching. In some cases, teachers managed the learning process well, and intrinsically motivated learning was the result. In others, the climate for learning was somehow different; students did not learn the principle of conservation by experimenting with the water jars, they just learned how to pour water back and forth. Other criticisms seem to me less valid. Some have blamed the decline on SAT scores on the new math and other self-directed curricula that made learning appear to be fun and lacking in disciplined practice of the basics. In spirit, these debates are strongly reminiscent of the controversy surrounding Dewey's progressive-education movement and the experience/theory conflicts concerning T-groups.

The cognitive-development tradition has had a less direct but equally powerful effect on adult learning. Although Piaget's stages of cognitive development terminated in adolescence, the idea that there are identifiable regularities in the development process has been extended into later adulthood by a number of researchers. In method and conceptual structure, these approaches owe a great deal to the Piagetian scheme. One of the first such approaches was Lawrence Kohlberg's extension of Piaget's early work on moral development (see Kurtines and Greif, 1974). Kohlberg began his research on schoolchildren but soon found that only the early stages of moral judgment that he had identified were actually achieved in childhood and that for many adults, the challenges of the later stages of moral judgment still lay before them. William Perry, in his outstanding book, *Forms of Intellectual and Ethical Development in the College Years* (1970), found similar patterns in the way Harvard students' systems of knowledge evolved through the college years, moving from absolutist, authority-centered, right/wrong views of knowledge in early college years, through stages of extreme relativism and, in their later college years, toward higher stages of personal commitment within relativism. Perry also found that these higher stages of development were not achieved by all students during college but, for many, posed developmental challenges that extended into their later lives. Jane Loevinger (1976) has attempted to integrate these and other cognitive developmental theories (for instance, Harvey, Hunt, and Schroder, 1961) with the socioemotional developmental theories of Erikson and others (described below) under the general rubric of ego development. Her six stages of ego development—impulsive, self-protective, conformist, conscientious, autonomous, and finally, integrated—clearly identify learning and development as a lifelong process.

The effects of these new conceptions of adult development are only now beginning to be felt. With the recognition that learning and development are lifelong processes, there comes a corresponding responsibility for social institutions and organizations to conduct their affairs in such a way that adults have experiences that facilitate their personal learning and development. One application of Kohlberg's work in moral development, for example, has been in prison reform (Hickey and Scharf, 1980), attempting in the management of prisons to build a climate that fosters development toward higher moral stages through the creation of a "just community" within the prison society. Although perhaps not as dramatic and obvious, there is a corresponding need in many public and private organizations to improve the climate for learning and development. It is not just in prisons that people feel they must adopt self-protective and conformist postures in order to survive, seeing little reward for conscientious, autonomous, and integrated behavior.

OTHER CONTRIBUTIONS TO EXPERIENTIAL LEARNING THEORY

Dewey, Lewin, and Piaget must stand as the foremost intellectual ancestors of experiential learning theory; however, there are other, related streams of thought that will contribute substantially to this inquiry. First among these are the therapeutic psychologies, stemming chiefly from psychoanalysis and reflected most particularly in the work of Carl Jung, although also including Erik Erikson, the humanistic traditions of Carl Rogers's client-centered therapy, Fritz Perls's gestalt therapy, and the self-actualization psychology of Abraham Maslow.

This school of thought brings two important dimensions to experiential learning. First is the concept of adaptation, which gives a central role to affective experience. The notion that healthy adaptation requires the effective integration of cognitive and affective processes is of course central to the practice of nearly all forms of psychotherapy. The second contribution of the therapeutic psychologies is the conception of socioemotional development throughout the life cycle. The developmental schemes of Erik Erikson, Carl Rogers, and Abraham Maslow give a consistent and articulated picture of the challenges of adult development, a picture that fits well with the cognitive schemes just discussed. Taken together, these socioemotional and cognitive-development models provide a holistic framework for describing the adult development process and the learning challenges it poses. It is Jung's theory, however, with its concept of psychological types representing different modes of adapting to the world, and his developmental theory of individuation that will be most useful for understanding learning from experience.

A second line of contribution to experiential learning theory comes from what might be called the radical educators—in particular, the work of Brazilian educator and revolutionary Paulo Freire (1973, 1974), and of Ivan Illich (1972), whose critique of Western education and plan to "deschool" society concretely applies many of Freire's ideas to contemporary American social problems. The core of these men's arguments is that the educational system is primarily an agency of social control, a control that is ultimately oppressive and conservative of the capitalist system of class discrimination. The means for changing this system is by instilling in the population what Freire calls "critical consciousness," the active exploration of the personal, experiential meaning of abstract concepts through dialogue among equals. If views of education and learning are to be cast on a political spectrum, then this viewpoint must be seen as the revolutionary extension of the liberal, humanistic perspective characteristic of the Deweyite progressive educators and laboratory-training practitioners. As such, these views serve to highlight the central role of the dialectic between abstract concepts and subjective personal experience in educational/political conflicts between the right, which places priority on maintenance of the social order, and the left, which values more highly individual freedom and expression.

Two further perspectives will be central to an inquiry helping to unravel the relationships between learning and knowledge. The first is the very active area of brain research, which is attempting to identify relationships between brain functioning and consciousness. Most relevant for our purpose is that line of research that seeks to identify and describe differences in cognitive functioning associated with the left and right hemispheres of the brain (Levy, 1980). The relevance of this work for experiential learning theory lies in the fact that the modes of knowing associated with the left and right hemispheres correspond directly with the distinction between concrete experiential and abstract cognitive approaches to learning. Thus, in his recent review of this literature, Corballis concludes:

> Such evidence may be taken as support for the idea that the left hemisphere is the more specialized for abstract or symbolic representation, in which the symbols need bear no physical resemblance to the objects they represent, while the right hemisphere maintains representations that are isomorphic with reality itself. . . . [Corballis, 1980, p. 288]

The implication here is that these two modes of knowing or grasping the world stand as equal and complementary processes. This position stands in sharp contrast to that of Piaget and other cognitive theorists, who consider concrete, experience-oriented forms of knowing as lower developmental manifestations of true knowledge, represented by abstract propositional reasoning.

A full exploration of this issue requires examination of the philosophical literature, particularly the domains of metaphysics and epistemology. Here also, the scientific rational traditions have been dominant, even though challenged since the early years of this century by the pragmatism of Dewey, James, and others, and certain scientists and mathematicians like Michael Polanyi and Albert Einstein, who in their own work came upon the limitations of rational scientific inquiry. Of special relevance is the work of the philosopher and metaphysician Stephen Pepper (1966, 1942), who developed a system of world hypotheses on which he bases a typology of knowledge systems. With this framework as a guide, we shall be able to explore the relationships between the learning process and the knowledge systems that flow from it.

Figure 1.2 summarizes seven themes that offer guidance and direction for programs of experiential learning. These themes stem from the work of Dewey, Lewin, and Piaget. From Kurt Lewin and his followers comes the theory and technology of T-groups and action research. The articulation of the democratic values guiding experiential learning is to be found in both Lewin's work and the educational philosophy of John Dewey. Dewey's pragmatism forms the

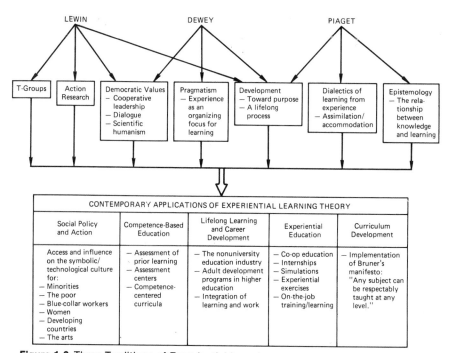

Figure 1.2 Three Traditions of Experiential Learning

philosophical rationale for the primary role of personal experience in experiential learning. Common to all three traditions of experiential learning is the emphasis on development toward a life of purpose and self-direction as the organizing principle for education. Piaget's distinctive contributions to experiential learning are his description of the learning process as a dialectic between assimilating experience into concepts and accommodating concepts to experience, and his work on epistemology—the relationship between the structure of knowledge and how it is learned.

These themes suggest guiding principles for current and emerging applications of experiential learning theory. In the case of social policy and action, experiential learning can be the basis for constructive efforts to promote access to and influence on the dominant technological/symbolic culture for those who have previously been excluded: minorities, the poor, workers, women, people in developing countries, and those in the arts. In competence-based education, experiential learning offers the theory of learning most appropriate for the assessment of prior learning and for the design of competence-centered curricula. Lifelong learning and career-development programs can find in experiential learning theory a conceptual rationale and guiding philosophy as well as practical educational tools. Finally, experiential learning suggests the principles for the conduct of experiential education in its many forms and for the design of curricula implementing Bruner's manifesto: "Any subject can be respectably taught at any level."

In all these applications it is important to recognize that experiential learning is not a series of techniques to be applied in current practice but a program for profoundly re-creating our personal lives and social systems. William Torbert puts the issue this way:

> In seeking to organize experiential learning, we must recognize that we are stepping beyond the personally, institutionally, and epistemologically preconstituted universe and that we deeply resist this initiative, no matter how often we have returned to it. We must recognize too that the art of organizing through living inquiry—the art of continually exploring beyond pre-constituted universes and continually constructing and enacting universes in concert with others—is as yet a publicly undiscovered art. To treat the dilemma of organizing experiential learning on any lesser scale is to doom ourselves to frustration, isolation or failure (1979, p. 42).

The Dewey, Lewin, and Piagetian traditions of experiential learning have produced a remarkable variety of vital and innovative programs. In their brief histories, these traditions have had a profound effect on education and the learning process. The influence of these ideas has been felt in formal education at all levels, in public and private organizations in this country and around the world, and in the personal lives of countless adult learners. Yet the future holds even greater challenges and opportunities. For these challenges to be successfully met, it is essential that these traditions learn from one another and cooperate to create a sound theoretical base from which to govern practice. Although in practice these traditions can appear very different—a student internship, a business simulation, a sensitivity training group, an action research project, a discovery curriculum in elementary science study—there is an underlying unity in the nature of the learning process on which they are based. It is to an examination of that process that we now turn.

two

The Process of Experiential Learning

*We shall not cease from exploration
And the end of all our exploring
Will be to arrive where we started
And know the place for the first time.*

T.S. Eliot, Four Quartets

Experiential learning theory offers a fundamentally different view of the learning process from that of the behavioral theories of learning based on an empirical epistemology or the more implicit theories of learning that underlie traditional educational methods, methods that for the most part are based on a rational, idealist epistemology. From this different perspective emerge some very different prescriptions for the conduct of education, the proper relationships among learning, work, and other life activities, and the creation of knowledge itself.

This perspective on learning is called "experiential" for two reasons. The first is to tie it clearly to its intellectual origins in the work of Dewey, Lewin, and Piaget. The second reason is to emphasize the central role that experience plays in the learning process. This differentiates experiential learning theory from rationalist and other cognitive theories of learning that tend to give primary emphasis to acquisition, manipulation, and recall of abstract symbols, and from behavioral learning theories that deny any role for consciousness and subjective experience in the learning process. It should be emphasized, however, that the aim of this work is not to pose experiential learning theory as a third alternative to behavioral and cognitive learning theories, but rather to suggest through experiential learning theory a holistic integrative perspective on learning that combines experience, perception, cognition, and behavior. This chapter will describe the learning models of Lewin, Dewey, and Piaget and identify the common characteristics they share—characteristics that serve to define the nature of experiential learning.

THREE MODELS OF THE EXPERIENTIAL LEARNING PROCESS

The Lewinian Model of Action Research and Laboratory Training

In the techniques of action research and the laboratory method, learning, change, and growth are seen to be facilitated best by an integrated process that begins with here-and-now experience followed by collection of data and observations about that experience. The data are then analyzed and the conclusions of this analysis are fed back to the actors in the experience for their use in the modification of their behavior and choice of new experiences. Learning is thus conceived as a four-stage cycle, as shown in Figure 2.1. Immediate concrete experience is the basis for observation and reflection. These observations are assimilated into a "theory" from which new implications for action can be deduced. These implications or hypotheses then serve as guides in acting to create new experiences.

Two aspects of this learning model are particularly noteworthy. First is its emphasis on *here-and-now concrete experience* to validate and test abstract concepts. Immediate personal experience is the focal point for learning, giving life, texture, and subjective personal meaning to abstract concepts and at the same time providing a concrete, publicly shared reference point for testing the implications and validity of ideas created during the learning process. When human beings share an experience, they can share it fully, concretely, *and* abstractly.

Second, action research and laboratory training are based on *feedback processes*. Lewin borrowed the concept of feedback from electrical engineering to describe a social learning and problem-solving process that generates valid

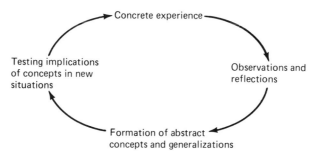

Figure 2.1 The Lewinian Experiential Learning Model

information to assess deviations from desired goals. This information feedback provides the basis for a continuous process of goal-directed action and evaluation of the consequences of that action. Lewin and his followers believed that much individual and organizational ineffectiveness could be traced ultimately to a lack of adequate feedback processes. This ineffectiveness results from an imbalance between observation and action—either from a tendency for individuals and organizations to emphasize decision and action at the expense of information gathering, or from a tendency to become bogged down by data collection and analysis. The aim of the laboratory method and action research is to integrate these two perspectives into an effective, goal-directed learning process.

Dewey's Model of Learning

John Dewey's model of the learning process is remarkably similar to the Lewinian model, although he makes more explicit the developmental nature of learning implied in Lewin's conception of it as a feedback process by describing how learning transforms the impulses, feelings, and desires of concrete experience into higher-order purposeful action.

> *The formation of purposes is, then, a rather complex intellectual operation. It involves: (1) observation of surrounding conditions; (2) knowledge of what has happened in similar situations in the past, a knowledge obtained partly by recollection and partly from the information, advice, and warning of those who have had a wider experience; and (3) judgment, which puts together what is observed and what is recalled to see what they signify. A purpose differs from an original impulse and desire through its translation into a plan and method of action based upon foresight of the consequences of action under given observed conditions in a certain way. . . . The crucial educational problem is that of procuring the postponement of immediate action upon desire until observation and judgment have intervened. . . . Mere foresight, even if it takes the form of accurate prediction, is not, of course, enough. The intellectual anticipation, the idea of consequences, must blend with desire and impulse to acquire moving force. It then gives direction to what otherwise is blind, while desire gives ideas impetus and momentum. [Dewey, 1938, p. 69]*

Dewey's model of experiential learning is graphically portrayed in Figure 2.2. We note in his description of learning a similarity with Lewin, in the emphasis on learning as a dialectic process integrating experience and concepts, observations, and action. The impulse of experience gives ideas their moving force, and ideas give direction to impulse. Postponement of immediate action is essential for observation and judgment to intervene, and action is essential for achievement of purpose. It is through the integration of these opposing but symbiotically related processes that sophisticated, mature purpose develops from blind impulse.

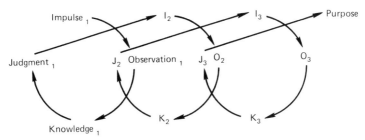

Figure 2.2 Dewey's Model of Experiential Learning

Piaget's Model of Learning and Cognitive Development

For Piaget, the dimensions of experience and concept, reflection, and action form the basic continua for the development of adult thought. Development from infancy to adulthood moves from a concrete phenomenal view of the world to an abstract constructionist view, from an active egocentric view to a reflective internalized mode of knowing. Piaget also maintained that these have been the major directions of development in scientific knowledge (Piaget, 1970). The learning process whereby this development takes place is a cycle of interaction between the individual and the environment that is similar to the learning models of Dewey and Lewin. In Piaget's terms, the key to learning lies in the mutual interaction of the process of *accommodation* of concepts or schemas to experience in the world and the process of *assimilation* of events and experiences from the world into existing concepts and schemas. Learning or, in Piaget's term, intelligent adaptation results from a balanced tension between these two processes. When accommodation processes dominate assimilation, we have imitation—the molding of oneself to environmental contours or constraints. When assimilation predominates over accommodation, we have play—the imposition of one's concept and images without regard to environmental realities. The process of cognitive growth from concrete to abstract and from active to reflective is based on this continual transaction between assimilation and accommodation, occurring in successive stages, each of which incorporates what has gone before into a new, higher level of cognitive functioning.

Piaget's work has identified four major stages of cognitive growth that emerge from birth to about the age of 14-16. In the first stage (0-2 years), the child is predominantly concrete and active in his learning style. This stage is called the sensory-motor stage. Learning is predominantly enactive through feeling, touching, and handling. Representation is based on action—for example, "a hole is to dig." Perhaps the greatest accomplishment of this period is the development of goal-oriented behavior: "The sensory-motor period shows a remarkable evolution from non-intentional habits to experimental and exploratory activity which is obviously intentional or goal oriented" (Flavell, 1963, p. 107). Yet the child has few schemes or theories into which he can assimilate events, and as a result, his primary stance toward the world is accommodative. Environment plays a major role in shaping his ideas and intentions. Learning occurs primarily through the association between stimulus and response.

In the second stage (2-6 years), the child retains his concrete orientation but begins to develop a reflective orientation as he begins to internalize actions, converting them to images. This is called the representational stage. Learning is now predominantly ikonic in nature, through the manipulation of observations and images. The child is now freed somewhat from his immersion in immediate experience and, as a result, is free to play with and manipulate his images of the world. At this stage, the child's primary stance toward the world is divergent. He is captivated with his ability to collect images and to view the world from different perspectives. Consider Bruner's description of the child at this stage:

> What appears next in development is a great achievement. Images develop an autonomous status, they become great summarizers of action. By age three the child has become a paragon of sensory distractibility. He is victim of the laws of vividness, and his action pattern is a series of encounters with this bright thing which is then replaced by that chromatically splendid one, which in turn gives way to the next noisy one. And so it goes. Visual memory at this stage seems to be highly concrete and specific. What is intriguing about this period is that the child is a creature of the moment; the image of the moment is sufficient and it is controlled by a single feature of the situation. [Bruner, 1966b, p. 13]

In the third stage (7-11 years), the intensive development of abstract symbolic powers begins. The first symbolic developmental stage Piaget calls the stage of concrete operations. Learning in this stage is governed by the logic of classes and relations. The child in this stage further increases his independence from his immediate experiential world through the development of inductive powers:

> The structures of concrete operations are, to use a homely analogy, rather like parking lots whose individual parking spaces are now occupied and now empty; the spaces themselves endure, however, and leave their owner to look beyond the cars actually present toward potential, future occupants of the vacant and to-be-vacant spaces. [Flavell, 1963, p. 203]

Thus, in contrast to the child in the sensory-motor stage whose learning style was dominated by accommodative processes, the child at the stage of concrete operations is more assimilative in his learning style. He relies on concepts and theories to select and give shape to his experiences.

Piaget's final stage of cognitive development comes with the onset of adolescence (12-15 years). In this stage, the adolescent moves from symbolic processes based on concrete operations to the symbolic processes of representational logic, the stage of formal operations. He now returns to a more active orientation, but it is an active orientation that is now modified by the development of the reflective and abstract power that preceded it. The

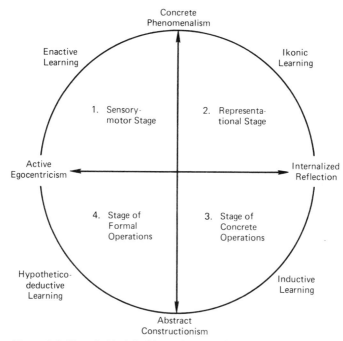

Figure 2.3 Piaget's Model of Learning and Cognitive Development

symbolic powers he now possesses enable him to engage in hypothetico-deductive reasoning. He develops the possible implications of his theories and proceeds to experimentally test which of these are true. Thus his basic learning style is convergent, in contrast to the divergent orientation of the child in the representational stage:

> We see, then, that formal thought is for Piaget not so much this or that specific behavior as it is a generalized orientation, sometimes explicit and sometimes implicit, towards problem solving; an orientation towards organizing data (combinatorial analysis), towards isolation and control of variables, towards the hypothetical, and towards logical justification and proof. [Flavell, 1963, p. 211]

This brief outline of Piaget's cognitive development theory identifies those basic developmental processes that shape the basic learning process of adults (see Figure 2.3).

CHARACTERISTICS OF EXPERIENTIAL LEARNING

There is a great deal of similarity among the models of the learning process discussed above.[1] Taken together, they form a unique perspective on learning

[1] There are also points of disagreement, which will be explored more fully in the next chapter.

and development, a perspective that can be characterized by the following propositions, which are shared by the three major traditions of experiential learning.

Learning Is Best Conceived as a Process, Not in Terms of Outcomes

The emphasis on the process of learning as opposed to the behavioral outcomes distinguishes experiential learning from the idealist approaches of traditional education and from the behavioral theories of learning created by Watson, Hull, Skinner, and others. The theory of experiential learning rests on a different philosophical and epistemological base from behaviorist theories of learning and idealist educational approaches. Modern versions of these latter approaches are based on the empiricist philosophies of Locke and others. This epistemology is based on the idea that there are elements of consciousness— mental atoms, or, in Locke's term "simple ideas"—that always remain the same. The various combinations and associations of these consistent elements form our varying patterns of thought. It is the notion of constant, fixed elements of thought that has had such a profound effect on prevailing approaches to learning and education, resulting in a tendency to define learning in terms of its outcomes, whether these be knowledge in an accumulated storehouse of facts or habits representing behavioral responses to specific stimulus conditions. If ideas are seen to be fixed and immutable, then it seems possible to measure how much someone has learned by the amount of these fixed ideas the person has accumulated.

Experiential learning theory, however, proceeds from a different set of assumptions. Ideas are not fixed and immutable elements of thought but are formed and re-formed through experience. In all three of the learning models just reviewed, learning is described as a process whereby concepts are derived from and continuously modified by experience. No two thoughts are ever the same, since experience always intervenes. Piaget (1970), for example, considers the creation of new knowledge to be the central problem of genetic epistemology, since each act of understanding is the result of a process of continuous construction and invention through the interaction processes of assimilation and accommodation (compare Chapter 5, p. 99). Learning is an emergent process whose outcomes represent only historical record, not knowledge of the future.

When viewed from the perspective of experiential learning, the tendency to define learning in terms of outcomes can become a definition of nonlearning, in the process sense that the failure to modify ideas and habits as a result of experience is maladaptive. The clearest example of this irony lies in the behaviorist axiom that the strength of a habit can be measured by its resistance to extinction. That is, the more I have "learned" a given habit, the longer I will persist in behaving that way when it is no longer rewarded. Similarly, there are those who feel that the orientations that conceive of learning in terms of outcomes as opposed to a process of adaptation have had a negative effect on the educational system. Jerome Bruner, in his influential book, *Toward a Theory of Instruction*, makes the point that the purpose of education is to stimulate inquiry and skill in the process of knowledge getting, not to memorize a body of knowledge: "Knowing is a process, not a product" (1966, p. 72). Paulo Freire calls the orientation that conceives of education as the transmission of fixed content the "banking" concept of education:

> *Education thus becomes an act of depositing, in which the students are the depositories and the teacher is the depositor. Instead of communicating, the teacher issues communiques and makes deposits which the students patiently receive, memorize, and repeat. This is the "banking" concept of education, in which the scope of action allowed to the students extends only as far as receiving, filing, and storing the deposits. They do, it is true, have the opportunity to become collectors or cataloguers of the things they store. But in the last analysis, it is men themselves who are filed away through the lack of creativity, transformation, and knowledge in this (at best) misguided system. For apart from inquiry, apart from the praxis, men cannot be truly human. Knowledge emerges only through invention and reinvention, through the restless, impatient, continuing, hopeful inquiry men pursue in the world, with the world, and with each other. [Friere, 1974, p. 58]*

Learning Is a Continuous Process Grounded in Experience

Knowledge is continuously derived from and tested out in the experiences of the learner. William James (1890), in his studies on the nature of human consciousness, marveled at the fact that consciousness is continuous. How is it, he asked, that I awake in the morning with the same consciousness, the same thoughts, feelings, memories, and sense of who I am that I went to sleep with the night before? Similarly for Dewey, continuity of experience was a powerful truth of human existence, central to the theory of learning:

> *. . . the principle of continuity of experience means that every experience both takes up something from those which have gone before and modifies in some way the quality of those which come after. . . . As an individual passes from one situation to another, his world, his environment, expands or contracts. He does not find himself living in another world but in a different part or aspect of one and the same world. What he has learned in the way of knowledge and skill in one situation becomes an instrument of understanding and dealing effectively with the situations which follow. The process goes on as long as life and learning continue. [Dewey, 1938, pp. 35, 44]*

Although we are all aware of the sense of continuity in consciousness and experience to which James and Dewey refer, and take comfort from the predictability and security it provides, there is on occasion in the penumbra of that awareness an element of doubt and uncertainty. How do I reconcile my own sense of continuity and predictability with what at times appears to be a chaotic and unpredictable world around me? I move through my daily round of tasks and meetings with a fair sense of what the issues are, of what others are saying and thinking, and with ideas about what actions to take. Yet I am occasionally upended by unforeseen circumstances, miscommunications, and dreadful miscalculations. It is in this interplay between expectation and experience that learning occurs. In Hegel's phrase, "Any experience that does not violate expectation is not worthy of the name experience." And yet somehow, the rents that these violations cause in the fabric of my experience are magically repaired, and I face the next day a bit changed but still the same person.

That this is a *learning* process is perhaps better illustrated by the nonlearning postures that can result from the interplay between expectation and experience. To focus so sharply on continuity and certainty that one is blinded to the shadowy penumbra of doubt and uncertainty is to risk dogmatism and rigidity, the inability to learn from new experiences. Or conversely, to have continuity continuously shaken by the vicissitudes of new experience is to be left paralyzed by insecurity, incapable of effective action. From the perspective of epistemological philosophy, Pepper (1942) shows that both these postures— dogmatism and absolute skepticism—are inadequate foundations for the creation of valid knowledge systems. He proposes instead that an attitude of provisionalism, or what he calls partial skepticism, be the guide for inquiry and learning (compare Chapter 5, p. 107).

The fact that learning is a continuous process grounded in experience has important educational implications. Put simply, it implies that all learning is *relearning*. How easy and tempting it is in designing a course to think of the learner's mind as being as blank as the paper on which we scratch our outline. Yet this is not the case. Everyone enters every learning situation with more or less articulate ideas about the topic at hand. We are all psychologists, historians, and atomic physicists. It is just that some of our theories are more crude and incorrect than others. But to focus solely on the refinement and validity of these theories misses the point. The important point is that the people we teach have held these beliefs whatever their quality and that until now they have used them whenever the situation called for them to be atomic physicists, historians, or whatever.

Thus, one's job as an educator is not only to implant new ideas but also to dispose of or modify old ones. In many cases, resistance to new ideas stems from their conflict with old beliefs that are inconsistent with them. If the education process begins by bringing out the learner's beliefs and theories, examining and testing them, and then integrating the new, more refined ideas into the person's belief systems, the learning process will be facilitated. Piaget (see Elkind, 1970, Chapter 3) has identified two mechanisms by which new ideas are adopted by an individual—integration and substitution. Ideas that evolve through integration tend to become highly stable parts of the person's conception of the world. On the other hand, when the content of a concept changes by means of substitution, there is always the possibility of a reversion to the earlier level of conceptualization and understanding, or to a dual theory of the world where espoused theories learned through substitution are incongruent with theories-in-use that are more integrated with the person's total conceptual and attitudinal view of the world. It is this latter outcome that stimulated Argyris and Schon's inquiry into the effectiveness of professional education:

> We thought the trouble people have in learning new theories may stem not so much from the inherent difficulty of the new theories as from the existing theories people have that already determine practices. We call their operational theories of action theories-in-use to distinguish them from the espoused theories that are used to describe and justify behavior. We wondered whether the difficulty in learning new theories of action is related to a disposition to protect the old theory-in-use. [Argyris and Schon, 1974, p. viii]

The Process of Learning Requires the Resolution of Conflicts Between Dialectically Opposed Modes of Adaptation to the World

Each of the three models of experiential learning describes conflicts between opposing ways of dealing with the world, suggesting that learning results from resolution of these conflicts. The Lewinian model emphasizes two such dialectics—the conflict between concrete experience and abstract concepts and the conflict between observation and action.[2] For Dewey, the major dialectic is between the impulse that gives ideas their "moving force" and reason that gives desire its direction. In Piaget's framework, the twin processes of accommodation of ideas to the external world and assimilation of experience into existing conceptual structures are the moving forces of cognitive development. In Paulo Freire's work, the dialectic nature of learning and adaptation is encompassed in his concept of *praxis*, which he defines as "reflection and action upon the world in order to transform it" (1974, p. 36). Central to the concept of praxis is the process of "naming the world," which is both active—in the sense that naming something transforms it—and reflective—in that our choice of words gives meaning to the world around us. This process of naming the world is accomplished through dialogue among equals, a joint process of inquiry and learning that Freire sets against the banking concept of education described earlier:

[2]The concept of dialectic relationship is used advisedly in this work. The long history and changing usages of this term, and particularly the emotional and ideological connotations attending its usage in some contexts, may cause some confusion for the reader. However, no other term expresses as well the relationship between learning orientations described here—that of mutually opposed and conflicting processes the results of each of which cannot be explained by the other, but whose merger through confrontation of the conflict between them results in a higher order process that transcends and encompasses them both. This definition comes closest to Hegel's use of the term but does not imply total acceptance of the Hegelian epistemology (compare Chapter 5, p. 117).

As we attempt to analyze dialogue as a human phenomenon, we discover something which is the essence of dialogue itself: the word. But the word is more than just an instrument which makes dialogue possible; accordingly, we must seek its constitutive elements. Within the word we find two dimensions, reflection and action, in such radical interaction that if one is sacrificed—even in part—the other immediately suffers. There is no true word that is not at the same time a praxis. Thus, to speak a true word is to transform the world.

An unauthentic word, one which is unable to transform reality, results when dichotomy is imposed upon its constitutive elements. When a word is deprived of its dimension of action, reflection automatically suffers as well; and the word is changed into idle chatter, into verbalism, into an alienated and alienating "blah." It becomes an empty word, one which cannot denounce the world, for denunciation is impossible without a commitment to transform, and there is no transformation without action.

On the other hand, if action is emphasized exclusively, to the detriment of reflection, the word is converted into activism. The latter—action for action's sake—negates the true praxis and makes dialogue impossible. Either dichotomy, by creating unauthentic forms of existence, creates also unauthentic forms of thought, which reinforce the original dichotomy.

Human existence cannot be silent, nor can it be nourished by false words, but only by true words, with which men transform the world. To exist, humanly, is to name the world, to change it. Once named, the world in its turn reappears to the namers as a problem and requires of them a new naming. Men are not built in silence, but in word, in work, in action-reflection.

But while to say the true word—which is work, which is praxis—is to transform the world, saying that word is not the privilege of some few men, but the right of every man. Consequently, no one can say a true word alone—nor can he say it for another, in a prescriptive act which robs others of their words. [Freire, 1974, pp. 75, 76]

All the models above suggest the idea that learning is by its very nature a tension- and conflict-filled process. New knowledge, skills, or attitudes are achieved through confrontation among four modes of experiential learning. Learners, if they are to be effective, need four different kinds of abilities— *concrete experience* abilities (CE), *reflective observation* abilities (RO), *abstract conceptualization* abilities (AC), and *active experimentation* (AE) abilities. That is, they must be able to involve themselves fully, openly, and without bias in new experiences (CE). They must be able to reflect on and observe their experiences from many perspectives (RO). They must be able to create concepts that integrate their observations into logically sound theories (AC), and they must be able to use these theories to make decisions and solve problems (AE). Yet this ideal is difficult to achieve. How can one act and reflect at the same time? How can one be concrete and immediate and still be theoretical? Learning requires abilities that are polar opposites, and the learner, as a result, must continually choose which set of learning abilities he or she will bring to bear in any specific learning situation. More specifically, there are two primary dimensions to the learning process. The first dimension represents the concrete experiencing of events at one end and abstract conceptualization at the other. The other dimension has active experimentation at one extreme and reflective observation at the other. Thus, in the process of learning, one moves in varying degrees from actor to observer, and from specific involvement to general analytic detachment.

In addition, the *way* in which the conflicts among the dialectically opposed modes of adaptation get resolved determines the level of learning that results. If conflicts are resolved by suppression of one mode and/or dominance by another, learning tends to be specialized around the dominant mode and limited in areas controlled by the dominated mode. For example, in Piaget's model, imitation is the result when accommodation processes dominate, and play results when assimilation dominates. Or for Freire, dominance of the active mode results in "activism," and dominance of the reflective mode results in "verbalism."

However, when we consider the higher forms of adaptation—the process of creativity and personal development—conflict among adaptive modes needs to be confronted and integrated into a creative synthesis. Nearly every account of the creative process, from Wallas's (1926) four-stage model of incorporation, incubation, insight, and verification, has recognized the dialectic conflicts involved in creativity. Bruner (1966a), in his essay on the conditions of creativity, emphasizes the dialectic tension between abstract detachment and concrete involvement. For him, the creative act is a product of detachment and commitment, of passion and decorum, and of a freedom to be dominated by the object of one's inquiry. At the highest stages of development. the adaptive commitment to learning and creativity produces a strong need for integration of the four adaptive modes. Development in one mode precipitates development in the others. Increases in symbolic complexity, for example, refine and sharpen both perceptual and behavioral possibilities. Thus, complexity and the integration of dialectic conflicts among the adaptive modes are the hallmarks of true creativity and growth.

Learning Is an Holistic Process of Adaptation to the World

Experiential learning is not a molecular educational concept but rather is a molar concept describing the central process of human adaptation to the social and physical environment. It is a holistic concept much akin to the Jungian theory of psychological types (Jung, 1923), in that it seeks to describe the emergence of basic life orientations as a function of dialectic tensions between basic modes of relating to the world. To learn is not the special province of a single specialized realm of human functioning such as cognition or perception. It involves the integrated functioning of the total organism—thinking, feeling, perceiving, and behaving.

This concept of holistic adaptation is somewhat out of step with current research trends in the behavioral sciences. Since the early years of this century and the decline of what Gordon Allport called the "simple and sovereign" theories of human behavior, the trend in the behavioral sciences has been away from theories such as those of Freud and his followers that proposed to explain the totality of human functioning by focusing on the interrelatedness among human processes such as thought, emotion, perception, and so on. Research has instead tended to specialize in more detailed exploration and description of particular processes and subprocesses of human adaptation—perception, person perception, attribution, achievement motivation, cognition, memory—the list could go on and on. The fruit of this labor has been bountiful. Because of this intensive specialized research, we now know a vast amount about human behavior, so much that any attempt to integrate and do justice to all this diverse knowledge seems impossible. Any holistic theory proposed today could not be simple and would certainly not be sovereign. Yet if we are to understand human behavior, particularly in any practical way, we must in some way put together all the pieces that have been so carefully analyzed. In addition to knowing how we think and how we feel, we must also know when behavior is governed by thought and when by feeling. In addition to addressing the nature of specialized human functions, experiential learning theory is also concerned with how these functions are integrated by the person into a holistic adaptive posture toward the world.

Learning is *the* major process of human adaptation. This concept of learning is considerably broader than that commonly associated with the school classroom. It occurs in all human settings, from schools to the workplace, from the research laboratory to the management board room, in personal relationships and the aisles of the local grocery. It encompasses all life stages, from childhood to adolescence, to middle and old age. Therefore it encompasses other, more limited adaptive concepts such as creativity, problem solving, decision making, and attitude change that focus heavily on one or another of the basic aspects of adaptation. Thus, creativity research has tended to focus on the divergent (concrete and reflective) factors in adaptation such as tolerance for ambiguity, metaphorical thinking, and flexibility, whereas research on decision making has emphasized more convergent (abstract and active) adaptive factors such as the rational evaluation of solution alternatives.

The cyclic description of the experiential learning process is mirrored in many of the specialized models of the adaptive process. The common theme in all these models is that all forms of human adaptation approximate scientific inquiry, a point of view articulated most thoroughly by the late George Kelly (1955). Dewey, Lewin, and Piaget in one way or another seem to take the scientific method as their model for the learning process; or to put it another way, they see in the scientific method the highest philosophical and technological refinement of the basic processes of human adaptation. The scientific method, thus, provides a means for describing the holistic integration of all human functions.

Figure 2.4 shows the experiential learning cycle in the center circle and a model of the scientific inquiry process in the outer circle (Kolb, 1978), with models of the problem-solving process (Pounds, 1965), the decision-making

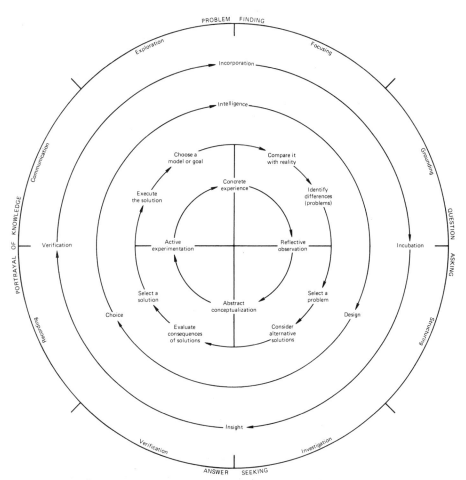

Figure 2.4 Similarities Among Conceptions of Basic Adaptive Processes: Inquiry/Research, Creativity, Decision Making, Problem Solving, Learning

process (Simon, 1947), and the creative process (Wallas, 1926) in between. Although the models all use different terms, there is a remarkable similarity in concept among them. This similarity suggests that there may be great payoff in the integration of findings from these specialized areas into a single general adaptive model such as that proposed by experiential learning theory. Bruner's work on a theory of instruction (1966b) shows one example of this potential payoff. His integration of research on cognitive processes, problem solving, and learning theory provided a rich new perspective for the conduct of education.

When learning is conceived as a holistic adaptive process, it provides conceptual bridges across life situations such as school and work, portraying learning as a continuous, lifelong process. Similarly, this perspective highlights the similarities among adaptive/learning activities that are commonly called by specialized names—learning, creativity, problem solving, decision making, and scientific research. Finally, learning conceived holistically includes adaptive activities that vary in their extension through time and space. Typically, an immediate reaction to a limited situation or problem is not thought of as learning but as *performance*. Similarly at the other extreme, we do not commonly think of long-term adaptations to one's total life situation as learning but as *development*. Yet performance, learning, and development, when viewed from the perspectives of experiential learning theory, form a continuum of adaptive postures to the environment, varying only in their degree of extension in time and space. Performance is limited to short-term adaptations to immediate circumstance, learning encompasses somewhat longer-term mastery of generic classes of situations, and development encompasses lifelong adaptations to one's total life situation (compare Chapter 6).

Learning Involves Transactions Between the Person and the Environment

So stated, this proposition must seem obvious. Yet strangely enough, its implications seem to have been widely ignored in research on learning and practice in education, replaced instead by a person-centered psychological view of learning. The casual observer of the traditional educational process would undoubtedly conclude that learning was primarily a personal, internal process requiring only the limited environment of books, teacher, and classroom. Indeed, the wider "real-world" environment at times seems to be actively rejected by educational systems at all levels.

There is an analogous situation in psychological research on learning and development. In theory, stimulus-response theories of learning describe relationships between environmental stimuli and responses of the organism. But in practice, most of this research involves treating the environmental stimuli as independent variables manipulated artificially by the experimenter to determine their effect on dependent response characteristics. This approach has had two outcomes. The first is a tendency to perceive the person-environment relationship as one-way, placing great emphasis on how environment shapes behavior with little regard for how behavior shapes the environment. Second, the models of learning are essentially decontextualized and lacking in what Egon Brunswick (1943) called ecological validity. In the emphasis on scientific control of environmental conditions, laboratory situations were created that bore little resemblance to the environment of real life, resulting in empirically validated models of learning that accurately described behavior in these artificial settings but could not easily be generalized to subjects in their natural environment. It is to me not surprising that the foremost proponent of this theory of learning would be fascinated by the creation of Utopian societies such as Walden II (Skinner, 1948); for the only way to apply the results of these studies is to make the world a laboratory, subject to "experimenter" control (compare Elms, 1981).

Similar criticisms have been made of developmental psychology. Piaget's work, for example, has been criticized for its failure to take account of environmental and cultural circumstances (Cole, 1971). Speaking of developmental psychology in general, Bronfenbrenner states, "Much of developmental psychology as it now exists is *the science of the strange behavior of children in strange situations with strange adults for the briefest possible periods of time*" (1977, p. 19).

In experiential learning theory, the transactional relationship between the person and the environment is symbolized in the dual meanings of the term *experience*—one subjective and personal, referring to the person's internal state, as in "the experience of joy and happiness," and the other objective and environmental, as in, "He has 20 years of experience on this job." These two forms of experience interpenetrate and interrelate in very complex ways, as, for example, in the old saw, "He doesn't have 20 years of experience, but one year repeated 20 times." Dewey describes the matter this way:

Experience does not go on simply inside a person. It does go on there, for it influences the formation of attitudes of desire and purpose. But this is not the whole of the story. Every genuine experience has an active side which changes in some degree the objective conditions under which experiences are had. The difference between civilization and savagery, to take an example on a large scale, is found in the degree in which previous experiences have changed the objective conditions under which subsequent experiences take place. The existence of roads, of means of rapid movement and transportation, tools, implements, furniture, electric light and power, are illustrations. Destroy the external conditions of present civilized experience, and for a time our experience would relapse into that of barbaric peoples. . . .

The word "interaction" assigns equal rights to both factors in experience— objective and internal conditions. Any normal experience is an interplay of these two sets of conditions. Taken together . . . they form what we call a situation.

The statement that individuals live in a world means, in the concrete, that they live in a series of situations. And when it is said that they live in these situations, the meaning of the word "in" is different from its meaning when it is said that pennies are "in" a pocket or paint is "in" a can. It means, once more, that interaction is going on between an individual and objects and other persons. The conceptions of situation *and of* interaction *are inseparable from each other. An experience is always what it is because of a transaction taking place between an individual and what, at the time, constitutes his environment, whether the latter consists of persons with whom he is talking about some topic or event, the subject talked about being also a part of the situation; the book he is reading (in which his environing conditions at the time may be England or ancient Greece or an imaginary region); or the materials of an experiment he is performing. The environment, in other words, is whatever conditions interact with personal needs, desires, purposes, and capacities to create the experience which is had. Even when a person builds a castle in the air he is interacting with the objects which he constructs in fancy. [Dewey, 1938, p. 39, 42-43]*

Although Dewey refers to the relationship between the objective and subjective conditions of experience as an "interaction," he is struggling in the last portion of the quote above to convey the special, complex nature of the relationship. The word *transaction* is more appropriate than *interaction* to describe the relationship between the person and the environment in experiential learning theory, because the connotation of interaction is somehow too mechanical, involving unchanging separate entities that become intertwined but retain their separate identities. This is why Dewey attempts to give special meaning to the word *in*. The concept of transaction implies a more fluid, interpenetrating relationship between objective conditions and subjective experience, such that once they become related, both are essentially changed.

Lewin recognized this complexity, even though he chose to sidestep it in his famous theoretical formulation, $B = f(P,E)$, indicating that behavior is a function of the person and the environment without any specification as to the specific mathematical nature of that function. The position taken in this work is similar to that of Bandura (1978)—namely, that personal characteristics, environmental influences, and behavior all operate in reciprocal determination, each factor influencing the others in an interlocking fashion. The concept of reciprocally determined transactions between person and learning environment is central to the laboratory-training method of experiential learning. Learning in T-groups is seen to result not simply from responding to a fixed environment but from the active creation by the learners of situations that meet their learning objectives:

> The essence of this learning experience is a transactional process in which the members negotiate as each attempts to influence or control the stream of events and to satisfy his personal needs. Individuals learn to the extent that they expose their needs, values, and behavior patterns so that perceptions and reactions can be exchanged. Behavior thus becomes the currency for transaction. The amount each invests helps to determine the return. [Bradford, 1964, p. 192]

Learning in this sense is an active, self-directed process that can be applied not only in the group setting but in everyday life.

Learning Is the Process of Creating Knowledge

To understand learning, we must understand the nature and forms of human knowledge and the processes whereby this knowledge is created. It has already been emphasized that this process of creation occurs at all levels of sophistication, from the most advanced forms of scientific research to the child's discovery that a rubber ball bounces. Knowledge is the result of the transaction between social knowledge and personal knowledge. The former, as Dewey noted, is the civilized objective accumulation of previous human cultural experience, whereas the latter is the accumulation of the individual person's subjective life experiences. Knowledge results from the transaction between these objective and subjective experiences in a process called learning. Hence, to understand knowledge, we must understand the psychology of the learning process, and to understand learning, we must understand epistemology—the origins, nature, methods, and limits of knowledge. Piaget makes the following comments on these last points:

> Psychology thus occupies a key position, and its implications become increasingly clear. The very simple reason for this is that if the sciences of nature explain the human species, humans in turn explain the sciences of nature, and it is up to psychology to show us how. Psychology, in fact, represents the junction of two opposite directions of scientific thought that are dialectically complementary. It follows that the system of sciences cannot be arranged in a linear order, as many people beginning with Auguste Comte have attempted to arrange them. The form that characterizes the system of sciences is that of a circle, or more precisely that of a spiral as it becomes ever larger. In fact, objects are known only through the subject, while the subject can know himself or herself only by acting on objects materially and mentally. Indeed, if objects are innumerable and science indefinitely diverse, all knowledge of the subject brings us back to psychology, the science of the subject and the subject's actions.
>   . . . it is impossible to dissociate psychology from epistemology . . . how is knowledge acquired, how does it increase, and how does it become organized or reorganized? . . . The answers we find, and from which we can only choose by more or less refining them, are necessarily of the following three types: Either knowledge comes exclusively from the object, or it is constructed by the subject alone, or it results from multiple interactions between the subject and the object— but what interactions and in what form? Indeed, we see at once that these are epistemological solutions stemming from empiricism, apriorism, or diverse interactionism. . . . [Piaget, 1978, p. 651]

It is surprising that few learning and cognitive researchers other than Piaget have recognized the intimate relationship between learning and knowledge and hence recognized the need for epistemological as well as psychological inquiry into these related processes. In my own research and practice with experiential learning, I have been impressed with the very practical ramifications of the epistemological perspective. In teaching, for example, I have found it essential to take into account the nature of the subject matter in deciding how to help students learn the material at hand. Trying to develop skills in empathic listening is a different educational task, requiring a different teaching approach from that of teaching fundamentals of statistics. Similarly, in consulting work with organizations, I have often seen barriers to communication and problem solving that at root are epistemologically based—that is, based on conflicting assumptions about the nature of knowledge and truth.

The theory of experiential learning provides a perspective from which to approach these practical problems, suggesting a typology of different knowledge systems that results from the way the dialectic conflicts between adaptive modes of concrete experience and abstract conceptualization and the modes of active experimentation and reflective observation are characteristically resolved in different fields of inquiry (compare Chapter 5). This approach draws on the work of Stephen Pepper (1942, 1966), who proposes a system for describing the different viable forms of social knowledge. This system is based on what Pepper calls world hypotheses. World hypotheses correspond to metaphysical systems that define assumptions and rules for the development of refined knowledge from common sense. Pepper maintains that all knowledge systems are refinements of common sense based on different assumptions about the nature of knowledge and truth. In this process of refinement he sees a basic dilemma. Although common sense is always applicable as a means of explaining an experience, it tends to be imprecise. Refined knowledge, on the other hand, is precise but limited in its application or generalizability because it is based on assumptions or world hypotheses. Thus, common sense requires the criticism of refined knowledge, and refined knowledge requires the security of common sense, suggesting that all social knowledge requires an attitude of partial skepticism in its interpretation.

SUMMARY: A DEFINITION OF LEARNING

Even though definitions have a way of making things seem more certain than they are, it may be useful to summarize this chapter on the characteristics of the experiential learning process by offering a working definition of learning.[3] *Learning is the process whereby knowledge is created through the transformation of experience.* This definition emphasizes several critical aspects of the learning process as viewed from the experiential perspective. First is the emphasis on the process of adaptation and learning as opposed to content or outcomes. Second is that knowledge is a transformation process, being continuously created and recreated, not an independent entity to be acquired or transmitted. Third, learning transforms experience in both its objective and subjective forms. Finally, to understand learning, we must understand the nature of knowledge, and vice versa.

---

[3]From this point on, I will drop the modifier "experiential" in referring to the learning process described in this chapter. When other theories of learning are discussed, they will be identified as such.

three

Structural Foundations of the Learning Process

Our intellectual process consists . . . in a rhythm of direct understanding—
technically called apprehension—with indirect mediated understanding
technically called comprehension.　　**John Dewey,** How We Think*

A term may be viewed in two ways, either as a class of objects . . . or as a
set of attributes or characteristics which determine the objects. The first
phase or aspect is called the denotation or extension of the term, while the
second is called the connotation or intension. Thus the extension of the term
"philosopher" is "Socrates," "Plato," "Thalus" and the like; its intension is
"lover of wisdom," "intelligent" and so on. . . . Why a term is applied to a set
of objects is indicated by its intension; the set of objects to which it is
applicable constitutes its extension.

Morris Cohen and Ernest Nagel
Introduction to Logic and Scientific Method

The models of learning that were described in the last chapter provided tantalizing suggestions as to the nature of the learning process, but they also raise many important questions. How, for example, does one move through stages of the learning cycles described? Is this process identical for everyone? What determines how the dialectic conflicts between adaptive modes get resolved? With what consequences for learning and development? To answer

---

*John Dewey, *How We Think*, Lexington, MA: D.C. Heath Co., 1910. Reprinted with the permission of the Center for Dewey Studies, Southern Illinois University at Carbondale.

these and other questions requires a more detailed examination and systematic formulation of the experiential learning process.

The approach taken in this chapter will be essentially structural. That is, the aim here is to identify the essential and enduring aspects of the learning process that determine its functioning, separating them from secondary, accidental aspects. In this sense, the structuralist approach seeks to draw the blueprints of how the "learning machine" functions ideally, not to document its actual functioning under varying conditions of circumstance, mood, culture, and the like. To achieve an adequate structural analysis of the learning process, we need to determine (1) its *holistic structure*, defining the interdependence of the internal components of the learning model without reliance on forces outside the model; (2) its *transformation process*, specifying the way in which structural components transact to maintain and elaborate themselves; and (3) its *process of self-regulation*, describing how the structural system maintains its identity and integrity (compare Piaget, 1968, p.5).

In a sense, this analysis is already under way, for we have seen in the last chapter how the more phenomenological, descriptive models of learning described by Lewin and Dewey are enriched and corroborated by Piaget's structural dimensions of cognitive development—phenomenalism/constructivism and egocentricism/reflectivism. However, the model proposed in this chapter will deviate in some respects from Piaget's formulation. For Piaget, these two dimensions represent a developmental continuum, in which phenomenalism and egocentricism are lower forms of knowing than are constructivism and reflection. I will propose here that the poles of these two dimensions are equipotent modes of knowing that through dialectic transformations result in learning. This learning proceeds along a third, developmental dimension that represents not the dominance of one learning mode over another but the integration of the four adaptive modes.[1] We will have occasion to examine the details of the points of disagreement between my perspective and that of Piaget in the course of a more complete elaboration of the structure of experiential learning.

PROCESS AND STRUCTURE IN EXPERIENTIAL LEARNING

As has been suggested, the process of experiential learning can be described as a four-stage cycle involving four adaptive learning modes—concrete experience, reflective observation, abstract conceptualization, and active experimentation. In this model, concrete experience/abstract conceptualization and active

---

[1] Those readers who are familiar with Piaget will already have noted this deviation from his linear idea of development in my description of the relationship between experiential learning and his model of development in Chapter 2. I there suggest an integrative developmental scheme by proposing that the stage of formal operations represents a return at a higher developmental level to the active orientation characteristic of stage 1.

experimentation/reflective observation are two distinct dimensions, each representing two dialectically opposed adaptive orientations. The structural bases of the learning process lie in the transactions among these four adaptive modes and the way in which the adaptive dialectics get resolved. To begin with, notice that the abstract/concrete dialectic is one of *prehension*, representing two different and opposed processes of grasping or taking hold of experience in the world—either through reliance on conceptual interpretation and symbolic representation, a process I will call *comprehension*, or through reliance on the tangible, felt qualities of immediate experience, what I will call *apprehension*. The active/reflective dialectic, on the other hand, is one of *transformation*, representing two opposed ways of transforming that grasp or "figurative representation" of experience—either through internal reflection, a process I will call *intention*, or active external manipulation of the external world, here called *extension*. These two dimensions of learning—*prehension* and *transformation*—correspond directly to Piaget's figurative and operative aspects of thought:[2]

> I shall begin by making a distinction between two aspects of thinking that are different, although complementary. One is the figurative aspect, and the other I call the operative aspect. The figurative aspect is an imitation of states taken as momentary and static. In the cognitive area the figurative functions are, above all, perception, imitation, and mental imagery, which is in fact interiorized imitation.
>
> The operative aspect of thought deals not with states but with transformations from one state to another. For instance, it includes actions themselves, which transform objects or states, and it also includes the intellectual operations, which are essentially systems of transformation. [Piaget, 1970, p.14]

In the figurative aspects, perception and imitation correspond roughly to the apprehension process, and mental imagery corresponds to the comprehension process. For the operative aspect, there is a rough correspondence between action and the process of extension and between intellectual operations and the intention process.

With this brief overview of our structural perspective, we are now in a position to give more substance to the definition of learning proposed in the last chapter—namely, that learning is the process whereby knowledge is created through the transformation of experience. Knowledge results from the combination of grasping experience and transforming it (see Figure 3.1). And since there are two dialectically opposed forms of prehension and, similarly, two opposed ways of transforming that prehension, the result is four different

---

[2]The concepts of prehension and transformation or figurative and operative aspects of thought have parallels in the computer modeling literature. For example, in Forrester's system-dynamics approach to model building, he distinguishes between rates and levels, specifying that in any model, rates can only directly influence levels and vice versa (Forrester, 1971). A level (e.g., population size at any given time) corresponds to the prehension or figurative aspect, and a rate (e.g., percent increase in a given time period) corresponds to the transformation or operative aspect.

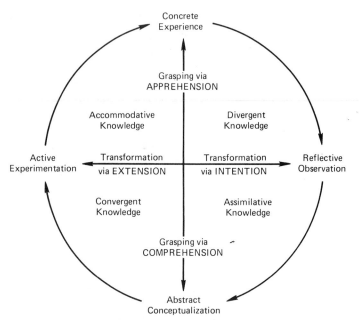

Figure 3.1 Structural Dimensions Underlying the Process of Experiential Learning and the Resulting Basic Knowledge Forms

elementary forms of knowledge. Experience grasped through apprehension and transformed through intention results in what will be called *divergent* knowledge. Experience grasped through comprehension and transformed through intention results in *assimilative* knowledge. When experience is grasped through comprehension and transformed through extension, the result is *convergent* knowledge. And finally, when experience is grasped by apprehension and transformed by extension, *accommodative* knowledge is the result. These elementary forms of knowledge, as will be shown in later chapters, become the building blocks for developmentally higher levels of knowing.

The central idea here is that learning, and therefore knowing, requires *both* a grasp or figurative representation of experience and some transformation of that representation. Either the figurative grasp or operative transformation alone is not sufficient. The simple perception of experience is not sufficient for learning; something must be done with it. Similarly, transformation alone cannot represent learning, for there must be something to be transformed, some state or experience that is being acted upon. This view is largely consistent with that of Piaget, although his work has tended to highlight the role of transformation processes over the prehension process, whereas I will seek in this exposition to give both aspects equal status (compare Piaget, 1970, p. 14-15).

In what follows, we will examine evidence for the prehension and transformation dimensions of learning from three different perspectives—

philosophy, psychology, and physiology. From these three fields there emerges a consistent picture of the structure and functioning of these two basic dimensions of the learning process.

THE PREHENSION DIMENSION-APPREHENSION VS. COMPREHENSION

That there are two distinct modes of grasping experience may not be readily apparent, but it is a fact that can be easily demonstrated with but a little effort. Pause in your reading for a moment and become aware of your surroundings. What you see, hear, and feel around you are those sensations, colors, textures, and sounds that are so basic and reliable that we call them reality. The continuous feel of your chair as it firmly supports your body, the smooth texture of the book and its pages, the muted mixture of sounds surrounding you—all these things and many others you know instantaneously without need for rational inquiry or analytical confirmation. They are simply there, grasped through a mode of knowing here called apprehension. Yet to describe these perceptions faithfully in words, as I have attempted here, is somewhat difficult. It is almost as though the words are vessels dipped in the sea of sensations we experience as reality, vessels that hold and give form to those sensations contained, while sensations left behind fade from awareness. The concept "chair," for example, probably describes where you are sitting (those of you in bed, standing in bookstore stalls, and so on notwithstanding). It is a convenient way to summarize a whole series of sensations you are having right now, although it tends to actively discourage attention to parts of that experience other than those associated with "chairness." The concept also ignores particular aspects of your chair that may be important to you, such as hardness or squeakiness.

In this sense, concepts and the associated mode of knowing called comprehension seem secondary and somewhat arbitrary ways of knowing. Through comprehension we introduce order into what would otherwise be a seamless, unpredictable flow of apprehended sensations, but at the price of shaping (distorting) and forever changing that flow. Yet knowing through comprehension has other qualities that have made it primary in human society—namely, that comprehensions of experience can be communicated and thereby transcend time and space. If you put down this book, get up from the chair, and leave the room, your apprehensions of that situation will vanish without trace (substituted for, of course, by new apprehensions of the hallway or whatever new immediate situation you are in). Your comprehension of that situation, however, will allow you to create for yourself and communicate to others a model of that situation that could last forever. Further, to the extent that the model was accurately constructed from your apprehensions, it allows you to predict and recreate those apprehensions. You can, for example, find again the comfortable chair you were sitting in, although if you did not attend to and comprehend the light source, you might not remember where the blue ceramic table lamp is. For these tremendous powers of communication, prediction, and control that symbolic comprehension brings, the loss of the nuance and security of raw apprehended experience seems a small price to pay. Yet, as Goethe notes in *Faust,* it is a price—"Gray are all theories,/And green alone Life's golden tree."

The relation between apprehension and comprehension has been an enduring philosophical concern. The philosophical distinction between these forms of knowing is perhaps best described by William James, whose *knowledge of acquaintance* and *knowledge-about* correspond to apprehension and comprehension respectively. The following quotation describes James's view of these two kinds of knowledge:

There are two kinds of knowledge *broadly and practically distinguishable: We may call them respectively* knowledge of acquaintance *and* knowledge-about. *Most languages express the distinction; thus,* γνῶναι, εἰδέναι; *noscere, scire; kennen, wissen; connâitre, savoir. I am acquainted with many people and things, which I know very little about, except their presence in the places where I have met them. I know the color blue when I see it, and the flavor of a pear when I taste it; I know an inch when I move my finger through it; a second of time, when I feel it pass; an effort of attention when I make it; a difference between two things when I notice it; but* about *the inner nature of these facts or what makes them what they are, I can say nothing at all. I cannot impart acquaintance with them to anyone who has not already made it himself. I cannot describe them, make a blind man guess what blue is like, define to a child a syllogism, or tell a philosopher in just what respect distance is just what it is, and differs from other forms of relation. At most, I can say to my friends, Go to certain places and act in certain ways, and these objects will probably come. All the elementary natures of the world, its highest genera, the simple qualities of matter and mind, together with the kinds of relation that subsist between them, must either not be known at all, or known in this dumb way of acquaintance without* knowledge-about. *In minds able to speak at all there is, it is true, some knowledge about everything. Things can at least be classed, and the times of their appearance told. But in general, the less we analyze a thing, and the fewer of its relations we perceive, the less we know about it and the more our familiarity with it is of the acquaintance-type. . . . We can relapse at will into a mere condition of acquaintance with an object by scattering our attention and staring at it in a vacuous trance-like way. We can ascend to* knowledge *about it by rallying our wits and proceeding to notice and analyze and think. What we are only acquainted with is only present to our minds; we* have *it, or the idea of it. But when we know* about *it, we do more than merely have it; we seem, as we think over its relations, to subject it to a sort of* treatment *and to operate upon it with our thought. The words* feeling *and* thought *give voice to the antithesis. Through feelings we become acquainted with things, but only by our thoughts do we know about them. Feelings are the germ and starting point of cognition, thoughts the developed tree. . . . The mental states usually distinguished as feelings are the emotions, and the sensations we get from skin, muscle, viscus, eye, ear, nose, and palate. The "thoughts," as recognized in popular parlance, are the conceptions and judgments. [James, 1890, Vol. I, pp. 221-22]*

Similar distinctions are made by Bertrand Russell (1912), Herbert Feigl (1958), and G.E. Moore, who describes two forms of actualized knowledge that parallel the apprehension and comprehension processes of grasping experience—apprehension (in direct and indirect forms) and knowledge proper (Klemke, 1969). Perkins distinguishes knowledge gained from physical concept formation and theory construction (comprehension) from what he calls "internal whatlike understanding" (apprehension), a process he defines as "that understanding of an experience that consists in knowing what an experience is like; and we know what an experience is like by virtue of having that experience" (1971, pp. 3-4). Whitehead distinguishes between two kinds of perception: perception by causal efficacy, in which one sees objects in terms of what can be done with them (comprehension), and perception by presentational immediacy, where one sees patches of color and hears patterns of sound (apprehension). Similarly, Pepper (1966, p. 68) distinguishes between conceptual knowledge and felt qualities.

Pepper and Feigl use the distinction between these two forms of grasping experience to propose a solution to a perennial question of philosophy—the mind-body problem. Feigl suggests that there are dual languages referring to the two forms of knowing: phenomenal language, referring to felt qualities of experience (apprehension), and physical language, referring to descriptive symbols (comprehension). Basing their ideas on research in neurophysiology, Pepper and Feigl maintained that the physical and phenomenal languages refer

Figure 3.2 René Magritte, *Les Idées Claires (Clear Ideas)*

to the same thing—namely, the object of acquaintance directly referred to in phenomenal language. Feigl puts his mind-body identity thesis this way:

> The identity thesis which I wish to clarify and defend asserts that the states of direct experience which conscious human beings "live through," and those which we confidently ascribe to some of the higher animals, are identical with certain (presumably configurational) aspects of the neural processes in those organisms. To put the same idea in the terminology explained previously, we may say what is had-in-experience, and (in the case of human beings) knowable by acquaintance, is identical with the object of knowledge by description provided first by molar behavior theory and this in turn is identical with what the science of neurophysiology describes (or, rather, will describe when sufficient progress has been achieved) as processes of the central nervous system, perhaps especially in the cerebral cortex. In its basic core this is a double knowledge theory. [Feigl, 1958, p. 446]

Since Feigl published that paragraph in 1958, research in neurophysiology has advanced greatly, providing enticing new evidence for the "double knowledge" theory. Recent research on the specialized functions of the left and right hemispheres of the neocortex has the most relevance for the distinction between apprehension and comprehension as dialectically opposed modes for grasping reality. The origins of this work stem from the research and clinical observation of Roger Sperry and his colleagues in the early 1960s (Sperry, Gazzaniga, and Bogen 1969). They studied the behavior of so-called split-brain patients who, in order to relieve the frequency and severity of epileptic seizures, had undergone surgical division of the *corpus callosum,* a complex bundle of neural fibers connecting the left and right hemispheres of the neocortex. These patients as a result possessed two relatively normal hemispheres whose functions could be separately identified. The resulting studies produced results that are at odds with conventional and ancient wisdom about brain function. Until that time, it had been assumed that it was the left hemisphere that was responsible for all cognitive functioning worthy of the name—consciousness, verbal reasoning, analytic ability, and so on. The right hemisphere was thought to be something of a cerebral spare tire, a nonconscious automaton whose function was only to transmit information to the executive left hemisphere. Sperry showed that this was not the case. In fact, the right hemisphere was superior to the left in its functioning on some tasks, such as the visual construction required in drawing.

It is worth describing some of these split-brain studies to illustrate how dramatic the results were. Since the left hemisphere controls vision in the right visual field and the right hand, while the right hemisphere controls the left visual field and the left hand (see Figure 3.3), it was possible to do experiments that gave information on problems to only one hemisphere or conflicting information to both hemispheres. Betty Edwards gives the following descriptions of the results of two such experiments:

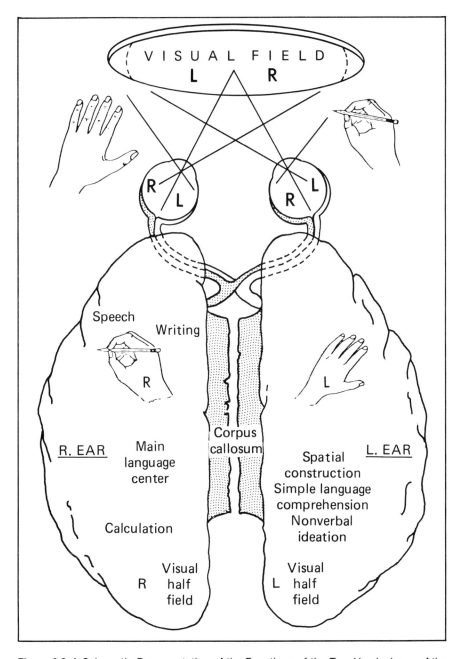

Figure 3.3 A Schematic Representation of the Functions of the Two Hemispheres of the Neocortex. The Right and Left Visual Fields Are Projected, Respectively, onto the Left and Right Occipital Lobes. Control of the Right and Left Sides of the Body Is Similarly Crossed, as is, Mainly, Hearing.

A few examples of the specially designed tests devised for use with the split-brain patients might illustrate the separate reality perceived by each hemisphere and the special modes of processing employed. In one test two different pictures were flashed for an instant on a screen, with a split-brain patient's eyes fixed on a midpoint so that scanning both images was prevented. Each hemisphere, then, received different pictures. A picture of a spoon on the left side of the screen went to the right brain; a picture of a knife on the right side of the screen went to the verbal left brain. When questioned, the patients gave different responses. If asked to name what had been flashed on the screen, the confidently articulate left hemisphere caused the patient to say, "knife." Then the patient was asked to reach behind a curtain with his left hand (right hemisphere) and pick out what had been flashed on the screen. The patient then picked out a spoon from a group of objects that included a spoon and a knife. If the experimenter asked the patient to identify what he held in his hand behind the curtain, the patient might look confused for a moment and then say, "a knife." The right hemisphere, knowing that the answer was wrong but not having sufficient words to correct the articulate left hemisphere, continued the dialogue by causing the patient to mutely shake his head. At that, the verbal left hemisphere wondered aloud, "Why am I shaking my head?"

In another test that demonstrated the right brain to be better at spatial problems, a male patient was given several wooden shapes to arrange to match a certain design. His attempts with his right hand (left hemisphere) failed again and again. His right hemisphere kept trying to help. The right hand would knock the left hand away; and finally, the man had to sit on his left hand to keep it away from the puzzle. When the scientists finally suggested that he use both hands, the spatially "smart" left hand had to shove the spatially "dumb" right hand away to keep it from interfering. [Edwards, 1979, pp. 30-31]

Further research with split-brain patients and later with normal subjects reinforced and elaborated the conclusion that the two hemispheres of the brain were specialized for two different modes of consciousness—the two different modes of knowing about the world that we are calling apprehension and comprehension.

Edwards (1979) has summarized the results of these studies in Figure 3.4. Left-mode functioning corresponds to the comprehension process. It is abstract, symbolic, analytical, and verbal. It functions in a linear sequential manner much like a digital computer. The right-mode function, corresponding to the apprehension process, is concrete, holistic, and spatial. Its functioning is analogic and synthetic, drawing together likenesses among things to recognize patterns. These different orientations to prehension of the world are apparent in many human activities. In music, for instance, the left hemisphere governs the ability to read music, but it is the right hemisphere with its holistic pattern recognition sense that controls the ability to recognize, appreciate, and remember melodies. The left hemisphere is specialized for understanding language communication, but it is the right hemisphere that is most adept at nonverbal understanding, such as recognizing facial expressions (Benton, 1980), emotion, and so on. It is not the assumed anatomical location of the

L— MODE	R— MODE
Verbal: Using words to name, describe, define.	Nonverbal: Awareness of things, but minimal connection with words.
Analytic: Figuring things out step-by-step and part-by-part.	Synthetic: Putting things together to form wholes.
Symbolic: Using a symbol to *stand for* something. For example, the drawn form ⟪◉⟫ stands for *eye*, the sign + stands for the process of addition.	Concrete: Relating to things as they are, at the present moment.
Abstract: Taking out a small bit of information and using it to represent the whole thing.	Analogic: Seeing likenesses between things; understanding metaphoric relationships.
Temporal: Keeping track of time, sequencing one thing after another: Doing first things first, second things second, etc.	Nontemporal: Without a sense of time.
Rational: Drawing conclusions based on *reason* and *facts*.	Nonrational: Not requiring a basis of reason or facts; willingness to suspend judgment.
Digital: Using numbers as in counting.	Spatial: Seeing where things are in relation to other things, and how parts go together to form a whole.
Logical: Drawing conclusions based on logic: one thing following another in logical order—for example, a mathematical theorem or a well-stated argument.	Intuitive: Making leaps of insight, often based on incomplete patterns, hunches, feelings, or visual images.
Linear: Thinking in terms of linked ideas, one thought directly following another, often leading to a convergent conclusion.	Holistic: Seeing whole things all at once; perceiving the overall patterns and structures, often leading to divergent conclusions.

Figure 3.4 A Comparison of Left-Mode and Right-Mode Characteristics [*Source:* Betty Edwards, *Drawing on the Right Side of the Brain* (Los Angeles: J.P. Tarcher, 1979)]

functions identified by this research that is primary, for this is currently highly speculative, but their description and recognition as representative of the dual-knowledge epistemology of experiential learning.

The hemisphere-dominance research provides compelling evidence for the theory that there are two distinct, coequal, and dialectically opposed ways of understanding the world. There is similar psychological evidence as well. In a recent *American Psychologist* article entitled, "Feeling and Thinking: Preferences Need No Inferences," Robert Zajonc (1980) summarizes evidence from the early studies of Wilhelm Wundt to his own present-day research indicating that feeling and thinking are separate processes. He further argues that affective responses are primary. Contrary to the accepted psychological doctrine that affective attributes are the result of cognitive analysis, Zajonc shows that in some cases, affective judgment occurs before cognitive analysis.

These findings suggest a basis for that mysterious process we call intuition—namely, that intuitive behavior is guided by affective judgment (the apprehension process) rather than cognitive judgment. For example, in one of his experimental studies, he showed that subjects were able to distinguish between old and new stimuli flashed for very short periods of time on the basis of affective judgment (like/dislike) before they were able to directly identify the stimuli as old and new. Zajonc suggests that cognitive judgments are based on *discriminanda,* the specific, analyzable, component features of a stimulus, whereas affective judgments are based on *preferenda,* which are more configural, vague, and global aspects of the stimulus.

> *. . . the separation being considered here is between an affective and a cognitive system—a separation that distinguishes between* discriminanda *and* preferenda *and that takes us back to Wundt and Bartlett, who speculated that the overall impression or attitude has an existence of its own, independent of the components that contributed to its emergence. The question that cannot be answered with the data thus far collected is whether the affect-content separation is simply a matter of separate storage . . . or whether there isn't some separation already at the point of registration and encoding. The rapid processing times of affect suggest a more complete separation of the two processes at several junctures.*
>
> *One is necessarily reminded in this context of the dual coding hypothesis proposed by Paivio (1975) for the processing of pictures and words. Paivio (1978a) suggested a number of differences between the processing of these types of content, for example, that representations of pictures emerge as perceptual isomorphs or analogs (imagens), whereas parallel units in the verbal system are linguistic components (logogens). He also proposed that pictorial information is organized in a synchronous and spatially parallel manner, whereas verbal information is discrete and sequential. Finally, he suggested that the processing of pictures is more likely to be the business of the right-brain hemisphere, whereas the processing of words is the business of the left. [Zajonc, 1980, p. 168]*

The view that concrete apprehension processes are coequal with comprehension processes represents a dramatic change from that of 40 years ago. Early research on brain damage viewed concreteness as a deficit, an indicator of brain damage (Goldstein and Scheerer, 1941). Piaget's work represents an intermediate position, considering concrete apprehension processes to be a sign of the young brain and immature thought. Now the theory of dual prehension processes has gained great credibility, based particularly on the hemisphere specialization research. It has been the basis for sharp critiques of the domination of comprehensive left-mode thinking throughout our society, particularly in education (Bogen, 1975). The process of apprehension as a mode of grasping experience and understanding the world is gaining scientific respectability, confirming the long-standing artistic recognition of these powers:

Lovers and madmen have such seething brains,
Such shaping fantasies, that apprehend
More than cool reason ever comprehends.
The lunatic, the lover and the poet
Are of imagination all compact. . . .

William Shakespeare
A Midsummer Night's Dream[3]

THE TRANSFORMATION DIMENSION-INTENTION AND EXTENSION

Although they are logical terms, and have thus been applied primarily to the symbolic processes of comprehension, I have chosen the terms *intention*[4] and *extension* to represent the basic transformation processes of learning as they apply to both the apprehensive and comprehensive modes of grasping experience. The dialectic nature of these dual transformation processes and their synergetic role in the creation of meaning has long been an accepted foundation of logical inquiry and the study of signs and symbols, the field of semiotics. The two major branches of semiotics—syntactics and semantics—correspond respectively to the study of the intentional formal characteristics of symbols and the extensional denotation of signs and symbols—that is, the objects in the world that signs and symbols refer to. The computer scientist, Douglas Hofstadter, describes the difference between these two processes and the central role that intention plays in thinking:

> *Not all descriptions of a person need be attached to some central symbol for that person, which stores the person's name. Descriptions can be manufactured and manipulated in themselves. We can invent nonexistent people by making descriptions of them; we can merge two descriptions when we find they represent a single entity; we can split one description into two when we find it represents two things, not one—and so on. The "calculus of descriptions" is at the heart of thinking. It is said to be intensional and not extensional, which means that descriptions can "float" without being anchored down to specific, known objects. The intensionality of thought is connected to its flexibility, it gives us the ability to imagine hypothetical worlds, to amalgamate different descriptions or chop one description into separate pieces, and so on. . . . Fantasy and fact intermingle very closely in our minds, and this is because thinking involves the manufacture and manipulation of complex descriptions, which need in no way be tied down to real events or things. [Hofstadter, 1979, pp. 338-39]*

[3]Shakespeare seemed fascinated with the distinction between apprehension and comprehension as two ways of knowing. Use of these terms is sprinkled appropriately throughout his works, including the humorous misuse of the distinction when the constable in *Much Ado About Nothing* reports, "Our watch, sir, have indeed comprehended two aspicious persons."

[4]The spelling is changed here from the logical term intension to include the broader psychological as well as logical meanings of intention (e.g., intent, purpose, meaning).

What I propose here is that the transformation processes of intention and extension can be applied to our concrete apprehensions of the world as well as to our symbolic comprehensions. We learn the meaning of our concrete immediate experiences by internally reflecting on their presymbolic impact on our feelings, and/or by acting on our apprehended experience and thus extending it. Take, for example, the rose lying on my desk. I transform my apprehension of the rose intentionally by deploying my attention to its different aspects, noting the delicate pink color that is not solid but alternates subtly from white to a deeper rose. I sense its delicate fragrance and experience a blossoming of brief reminiscences. Here I cannot resist the impulse to transform the experience extensionally, to pick up the rose and hold it to my nose. In so doing, I prick my finger on the thorny stem and extend my apprehension of this rose still further. Now this new extended apprehension further stimulates my internal reflections and feelings. . . .

Learning, the creation of knowledge and meaning, occurs through the active extension and grounding of ideas *and* experiences in the external world and through internal reflection about the attributes of these experiences and ideas. As Yeats put it, "The human soul is always moving outward into the external world and inward into itself, and this movement is double because the human soul would not be conscious were it not suspended between contraries. The greater the contrast, the more intense the consciousness."

As previously indicated, the conception that extension and intention are the basic transformation processes in learning is largely consistent with Piaget's emphasis on the operative aspects of thought, which he divides into behavioral actions (extension) that transform objects or states, and intellectual operations (intention) that are internalized actions or systems of transformation (see Piaget, 1971, p. 67). It should be noted that Piaget seems to associate extensional transformation (individual actions) primarily with concrete apprehensions of the world, whereas intentional transformation (reflective abstraction) is reserved for logical and mathematical knowledge. This is perhaps a function of his focus on child development, where we see as the child matures that reflection and abstraction together do replace overt action and concrete apprehension. In addition, Piaget's tendency to view transformation by reflective abstraction as superior to overt action transformation also reflects this developmental focus. It will be argued here, however, that although the figurative and operative aspects develop together in childhood, in the mature adult the two dimensions are independent, producing four equipotent combinations of prehension and transformation (see Chapter 6, pp. 136-140).

In this sense, the transformation dimension is perhaps best described by the concepts of introversion (intention) and extraversion (extension), the primary concepts in the theory of types developed by Carl Jung:

> . . . one could describe the introverted standpoint as one that under all circumstances sets the self and the subjective psychological process above the object and the objective process, or at any rate holds its ground against the

object. This attitude, therefore, gives the subject a higher value than the object. As a result, the object always possesses a lower value; it has secondary importance; occasionally it even represents merely an outward objective token of a subjective content, the embodiment of an idea in other words, in which, however, the idea is the essential factor; or it is the object of a feeling, where, however, the feeling experience is the chief thing, and not the object in its own individuality. The extroverted standpoint, on the contrary, sets the subject below the object, whereby the object receives the predominant value. The subject always has secondary importance; the subjective process appears at times merely as a disturbing or superfluous accessory to objective events. It is plain that the psychology resulting from these antagonistic standpoints must be distinguished as two totally different orientations. The one sees everything from the angle of his conception, the other from the viewpoint of the objective occurrence.

These opposite attitudes are merely opposite mechanisms—a diastolic going out and seizing of the object, and a systolic concentration and release of energy from the object seized. Every human being possesses both mechanisms as an expression of his natural life-rhythm. . . . [Jung, 1923, pp. 12-13]

In this original conception, Jung laid great emphasis on the epistimological aspects of introversion and extraversion. He saw in the distinction the psychological underpinning of the philosophical debate between *nominalism*, the view that universals and ideas exist in name only, and *realism*, the doctrine that universals have a real objective existence. For Jung, truth lay neither in the nominalist or realist positions but in the dynamic integration of the introverted and extraverted attitudes:

Every logico-intellectual formulation, however embracing it may be, divests the objective impression of its living and immediate quality. It must do this in order to reach any formulation whatsoever. But, in so doing, just that is lost which to the extraverted attitude seems absolutely essential, namely, the relationship to the real object. No possibility exists, therefore, that we shall find upon the line of either attitude any satisfactory and reconciling formula. And yet man cannot remain in this division—even if his mind could—for this discussion is not merely a matter of remote philosophy; it is the daily repeated problem of the relations of man to himself and to the world. And, because this at bottom is the problem at issue, the division cannot be resolved by a discussion of nominalist and realist arguments. For its solution a third, intermediate standpoint is needed. To the "esse in intellectu" tangible reality is lacking; to the "esse in re" the mind.

Idea and thing come together, however, in the psyche of man, which holds the balance between them. What would the idea amount to if the psyche did not provide its living value? What would the objective thing be worth if the psyche withheld from it the determining force of the sense impression? What indeed is reality if it is not a reality in ourselves, an "esse in anima?" Living reality is the exclusive product neither of the actual, objective behavior of things, nor of the formulated idea; rather does it come through the gathering up of both in the living psychological process, through the "esse in anima." Only through the specific vital activity of the psyche does the sense-perception attain that intensity, and the idea that effective force, which are the two indispensable constituents of living reality. [Jung, 1923, p. 68]

In proposing *esse in anima* as the dialectic integration of *esse in re* and *esse in intellectu*, Jung was at great pains to assert the reality of the internal world of ideas and fantasy, placing it in an equal or perhaps even superior status with the demonstrable reality of the external world. He saw, in his time, that both the church and modern science had fostered attitudes that denied the reality of the inner world in favor of objective, publicly confirmable external events and objects. For the basic dialectic of introversion and extraversion to work, however, internal experience could not merely be reflections of the external world. The assertion of the validity and independent status of internal experiences in the face of the powerful social forces denying them was to become a central mission of Jung's work, reflected in his later inquiries into mysticism, alchemy, and religion for the fundamental symbols or archetypes that constitute what he called the collective unconscious. Jung defined these archetypes as "active living dispositions, ideas in the Platonic sense, that preform and continually influence our thoughts, feelings, and actions" (Read et al. eds., 1961-67, Vol. 8, p. 154). For Jung, the role of personal experience was to actualize the potential that existed in the archetypes born within each and every living individual, inherited in the same way that physical characteristics are. By thus developing and playing our archetypes in personal life experiences, one achieved individuation or self-actualization by realizing one's genetic potential. Personal development was not the result of accumulated life experiences that shaped the personality (the Freudian/behaviorist view), but rather resulted from the interaction of internal subjective archetypical potentials and external circumstance.

I have included original excerpts from Jung here because as successive generations of researchers have explored introversion and extraversion, a kind of conceptual "genetic drift" has taken place, such that Jung's original epistomological concerns and his conception of the dialectic relationship between introversion and extraversion has been lost. Psychometricians have consistently conceived of introversion/extraversion (I/E) as a single dimension in spite of Jung's clear conception of introversion and extraversion as independent entities in dialectic opposition (for example, Eaves and Eysenck, 1975). Most research studies have been unable to demonstrate a single I/E factor, and this has often been considered evidence for doubting the validity of the concept (Carrigan, 1960) rather than as a failure to properly operationalize it. What these studies do show is that at least two independent factors are required to account for the intercorrelations between I/E variables. One factor, emphasizing the strengths of introversion skills, seems to coincide with the common European view of the dimension, with its emphasis on impulsiveness and weak-superego controls in the extravert; the other, emphasizing the positive skills of the extravert, fits the American conception that views extraverts as sociable and comfortable in interpersonal relations. Although both these conceptions reflect meaningful aspects of introversion and extraversion, I prefer to think of them as secondary to the basic epistemological dynamics emphasized by Jung, at least for the present purposes of inquiry about learning.

Another facet of the psychological perspective on the processes of intention and extension is provided by a contemporary of Jung's, Hermann Rorschach. The creator of the famous ink-blot projective test developed a measure of subjects' responses to the test that he called *experience balance*. This measure is the ratio of responses to the test that are judged to be determined by the colors of the ink, divided into those responses that describe movement (for instance, two dancing women). Those persons labeled *extratensive* by Rorschach, with a ratio favoring color, are said to be outwardly oriented, by virtue of their responsiveness to objective reality—color stimuli present in the blots. The perception of movement, on the other hand, has no corresponding external reality, and thus requires an intervening subjective process. Consequently, *intratensive* subjects, with a preponderance of movement responses, are described as having a more active "inner life" and less concern with external, objective reality.

Although Rorschach (1951) denied any relation between his experience balance concept and Jung's extraversion-introversion, the two viewpoints seem to have much in common (compare Bash, 1955). Rorschach's distinction between objective and subjective orientation is the crux of Jung's theory, and descriptions of the two Rorschach "experience types" are remarkably like Jung's characterizations of the extravert and introvert. Moreover, evidence from several studies indicates that some of the empirical differences between extratensive and intratensive subjects correspond to hypothesized or observed differences between extraverts and introverts. Intratensives are more cognitively complex than extratensives (Bieri and Messerley, 1957); they are more imaginative, have more active fantasy lives, and are more capable of motor inhibition (Singer, Wilensky, and McCraven, 1956); they have few doubts "that the self is a reasonably stable basis from which experience may be interpreted" (Palmer, 1956, p. 209; compare Mann, 1956; Singer and Spohn, 1954).

The contemporary work of Jerome Kagan adds further insights into the dynamics of intention and extension. His research on cognitive processes in children has identified a dimension that he calls impulsivity-reflection. This dimension, which he defines as "the degree to which the subject reflects on the validity of his solution hypothesis" (Kagan and Kogan, 1970, p. 1309), is very similar to the European view of introversion in its tendency to emphasize the positive skills of introversion, impulse control, and reflection. Kagan has used several tests to assess this dimension, the most common of which is the Matching Familiar Figures Test. This test asks the child to select one figure from a group of six that is identical with a given standard. Impulsive children tend to make more errors and respond more quickly on this task than do reflective children. Kagan finds that reflection increases with age from 5 to 11 years; that people have fairly stable dispositions toward impulsivity or reflection over time—that is, they maintain their position on this dimension relative to their age mates; and that a given person's tendency to be reflective or impulsive generalizes across different kinds of tasks. Kagan also finds, however, that people modify their orientations as a function of environmental demands; that is, when they are encouraged to take their time and be sure of answers, reflection increases (Kagan and Kogan, 1970). His interpretation of these and other findings suggests that impulsive and reflective people have different underlying motivational dynamics:

> . . . the greater the fear of making a mistake, the more reflective and cautious the performance. Minimal anxiety over a potentially inaccurate answer is likely to be a primary determinant of an impulsive performance. Reflectives seem to be overly concerned with making a mistake and wish to avoid error at all costs. Impulsives seem minimally apprehensive about error and consequently respond quickly. It will be recalled that impulsive subjects did not scan all the alternatives before offering a solution hypothesis and reported words they did not hear in a serial recall procedures. [Kagan and Kogan, 1970, pp. 13-14]

Thus, those with an orientation toward extensional transformation are primarily concerned with maximizing success, with little concern about failure or error; being oriented toward intentional transformation is associated with primary concern about avoiding failure and error and a willingness to sacrifice opportunities for successful performance in order to do so. The differences in these two definitions of successful performance are not only useful for understanding the behavior of children; they also shed light on basic conflicts between intentional and extensional orientations in the adult world. Many of the conflicts between science and government or between professionals and academics have their origin in these differences. The scientist, for example, seeks the best approximation of absolute truth and is socialized to avoid "irresponsible" errors, whereas the politician is perpetually faced with the imperative of action under uncertainty. Here, doing something takes priority over doing what is ideal.

As with the prehension modes of apprehension and comprehension, there is evidence, although more tentative, of physiological bases for the transformation modes of intention and extension. Whereas the control of prehension modes seems to reside primarily in the left and right hemispheres of the neocortex, Bogen (in press) has suggested that transformation processes may be reflected in a front-to-back placement in the brain: "If there is a manipulative (extension) vs. perceptual (intention) gradient in the brain, it is more likely from front to back than from left to right." Other evidence suggests that orientations toward intention and extension are associated with changes in the limbic system, driven primarily by the arousal of parasympathetic and sympathetic nervous systems. The sympathetic nervous system is considered to have a generally mobilizing function in preparation for action and coping with the external world, whereas the parasympathetic nervous system is thought to work toward the person's protection, conservation, and relaxation when dealing with the external world is not required. These two portions of the limbic systems are somewhat independent but frequently are in competition, so that a person's extensional or intentional orientation would be a function of the joint momentary activity of the two systems.

The effect of the activation or inhibition of these two systems on performance and learning is illustrated by Broverman et al.'s (1968) review of the effects of drug-induced arousal or inhibition of these two systems. From their literature review of the effects of drugs on performance, they concluded that those substances that increased the organism's level of activation (extensional orientation), either by stimulating the sympathetic nervous system or by depressing the functioning of the parasympathetic system, result in increased effectiveness in dealing with simple perceptual-motor tasks such as visual acuity or reading and writing speed, but result in poorer performance on more complex perceptual restructuring tasks that require inhibition of action and higher-order thought processes. Those substances that tended to increase the organism's level of inhibition (intentional orientation) by depressing sympathetic nervous system functioning or by stimulating parasympathetic functioning produce the reverse pattern—poorer performance on the simple tasks and improved performance on the complex tasks. This symmetrical but rather complex pattern of results is portrayed in Table 3.1.

Table 3.1 The Effects of Stimulation and Depression of Sympathetic and Parasympathetic Nervous Systems on Simple Perceptual-Motor and Perceptual-Restructuring Task Performances

| | Increased Activation (extensional orientation) | | Increased Inhibition (intentional orientation) | |
	Sympathetic Stimulation	Para-sympathetic Depression	Sympathetic Depression	Para-sympathetic Stimulation
Simple perceptual-motor tasks	Improvement	Improvement	Impairment	Impairment
Perceptual-restructuring tasks	Impairment	Impairment	Improvement	Improvement

Source: Donald Broverman et al., "Roles of Activation and Inhibition in Sex Differences in Cognitive Abilities," *Psychological Review*, 75 (1968), pp. 23–50.

Overall, the evidence suggests that it is not the sympathetic/and/parasympathetic nervous systems alone that determine the individual's orientation toward intentional or extensional transformation of experience, but that these systems are major forces in determining a holistic pattern of psychological and physiological processes governing the person's orientation toward action or reflection. Arthur Diekman has described these two orientations as an action

mode and a receptive mode of consciousness. He describes the components of
these two holistic orientations as follows:

> The action mode is a state organized to manipulate the environment. The
> striate muscle system and the sympathetic nervous system are the dominant
> physiological agencies. The EEG shows beta waves, and baseline muscle tension
> is increased. The principle psychological manifestations of this state are focal
> attention, object-based logic, heightened boundary perception, and the dom-
> inance of formal characteristics over the sensory; shapes and meanings have a
> preference over colors and textures. The action mode is a state of striving,
> oriented toward achieving personal goals that range from nutrition to defense to
> obtaining social rewards, plus a variety of symbolic and sensual pleasures, as well
> as the avoidance of a comparable variety of pain. . . .
> In contrast, the receptive mode is a state organized around intake of the
> environment rather than manipulation. The sensory-perceptual system is the
> dominant agency rather than the muscle system, and parasympathetic functions
> tend to be most prominent. The EEG tends toward alpha waves, and baseline
> muscle tension is decreased. Other attributes of the receptive mode are diffuse
> attending, paralogical thought processes, decreased boundary perception, and
> the dominance of the sensory over the formal. [Diekman, 1971, p. 481]

With Jung, Diekman argues that the action mode has come to dominate
the reflection mode in human society. The obvious survival value of orienting
toward and coping with the external environment tends to overshadow the
values of perception and experiencing, in the receptive mode, an orientation
that tends to be commonly associated with infancy, passivity, and regression.
This domination is particularly prominent in Western technological societies,
whereas Eastern cultures have tended to give more emphasis to the receptive
mode and have developed reflective adaptive skills highly in such disciplines as
yoga and Zen meditation. Certain forms of yoga can develop demonstrable
voluntary control over parasympathetically controlled processes such as
heartbeat and respiration rate. Currently, there is great interest in developing
introverted reflective functioning by using yogic meditative activities and other
Eastern disciplines, such as the martial arts, as well as such Western
technological variations as biofeedback, to cope with the stress and tension
created by the overemphasis on the extraverted action mode and its attendant
arousal of the sympathetic nervous system (for example, Ornstein, 1972).

SUMMARY

This chapter has reported a convergence of evidence from the fields of
philosophy, psychology, and physiology describing two basic structural
dimensions of the learning process. The first is a prehension dimension that
includes two dialectically opposed modes of grasping experience, one via direct
apprehension of immediate concrete experience, the other through indirect
comprehension of symbolic representations of experience. The second is a

transformation dimension, which includes two dialectically opposed modes of transforming experience, one via intentional reflection, the other via extensional action.

Previous thinking has tended to confuse the grasping and transformation dimensions by collapsing them into one dimension. Thus, Jung first saw extraversion as associated with the feeling orientation and introversion with the thinking orientation (Bash, 1955). Only later did his research separate these as independent dimensions. Similarly, Piaget sees the dimension of phenomenalism/constructivism and the operative dimension of egocentricism/reflection as correlated throughout the developmental process, although he does emphasize the differences between the figurative and operative aspects of thought in his structural analysis of cognitive development. Much of the literature on left/right brain functions has, in my own opinion, also confused the grasping dimension with the prehension dimension and as a result attributed to the left and right hemispheres psychological functions that are controlled elsewhere (see Ornstein, 1972; or Diekman, 1971, quoted above). The position taken here is that it is useful to keep these dimensions analytically separate even though in some circumstances they are empirically correlated (such as in successive stages of child development).

In addition, it is important to note that these two basic dimensions are not unitary continua; rather, each represents a dialectic opposition between two independent but mutually enhancing orientations. Apprehension and comprehension are each independent modes of grasping experience. Physiological evidence suggests separate locations of these functions in the right and left cerebral hemispheres and an integrative mechanism in the *corpus callosum.*

Figure 3.5 Escher, *Dag en nacht—Day and night—Tag und Nacht—Jour et nuit*

Similarly, intention and extension are independent modes of transforming experience and appear to be controlled in part by the separate and interrelated parasympathetic and sympathetic nervous systems. Finally, it is maintained that apprehension and comprehension as prehension processes, and intention and extension as transformation processes, are equipotent contributions to the learning process. This is in disagreement with Piaget's view that comprehension and intention are superior processes. This relationship between apprehension and comprehension and between intention and extension is captured (at an admittedly intuitive, apprehension level) by Escher's etching, *Day and Night* (Figure 3.5).

After the description of the basic underlying structures of the experiential learning process, it now remains for us to describe how these structures function in the learning process. In the next chapter, we will examine patterns and vicissitudes in the learning process and the concept of individual learning styles.

four

Individuality
in Learning
and the Concept
of Learning Styles

But the complicated external conditions under which we live, as well as the presumably even more complex conditions of our individual psychic disposition, seldom permit a completely undisturbed flow of our psychic activity. Outer circumstances and inner disposition frequently favor the one mechanism, and restrict or hinder the other; whereby a predominance of one mechanism naturally arises. If this condition becomes in any way chronic, a type is produced, namely an habitual attitude, in which the one mechanism permanently dominates; not, of course, that the other can ever be completely suppressed, inasmuch as it also is an integral factor in psychic activity. Hence, there can never occur a pure type in the sense that he is entirely possessed of the one mechanism with a complete atrophy of the other. A typical attitude always signifies the merely relative predominance of one mechanism. **Carl Jung,** Psychological Types*

The structural model of the learning process described in the last chapter is a complex one, capable of producing a rich variety of learning processes that vary widely in subtlety and complexity. The model gives the basic prehension processes of apprehension and comprehension independent structural status. The same is true for the transformation processes of intention and extension. In addition, apprehension and comprehension as well as intention and extension are dialectically related to one another, such that their synthesis produces higher levels of learning. Thus, the learning process at any given moment in time may be governed by one or all of these processes interacting simultaneously. Over time, control of the learning process may shift from one of these structural bases for learning to another. Thus, the structural model of learning can be likened to a musical instrument and the process of learning to a musical score that depicts a succession and combination of notes played on the instrument over time. The melodies and themes of a single score form distinctive individual patterns that we will call learning styles.

THE SCIENTIFIC STUDY OF INDIVIDUALITY

In this analogy, I am suggesting that the learning process is not identical for all human beings. Rather, it appears that the physiological structures that govern learning allow for the emergence of unique individual adaptive processes that tend to emphasize some adaptive orientations over others. When the matter is viewed from an evolutionary perspective, there appears to be good reason for this variability and individuality in human learning processes.

Human individuality does not just result from random deviations from a single normative blueprint; it is a positive, adaptive adjustment of the human species. If there are evolutionary pressures toward "the survival of the fittest" in the human species, these apply not to individuals but to the human community as a whole. Survival depends not on the evolution of a race of identical supermen but on the emergence of a cooperative human community that cherishes and utilizes individual uniqueness (compare Levy, 1980).

Attempts to understand the nature of human individuality and to describe the essential dimensions along which individuals vary began long before psychology was a recognized field of inquiry. For example, gnostic philosophers of the second century conceived of human variability as occurring along three dimensions: the *pneumatici* (thinking orientation), the *psychici* (feeling orientation), and the *hylici* (sensation orientation). In the eighteenth century, the poet and philosopher Fredrich Schiller divided people into "naive" and sentimental types, paralleling realist and idealist philosophical orientations. In the century that followed, Nietzsche developed the famous Apollonian and Dionysian typology. In 1923, Carl Jung combined these and other approaches to individuality into what must be considered one of the most important books on individual differences ever written, *Psychological Types*. Today, psychology abounds with every type of individual difference measures—in traits, values, motives, attitudes, cognitive styles, and so on (compare Tyler, 1978).

The scientific study of human individuality poses some fundamental dilemmas. The human sciences, unlike the physical sciences, place an equal emphasis on the discovery of general laws that apply to all human beings and on the understanding of the functioning of the individual case. In chemistry, for example, a researcher is apt to discard a sample of a given compound if it does not perform as the general laws of chemistry indicate it should. Impurities or contaminants in the sample are usually seen as irrelevant-error variance to be eliminated. In the human sciences, however, each sample is a human being whose uniqueness and individuality are highly prized, particularly by the person him- or herself. We are interested, therefore, not only in general laws of behavior, but in their specific relevance and application for each individual case.

The basic dilemma for the scientific study of individual differences, therefore, is how to conceive of general laws or categories for describing human individuality that do justice to the full array of human uniqueness.

Theories describing psychological types or personality styles have been much criticized in this regard. Psychological categorizations of people such as those depicted by psychological "types" can too easily become stereotypes that tend to trivialize human complexity and thus end up denying human individuality rather than characterizing it. In addition, type theories often have a static and fixed connotation to their descriptions of individuals, lending a fatalistic view of human change and development. This view often gets translated into a self-fulfilling prophecy, as with the common educational strategy of "tracking" students on the basis of individual differences and thereby perhaps reinforcing those differences. Another problem with type theories is that they tend to become somewhat idealized. Descriptions tend to be cast in the form of "pure" types, with the caveat that no person actually represents a pure type. We are thus left with the problem of describing and attempting to research an ideal profile that does not exist empirically.

These problems with type theories seem to stem from the underlying epistemology on which they are based. Type theories, like many scientific theories, have tended to be based on the epistemological root metaphor of formism (see Chapter 5 for further elaboration of the role of root metaphors in epistemology). In the formist epistemology, forms or types are the ultimate reality, and individual particulars are simply imperfect representations of the universal form or type. Type theories thus easily fall into the problems identified above. An alternative epistemological root metaphor, one that we will use in our approach to understanding human individuality, is that of contextualism. In contextualism, the person is examined in the context of the emerging historical event, in the processes by which both the person and event are shaped. In the contextualist view, reality is constantly being created by the person's experience. As Dewey notes, "an individual is no longer just a particular, a part without meaning save in an inclusive whole, but is a subject, self, a distinctive centre of desire, thinking and aspiration" (1958, p. 216).

The implication of the contextualist world view for the study of human individuality is that psychological types or styles are not fixed *traits* but stable *states*. The stability and the endurance of these states in individuals comes not solely from fixed genetic qualities or characteristics of human beings; nor, for that matter, does it come solely from the stable, fixed demands of environmental circumstances. Rather, stable and enduring patterns of human individuality arise from consistent patterns of transaction between the individual and his or her environment. Leona Tyler calls these patterns of transaction *possibility processing structures*.

We can use the general term possibility processing structures *to cover all of these concepts having to do with the ways in which the person controls the selection of perceptions, activities, and learning situations. Any individual can carry out, simultaneously or successively, only a small fraction of the acts for which his sense organs, nervous system, and muscles equip him. Only a small fraction of the energies constantly bombarding the individual can be responded to. If from moment to moment a person had to be aware of all of these stimulating energies, all of these possible responses, life would be unbearably complicated and confusing. The reason that one can proceed in most situations to act sensibly without having to make hundreds of conscious choices is that one develops organized ways of automatically processing most of the kinds of information encountered. In computer terms, one does what one is "programmed" to do. Much of the programming is the same for all or most of the human race; much is imposed by the structure of particular culture and subcultures. But in addition there are programs unique to individuals, and these are fundamental to psychological individuality (Tyler, 1978, pp. 106-7).*

The concept of possibility-processing structure gives central importance to the role of individual choice in decision making. The way we process the possibilities of each new emerging event determines the range of choices and decisions we see. The choices and decisions we make, to some extent, determine the events we live through, and these events influence our future choices. Thus, people create themselves through their choice of the actual occasions they live through. In Tyler's words, to some degree we write our own "programs." Human individuality results from the pattern or "program" created by our choices and their consequences.

LEARNING STYLES AS POSSIBILITY-PROCESSING STRUCTURES

The complex structure of learning allows for the emergence of individual, unique possibility-processing structures or styles of learning. Through their choices of experience, people program themselves to grasp reality through varying degrees of emphasis on apprehension or comprehension. Similarly, they program themselves to transform these prehensions via extension and/or intention. This self-programming conditioned by experience determines the extent to which the person emphasizes the four modes of the learning process: concrete experience, reflective observation, abstract conceptualization, and active experimentation (see Figures 4.1 and 4.2 for examples).

To illustrate the variety and complexity of the learning process, let us examine in some detail how these processes unfold in the specific situation of playing and learning the game of pool. Pool players, be they novice or expert, use a variety of learning strategies in the course of their play. In some of these strategies, we see very clearly the four basic elemental forms of learning: $A\Delta I$, apprehension transformed by intention; $A\Delta E$, apprehension transformed by extension; $C\Delta I$, comprehension transformed by intention; and $C\Delta E$, comprehension transformed by extension. In addition, we also see higher-order combinations of these basic elemental forms—for example, $A\Delta I\Delta C$, apprehension linked via intentional transformation with comprehension.

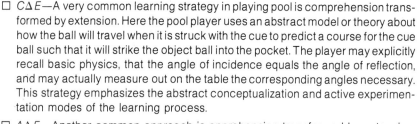

☐ *C∆E*—A very common learning strategy in playing pool is comprehension transformed by extension. Here the pool player uses an abstract model or theory about how the ball will travel when it is struck with the cue to predict a course for the cue ball such that it will strike the object ball into the pocket. The player may explicitly recall basic physics, that the angle of incidence equals the angle of reflection, and may actually measure out on the table the corresponding angles necessary. This strategy emphasizes the abstract conceptualization and active experimentation modes of the learning process.

☐ *A∆E*—Another common approach is apprehension transformed by extension. This learning strategy does not rely on a theoretical model about how the cue ball and object ball will travel, but rather focuses on the concrete position of the balls on the table. The player relies on a global intuitive feel of the situation. In this situation, the player often seems to be making minor adjustments before hitting the ball, with the criteria for these adjustments being not some theoretical calculation but the finding of a position that "feels right." Here, concrete experience and active experimentation are the dominant learning modes used.

☐ *A∆I*—Since pool is an active game, learning through intentional transformations is less obvious. Intentional transformation of apprehensions may take the form of watching one's opponent or partner as he or she shoots, or of reflecting on the course of one's own shots. Here, one learns in fairly concrete ways by modeling or picking up hints from someone else's approach to the game or trying to do again what one did on the last shot. This strategy relies on reflective observation and concrete experience.

☐ *C∆I*—Intentional transformation of comprehensions, on the other hand, is a kind of inductive model-building process relying on abstract conceptualization and reflective observation. For example, one might try to understand the consequences of applying "English" to the ball by compiling and organizing into laws one's observations of the various attempts by oneself and others.

All the learning strategies above taken separately have a certain incompleteness to them. Although one can analytically identify certain learning achievements in each of the four elementary learning modes just described, more powerful and adaptive forms of learning emerge when these strategies are used in combination. For example, if the theory of "English" that I develop through comprehension transformed by intension—*C∆I*—is combined with the empirical testing of hypotheses derived from that theory—*C∆E*—I have developed a way of checking the validity of my inductive process that uses three of the four modes of the learning process: reflective observation, abstract conceptualization and active experimentation (*I∆C∆E*). Similarly, if I combine these hypotheses about the effects of "English" (*C∆E*) with my concrete feel of the situation (*A∆E*), these abstract ideas about how to impart English to the ball will be translated into the appropriate motor and perceptual behavior: I will increase my confidence that my hypotheses about "English" have in fact been adequately tested; that is, I did actually hit the ball the way I had planned to (*C∆E∆A*). Thus, these pairwise combinations of elementary learning strategies that share a common prehension or transformation mode produce a somewhat higher level of learning beyond the elementary forms. This second-order learning includes not only some goal-directed behavior such as deriving a hypothesis from a theory or garnering observations from a specific experience, but also some process for testing out how adequately that goal-directed activity has been carried out. This second-order feedback loop stimulates the development of the learning modality in common between the two elementary learning modes. Thus, in the example just cited, the linking of apprehension and comprehension through extension allows for increasing sophistication in extensional learning skills. When apprehension/extension ($A \Delta E$) is combined with apprehension/intention ($A \Delta I$), a similar result occurs. That is, when I relax and hit the ball ($A \Delta E$) and then watch carefully where it goes ($A \Delta I$), my awareness of the situation becomes more sophisticated and higher-level ($E \Delta A \Delta I$).

The combination of all four of the elementary learning forms produces the highest level of learning, emphasizing and developing all four modes of the learning process. Here, the specialized achievements of the four elementary learning strategies combine in a unified adaptive process. Here our pool player observes the events around him/her ($A \Delta I$), integrates these into theories ($I \Delta C$) from which he or she derives hypotheses, which are then tested out in action ($C \Delta E$), creating new events and experiences ($E \Delta A$). Any new observations are used to modify theories and adjust action, thereby creating an increasingly sophisticated adaptive process that is progressively attuned to the requirement of the game:

$$\Delta \overset{A}{} \Delta$$
$$E \qquad I$$
$$\Delta \underset{C}{} \Delta$$

If you were to analyze your own approach to learning the game of pool or to spend some time observing players at your local pool hall, I suspect you would find that very few people follow this highest level of learning much of the time. Some people just step up and hit the ball without bothering to look very carefully at where their shot went unless it went in the pocket. Others seem to go through a great deal of analysis and measurement but seem a bit hesitant on the execution. Thus there seem to be distinctive styles or strategies for learning and playing the game. Yet even when people have distinctive styles that rely heavily on one of the elementary learning strategies, there are occasions in their learning process when they rely on other of the elementary forms and combine these with their preferred orientation into the second and third orders of learning.

Individual styles of learning are complex and not easily reducible into simple typologies—a point to bear in mind as we attempt to describe general patterns of individuality in learning. Perhaps the greatest contribution of cognitive-style research has been the documentation of the diversity and complexity of cognitive processes and their manifestation in behavior. Three important dimensions of diversity have been identified:

☐ Within any single theoretical dimension of cognitive functioning, it is possible to identify consistent subtypes. For example, it appears that the dimension of cognitive complexity/simplicity can be further divided into at least three distinct subtypes: the tendency to judge events with few variables vs. many; the tendency to make fine vs. gross distinctions on a given dimension; and the tendency to prefer order and structure vs. tolerance of ambiguity (Vannoy, 1965).

☐ Cognitive functioning will vary among people as a function of the area of content it is focused on, the so-called cognitive domain. Thus, a person may be concrete in his interaction with people and abstract in his work (Stabel, 1973), or children will analyze and classify persons differently from nations (Signell, 1966).

☐ Cultural experience plays a major role in the development and expression of cognitive functioning. Lessor (1976) has shown consistent differences in thinking style across different American ethnic groups; Witkin (1976) has shown differences in global and abstract functioning in different cultures; and Bruner et al. (1966) have shown differences in the rate and direction of cognitive development across cultures. Although the evidence is not conclusive, it would appear that these cultural differences in cognition, in Michael Cole's words, "reside more in the situations to which cognitive processes are applied than in the existence of a process in one cultural group and its absence in another" (1971, p. 233). Thus, Cole found that African Kpelle tribesmen were skillful at measuring rice but not at measuring distance. Similarly, Wober (1967) found that Nigerians function more analytically than Americans when measured by a test that emphasizes proprioceptive cues, whereas they were less skilled at visual analysis.

Our investigation of learning styles will begin with an examination of generalized differences in learning orientations based on the degree to which people emphasize the four modes of the learning process as measured by a self-report test called the Learning Style Inventory. From these investigations we will draw a clearer picture of the programs or patterns of behavior that characterize the four elementary forms of learning. With these patterns as a rough map of the terrain of individuality in learning, the next chapter will examine the relationships among these styles of learning and the structure of knowledge. Chapter 6 will consider the higher levels of learning and the relation between learning and development.

ASSESSING INDIVIDUAL LEARNING STYLES: THE LEARNING STYLE INVENTORY

To assess individual orientations toward learning, the Learning Style Inventory (LSI) was created. The development of this instrument was guided by four design objectives: First, the test should be constructed in such a way that people would respond to it in somewhat the same way as they would a learning situation; that is, it should require one to resolve the opposing tensions between abstract-concrete and active-reflective orientations. In technical testing terms, we were seeking a test that was both *normative,* allowing comparisons between individuals in their relative emphasis on a given learning mode such as abstract conceptualization, and *ipsative,* allowing comparisons within individuals on their relative emphasis on the four learning modes—for instance, whether they emphasized abstract conceptualization more than the other three learning modes in their individual approach to learning.

Second, a self-description format was chosen for the inventory, since the notion of possibility-processing structure relies heavily on conscious choice and decision. It was felt that self-image descriptions might be more powerful determinants of behavioral choices and decisions than would performance tests. Third, the inventory was constructed with the hope that it would prove to be valid—that the measures of learning styles would predict behavior in a way that was consistent with the theory of experiential learning. A final consideration was a practical one. The test should be brief and straightforward, so that in addition to research uses, it could be used as a means of discussing the learning process with those tested and giving them feedback on their own learning styles.

The final form of the test is a nine-item self-description questionnaire. Each item asks the respondent to rank-order four words in a way that best describes his or her learning style. One word in each item corresponds to one of the four learning modes—concrete experience (sample word, *feeling*), reflective observation (*watching*), abstract conceptualization (*thinking*), and active experimentation (*doing*). The LSI measures a person's relative emphasis on each of the four modes of the learning process—concrete experience *(CE)*, reflective observation *(RO)*, abstract conceptualization *(AC)*, and active experimentation *(AE)*—plus two combination scores that indicate the extent to which the person emphasizes abstractness over concreteness *(AC-CE)* and the extent to which the person emphasizes action over reflection *(AE-RO)*. The four basic learning modes are defined as follows:

☐ An orientation toward *concrete experience* focuses on being involved in experiences and dealing with immediate human situations in a personal way. It emphasizes feeling as opposed to thinking; a concern with the uniqueness and complexity of present reality as opposed to theories and generalizations; an intuitive, "artistic" approach as opposed to the systematic, scientific approach to problems. People with concrete-experience orientation enjoy and are good at relating to others. They are often good intuitive decision makers and function well in unstructured situations. The person with this orientation values relating to people and being involved in real situations, and has an open-minded approach to life.

☐ An orientation toward *reflective observation* focuses on understanding the meaning of ideas and situations by carefully observing and impartially describing them. It emphasizes understanding as opposed to practical application; a concern with what is true or how things happen as opposed to what will work; an emphasis on reflection as opposed to action. People with a reflective orientation enjoy intuiting the meaning of situations and ideas and are good at seeing their implications. They are good at looking at things from different perspectives and at appreciating different points of view. They like to rely on their own thoughts and feelings to form opinions. People with this orientation value patience, impartiality, and considered, thoughtful judgment.

☐ An orientation toward *abstract conceptualization* focuses on using logic, ideas, and concepts. It emphasizes thinking as opposed to feeling; a concern with building general theories as opposed to intuitively understanding unique, specific areas; a scientific as opposed to an artistic approach to problems. A person with an abstract-conceptual orientation enjoys and is good at systematic planning, manipulation of abstract symbols, and quantitative analysis. People with this orientation value precision, the rigor and discipline of analyzing ideas, and the aesthetic quality of a neat conceptual system.

☐ An orientation toward *active experimentation* focuses on actively influencing people and changing situations. It emphasizes practical applications as opposed to reflective understanding; a pragmatic concern with what works as opposed to what is absolute truth; an emphasis on doing as opposed to observing. People with an active-experimentation orientation enjoy and are good at getting things accomplished. They are willing to take some risk in order to achieve their objectives. They also value having an influence on the environment around them and like to see results.

Norms for scores on the LSI were developed from a sample of 1,933 men and women ranging in age from 18 to 60 and representing a wide variety of occupations. These norms, along with reliability and validity data for the LSI, are reported in detail elsewhere (Kolb, 1976, 1981). The following sample LSI profiles are included along with the respondents' self-descriptions to illustrate the kind of self-assessment information generated by the inventory. The first profile is that of a 20-year-old female social worker currently completing a graduate degree in social work. Her high scores on concrete experience and active experimentation are evident not only in the content of the following excerpts from her self-analysis but also in the way the analysis is written, with its strong feeling tone:

> The Learning Style exercise and assignment had a tremendous effect on me, forcing me to take stock of my standard learning and problem solving pattern. And, obviously, these patterns more or less represent my general life patterns and attitudes. In the past, I have noted my methods of handling specific problems, but the assignment really pulled it all together, which was more than a little terrifying. . . . [She describes her recent experience in choosing an apartment.]
>
> Those are the specifics. I can recall many other examples where my learning and problem solving style was exactly the same. In fact, I'm writing this paper right now, twenty minutes after class, as a direct result of my poor score on the paper just returned to me. If I sat and analyzed what it meant to receive a poor mark, I would become too upset. I had to do something about it, to fix it, so I immediately went home and sat down to write a good paper to prove I could do better.
>
> The general process is clear: When I first become emotionally concerned with a problem, the only way I can see to relieve the worry is to jump into action, "solving" the problem as quickly as possible. It's too hard, too hurting, to sit and

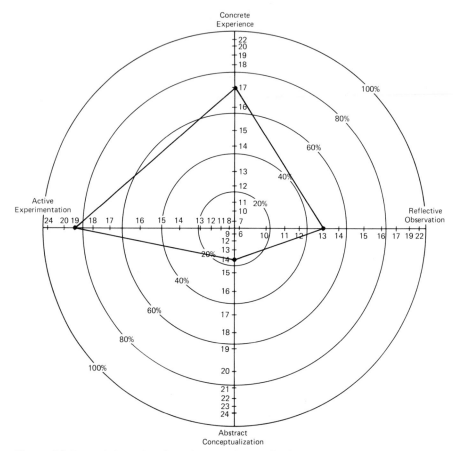

Figure 4.1 Example Learning-Style Profile—Female Social Worker

think and analyze. When a problem touches me on a gut level, be it a love affair or a beautiful pair of shoes in a store window, I jump to concrete action; I accommodate.

During the aforementioned apartment search, as during most of my escapades, a little voice in the back of my head knew what was going on and warned and cautioned me. Yet I proceeded just the same. It's as if my process is compulsive and inevitable; I feel it to be almost beyond any conscious control on my part.

I realize that my problem solving process is not 100% destructive. My instincts are often very good, and I'm just as likely to make the right decision as not, based on my experience. In fact, this same compulsive need to act has led me into many beautiful and exciting adventures which I wouldn't have missed for the world. What frightens me is my apparent inability to try out other problem solving techniques.

My accommodator style [see below, under "Characteristics of the Basic Learning Styles"] most concerns me in the context of professional situations.

When working with a client, I tend to promote and encourage action choices or solutions before we have fully analyzed the problem at hand; it breaks my heart to see a client suffer, so I want to relieve his or her pain with the same medicine I use on myself. I am always trying to slow down, to check and double check, to consider a wide range of options. But on the other hand, my action instincts have many times procured immediate vital services for a client, while my more reflective colleagues were still putzing around on paper.

I'm also concerned about the effect of this style on my life plans. I've jumped from major to major in college, and recently from career to career, without much careful, consistent reflection and analysis. Again, the benefits are a variety of rich experiences at a relatively young age; I have never felt stagnant or bored. The consequences are that, up to now, I've never allowed myself to realize potential in any field. I am presently trying very hard to break that pattern. I am focusing in, to the best of my ability, on social work, both academic and practical. I'm attempting to discover the joys of thoroughness. It's not easy. I'm tempted to jump around like a little flea. . . .

The process of sorting my thoughts for this paper has meant a great deal to me. It took me an hour to sort it out. That may not be much for most people, but a concentrated hour of attempting to calmly and reflectively sort my thoughts represents a minor miracle for me! And I must admit that it feels good.

The second example is a very different one. It is from a 32-year-old M.B.A. student. This man's high scores on abstract conceptualization and reflective observation are reflected in a self-interpretation report that is more formal and academic in its tone. In addition, he describes his difficulties in valuing and learning from the experiential learning approach taken in the organization behavior course where he completed the LSI. In a rather dramatic way, this case demonstrates the powerful effect that learning styles can have on the learning process and at the same time reminds us that experiential learning techniques per se are not preferred by everyone:

"They, assimilators [see below], are often frustrated and benefit little from unstructured 'discover' learning approaches such as exercises and simulations." Falling onto the extreme edge of the assimilator category, I, too, have experienced frustration with the experiential learning approach and much of the content of the course to date. This first conceptual paper will briefly describe my learning style, recount some of my experiences in the course, relate my feelings, present my intellectual reactions to those experiences and feelings, and outline my expected future course of action.

Since the learning process is a dynamic, circular one of building on past experience and learning, some description of my background is needed to understand my learning style preference. The Learning Styles Inventory very clearly identified my assimilator predisposition. Both concrete experience and active experimentation scores were inside the twentieth percentile circle. Reflective observation was in the middle range, while abstract conceptualization fell on the outer circle. This result corresponds well with my formal educational and professional experience. Typically, both mathematicians and economists are assimilators, drawing on theoretical models to describe reality. My degrees in

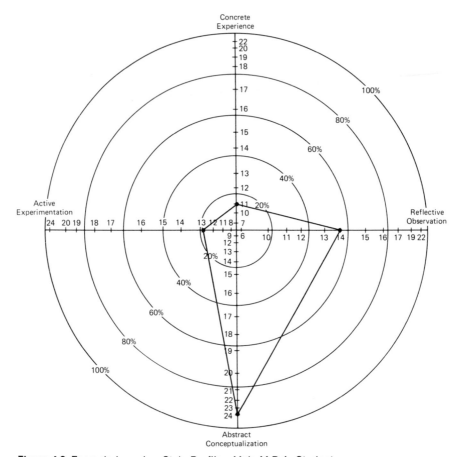

Figure 4.2 Example Learning-Style Profile—Male M.B.A. Student

these areas reflect my strength in and affinity for that style of learning. Kolb reports that members of the research and planning departments of organizations tend to be the most assimilative group. Prior to entering the M.B.A. program, I had spent two years in such a capacity, leaving _____ college as Associate Director of Institutional Research and Planning.

    Entering the organizational behavior class, I anticipated difficulty, but did not anticipate the wholesale assault on my value system which I encountered. Detailing those incidents and my reactions comprises the body of this essay. Prior to describing concrete situations, I need to present my definition of concrete and active as they apply to learning. Basically, I propose to generalize from the physical definitions to include those activities of the mind which are active and concrete, rather than passive and imprecise. For example, much of the active part of active listening is a mental, rather than a physical activity. Similarly, for me, active participation in a novel, textbook, or journal article is more "active" than engaging in typical sporting activities. To view my learning as balanced, *rather than ivory-towerish, one must surmount what economists term the "fallacy of misplaced concreteness." Cerebral as well as sensual participation in life can be concrete and active.*

Experiences with classmates, instructors, and the texts have all contributed to my feelings of isolation, defensiveness, and frustration. During my group's first discussion session I expressed my distaste for experiential learning. I noted that it seemed to be the opposite of normal science or education, where the goal of furthering man's knowledge required building upon the work and achievements of others, rather than egocentrically assuming that individuals would be able to replicate past acts of genius. I was motivated to get my views on the table so that future discussion on my part would be understood in the proper light. Unwittingly, I was combatting what Argyris terms "double loop learning." I was immediately questioning the rules of the game by putting my views forward.

Reaction by some other members of the group was swift and harsh. Replies such as, "You can't learn anything from books," and "Books are irrelevant to business, you learn by doing," shocked me. Coming from an institution (_____ College) where life revolved almost entirely around intellectual activities, I was surprised to find that students at an apparently similar school possessed anti-intellectual attitudes.

Our group leader reported this discussion as, "One of our members said that he preferred passive learning, had gone to a school where experiential learning was used, and did not like it." The whole group's reaction was surprise. I felt embarrassed and misunderstood, wanted to defend my views and straighten out the group leader. Feelings of isolation and serious questioning of my reasons for being in business school followed that session.

During the second group session, a number of our group members discussed the Learning Styles Inventory. One member questioned the validity of the measurement and what it really measured. I presented my views on inductive versus deductive reasoning and the difficulty of constructing an index which is unidimensional. One group member remarked, "I never know what he's talking about," leading to snickers from the group. Score crushed ego and feelings a third time.

The physical placement of students on the Learning Styles Inventory grid in the lounge further confirmed my feelings of isolation. From my perspective, four students were extreme assimilators, eight others were assimilators near the center, ten were convergers, twelve were divergers, and twenty were accommodators. The four members of our group discussed the advantages and disadvantages of assimilation as a learning style, questioned the realism of our goals in management vis-à-vis our learning orientation, and related the LSI to our majors and computer programming. I felt a sense of community and cohesion forming in the group. In particular, a lawyer and I confirmed our commonality of vision.

This activity did result in constructive reflection on my part. It appears to me that people under stress or feeling isolated seek others with similar feelings for security. In addition, the experience spurred me to look in the reader for more information. The last article presented findings on the distribution of academics majors on the LSI grid which satisfied some of my curiousity about the applicability of the inventory. . . .

EVIDENCE FOR THE STRUCTURE OF LEARNING

The structural model of learning developed in the preceding chapter postulates two fundamental dimensions of the learning process, each describing basic adaptive processes standing in dialectical opposition. The prehension dimension opposes the process of apprehension and an orientation toward concrete experience against the comprehension process and an orientation toward abstract conceptualization. The transformation dimension opposes the process of intention and reflective observation against the process of extension and active experimentation. We have emphasized that these dimensions are not unitary theoretically, such that a high score on one orientation would automatically imply a low score on its opposite, but rather that they are dialectically opposed, implying that a higher-order synthesis of opposing orientations makes highly developed strengths in opposing orientations possible. If this reasoning is applied to scores on the Learning Style Inventory, we would predict a moderate (but not perfect) negative relation between abstract conceptualization and concrete experience and a similar negative relation between active experimentation and reflective observation. Other correlations should be near zero. Intercorrelations of the scale scores for a sample of 807 people shows this to be the case (see Kolb, 1976, for details). CE and AC were negatively correlated ($-.57$, $p < .001$). RO and AE were negatively correlated ($-.50$, $p < .001$). Other correlations were low but significant because of the large sample size (CE) with $RO = .13$, RO with $AC = -.19$, AC with $AE = -.12$, and AE with $CE = -.02$). All but the last are significant ($p < .001$). As a result of the intercorrelations, we felt justified in creating two combination scores to measure the abstract/concrete dimension (AE-CE) and active/reflective dimension (AE-RO). With the abstract/concrete dimension, CE correlated $-.85$ and AC correlated $.90$. With the active/reflective dimension, AE correlated $.85$ and RO correlated $-.84$. Subsequent studies with more limited and specialized populations have shown patterns of correlation similar to those described above. One longitudinal study of changes in learning style during college examined the relationship between the Learning Style Inventory and commonly used instruments designed to measure cognitive development according to Piaget, Kohlberg, Loevinger and Perry theoretical descriptions of growth. Analyses of the interrelationships of college student performance on these measures found that the concrete/abstract dimension correlated with these measures. The reflective/active dimension did not. For these college students, dimensions of learning and development designed to tap cognitive growth do not reflect movement on the reflective/active dimension. The latter dimension also does not correlate with age at entrance to college for younger or older students, which supports the idea that the two dimensions are independent (Mentkowski and Strait, 1983).

    A more rigorous test of these hypothesized relationships requires controlling for the built-in negative correlations in the LSI caused by the forced-ranking procedure and validation of the scales against external criteria. It is possible to control for the "bias" introduced by the forced-choice format of the LSI by using data from a study by Certo and Lamb (1979), who generated 1,000 random responses to the LSI instrument and intercorrelated the resulting scale scores. The resulting correlations measure the magnitude of the inbuilt negative correlations in the LSI. If these correlations are used as the null hypothesis instead of the traditional zero point to test for significance of difference, the hypothesized negative relationships between AC and CE and between AE and RO can be tested with the forced-ranking effect partialed out. Thus, when Certo and Lamb's random correlations are compared to the empirical correlations obtained from 807 subjects using the formula provided by McNemar (1957, p. 148), both the AC/CE correlations and AE/RO correlations are significantly *more* negative than the random correlations (random $AC/CE = -.26$, empirical $= -.57$, p of difference $< .001$; random $AE/RO = -.35$, empirical $= -.50$, p of difference $< .001$).

External validation of these negative relationships comes from a recent study by Gypen (1980). He correlated ratings by professional social workers and engineers of the extent to which they were oriented toward each of the four learning modes in their current job with their LSI scores obtained four to six months earlier. Each mode was rated separately on a seven-point scale describing the learning mode in a way that attempted to minimize social-desirability bias. Table 4.1 shows the correlations between the subjects' LSI

Table 4.1 Pearson Correlation Coefficients Between the Learning Style Inventory Scales and Ratings of Learning Orientations at Work *(N = 58)*

| LSI Scales | Learning Orientation on Current Job | | | |
	Concrete Experience	Reflective Observation	Abstract Conceptualization	Active Experimentation
Concrete Experience *(CE)*	.49 p < .001	−.17 n.s.	−.37 p < .01	.08 n.s.
Reflective Observation *(RO)*	.03 n.s.	.22 p < .05	.12 n.s.	−.34 p < .01
Abstract Conceptualization *(AC)*	−.30 p < .05	−.04 n.s.	.27 p < .05	−.09 n.s.
Active Experimentation *(AE)*	.01 n.s.	−.09 n.s.	−.06 n.s.	.37 p < .01
Abstract-Concrete *(AC-CE)*	−.42 p < .001	.06 n.s.	.36 p < .003	−.07 n.s.
Active-Reflective *(AE-RO)*	−.02 n.s.	−.18 p < .08	−.07 n.s.	.43 p < .001

scores and self-ratings of their current job orientation. These results provide strong support for the negative relation between concrete experience and abstract conceptualization, and somewhat weaker support for the negative relation between active experimentation and reflective observation. The Gypen study and the "corrected" internal correlations among LSI scales both demonstrate empirical support for the bipolar nature of the experiential learning model that is independent of the forced-ranking method used in the LSI.

Although these data do not prove validity of the structural learning model, they do suggest an analytic heuristic for exploring with the LSI the characteristics of the four elemental forms of knowing proposed by the model (see Figure 3.1). If for purposes of analysis we treat the abstract-concrete (AC-CE) and active-reflective (AE-RO) dimensions as negatively related in a unidimensional sense, it is possible to create a two-dimensional map of learning space that can be used to empirically characterize differences in the four elementary forms of knowing: convergence, divergence, assimilation, and accommodation. In so doing, I will save the third dimension for depicting in Chapter 6 the process of development and higher forms of knowing achieved through the dialectic synthesis of action/reflection and abstract/concrete orientations.

Since the AC and CE scales and AE and RO scales are not perfectly negatively correlated, two other types of LSI scores do in fact occur occasionally: those that are highest on AC and CE, and those that are highest on AE and RO. These so-called "mixed" types of people, on the basis of what fragmentary evidence we have, seem to be those who rely on the second- and third-order levels of learning. Thus, through integrative learning experiences, these people have developed styles that emphasize the dialectically opposed orientations. Some support for this argument comes from Rita Weathersby's study of adult learners at Goddard College (1977). The important point, however, is that the LSI measures differences only in the elementary knowledge orientations, since the forced-ranking format of the inventory precludes integrative responses.

CHARACTERISTICS OF THE BASIC LEARNING STYLES

In using the analytic heuristic of a two-dimensional-learning-style map, it is proposed that a major source of pattern and coherence in individual styles of learning is the underlying structure of the learning process. Over time, individuals develop unique possibility-processing structures such that the dialectic tensions between the prehension and transformation dimensions are consistently resolved in a characteristic fashion. As a result of our hereditary equipment, our particular past life experience, and the demands of our present environment, most people develop learning styles that emphasize some learning abilities over others. Through socialization experiences in family, school, and work, we come to resolve the conflicts between being active and reflective and between being immediate and analytical in characteristic ways, thus lending to reliance on one of the four basic forms of knowing: *divergence*, achieved by reliance on apprehension transformed by intention; *assimilation*, achieved by comprehension transformed by intention; *convergence*, achieved through extensive transformation of comprehension; and *accommodation*, achieved through extensive transformation of apprehension.

Some people develop minds that excel at assimilating disparate facts into coherent theories, yet these same people are incapable of or uninterested in deducing hypotheses from the theory. Others are logical geniuses but find it impossible to involve and surrender themselves to an experience. And so on. A mathematician may come to place great emphasis on abstract concepts, whereas a poet may value concrete experience more highly. A manager may be primarily concerned with the active application of ideas, whereas a naturalist may develop his observational skills highly. Each of us in a unique way develops a learning style that has some weak and some strong points. Evidence for the existence of such consistent unique learning styles can be found in the research of Kagan and Witkin (Kagan and Kogan, 1970). They find, in support of Piaget, that there is a general tendency to become more analytic and reflective with age, *but* that individual rankings within the population tested remain highly stable from early years to adulthood. Similar results have been found for measures of introversion/extraversion. Several longitudinal studies have shown introversion/extraversion to be one of the most stable characteristics of personality from childhood to old age. Although there is a general tendency toward introversion in old age, studies show that people tend to retain their relative ranking throughout their life span (Rubin, 1981). Thus, they seem to develop consistent stable learning or cognitive styles relative to their age mates. The following is a description of the characteristics of the four basic learning styles based on both research and clinical observation of these patterns of LSI scores.

☐ The *convergent* learning style relies primarily on the dominant learning abilities of abstract conceptualization and active experimentation. The greatest strength of this approach lies in problem solving, decision making, and the practical application of ideas. We have called this learning style the *converger* because a person with this style seems to do best in situations like conventional intelligence tests, where there is a single correct answer or solution to a question or problem (Torrealba, 1972; Kolb, 1976). In this learning style, knowledge is organized in such a way that through hypothetical-deductive reasoning, it can be focused on specific problems. Liam Hudson's (1966) research on those with this style of learning (using other measures than the LSI) shows that convergent people are controlled in their expression of emotion. They prefer dealing with technical tasks and problems rather than social and interpersonal issues.

☐ The *divergent* learning style has the opposite learning strengths from convergence, emphasizing concrete experience and reflective observation. The greatest strength of this orientation lies in imaginative ability and awareness of meaning and values. The primary adaptive ability of divergence is to view concrete situations from many perspectives and to organize many relationships into a meaningful "gestalt." The emphasis in this orientation is on adaptation by observation rather than action. This style is called *diverger* because a person of this type performs better in situations that call for generation of alternative ideas and implications, such as a "brainstorming" idea session. Those oriented toward divergence are interested in people and tend to be imaginative and feeling-oriented.

☐ In *assimilation,* the dominant learning abilities are abstract conceptualization and reflective observation. The greatest strength of this orientation lies in inductive reasoning and the ability to create theoretical models, in assimilating disparate observations into an integrated explanation (Grochow, 1973). As in convergence, this orientation is less focused on people and more concerned with ideas and abstract concepts. Ideas, however, are judged less in this orientation by their practical value. Here, it is more important that the theory be logically sound and precise.

☐ The *accommodative* learning style has the opposite strengths from assimilation, emphasizing concrete experience and active experimentation. The greatest strength of this orientation lies in doing things, in carrying out plans and tasks and getting involved in new experiences. The adaptive emphasis of this orientation is on opportunity seeking, risk taking, and action. This style is called *accommodation* because it is best suited for those situations where one must adapt oneself to changing immediate circumstances. In situations where the theory or plans do not fit the facts, those with an accommodative style will most likely discard the plan or theory. (With the opposite learning style, assimilation, one would be more likely to disregard or reexamine the facts.) People with an accommodative orientation tend to solve problems in an intuitive trial-and-error manner (Grochow, 1973), relying heavily on other people for information rather than on their own analytic ability (Stabell, 1973). Those with accommodative learning styles are at ease with people but are sometimes seen as impatient and "pushy."

The patterns of behavior associated with these four learning styles are shown consistently at various levels of behavior, from personality type to specific task-oriented skills and behaviors. We will examine these patterns at five such levels: (1) Jungian personality type, (2) early educational specialization, (3) professional career, (4) current job, and (5) adaptive competencies.

Personality Type and Learning Style

We have already acknowledged and examined to some extent the indebtedness of experiential learning theory to Jung's theory of psychological types. Now we examine more specifically the relations between Jung's types and the four basic learning styles. In his theory of psychological types, Jung developed a holistic framework for describing differences in human adaptive processes. He began by distinguishing between those people who are oriented toward the external world and those oriented toward the internal world—the distinction between extravert and introvert examined in the last chapter. He then proceeded to identify four basic functions of human adaptation—two describing alternative ways of perceiving, sensation and intuition; and two that describe alternative ways of making judgments about the world, thinking and feeling. In his view, human individuality develops through transactions with the social environment that reward and develop one function over another. He saw that this specialized adaptation is in service of society's need for specialized skills to meet the differentiated, specialized role demands required for the survival of and development of culture. Jung saw a basic conflict between the specialized psychological orientations required for the development of society and the need for people to develop and express all the psychological functions for their own individual fulfillment. His concept of individuation describes the process whereby people achieve personal integrity through the development and reassertion of the nonexpressed and nondominant functions integrating them with their dominant specialized orientation into a fluid, holistic adaptive process. He describes the conflict between specialized types and individual development in this way:

> The natural, instinctive course, like everything in nature, follows the principle of least resistance. One man is rather more gifted here, another there; or, again, adaptation to the early environment of childhood may demand either relatively more restraint and reflection or relatively more sympathy and participation, according to the nature of the parents and other circumstances. Thereby a certain preferential attitude is automatically moulded, which results in different types. Insofar then as every man, as a relatively stable being, possesses all the basic psychological functions, it would be a psychological necessity with a view to perfect adaptation that he should also employ them in equal measure. For there must be a reason why there are different ways of psychological adaptation: Evidently one alone is not sufficient, since the object seems to be only partially comprehended when, for example, it is either merely thought or merely felt. Through a one-sided (typical) attitude there remains a deficit in the resulting psychological adaptation, which accumulates during the course of life; from this deficiency a derangement of adaptation develops, which forces the subject towards a compensation. [Jung, 1923, p.28]

Thus, his conception of types or styles is identical to that proposed here—a basic but incomplete form of adaptation with the potential for development via integration with other basic types into a fluid, holistic adaptive process.

Jung's typology of psychological types includes four such pairs of dialectically opposed adaptive orientations, describing individuals' (1) mode of relation to the world via introversion or extroversion, (2) mode of decision making via perception or judgement, (3) preferred way of perceiving via sensing or intuition, and (4) preferred way of judging via thinking or feeling. These opposing orientations are described in Table 4.2.

As was indicated in the preceding chapter, there is a correspondence between the Jungian concepts of introversion and the experiential learning mode of reflective observation via intentional transformation, and between

Table 4.2 Jung's Psychological Types

Mode of relation to the world	E EXTROVERT TYPE Oriented toward external world of other people and things	I INTROVERT TYPE Oriented toward inner world of ideas and feelings
Mode of decision making	J JUDGING TYPE Emphasis on order through reaching decision and resolving issues	P PERCEIVING TYPE Emphasis on gathering information and obtaining as much data as possible
Mode of perceiving	S SENSING TYPE Emphasis on sense perception, on facts, details, and concrete events	N INTUITION TYPE Emphasis on possibilities, imagination, meaning, and seeing things as a whole
Mode of judging	T THINKING TYPE Emphasis on analysis, using logic and rationality	F FEELING TYPE Emphasis on human values, establishing personal friendships, decisions made mainly on beliefs and likes

extraversion and active experimentation via extension. In addition, concrete experience and the apprehension process are clearly associated with both the sensing approach to perception and the feeling approach to judging. Abstract conceptualization and the comprehension process, on the other hand, are related to the intuition approach to perceiving and the thinking approach to judging. Predictions about perception and judgment types are difficult to make, since this preference is a second-order one; for instance, if I prefer perception, I could perform it via sensing or intuition. Myers-Briggs states, "In practice the JP preference is a by-product of the choice as to which process, of the two liked best (N over S or T over F), shall govern one's life" (1962, p. 59).

The Myers-Briggs Type Indicator (MBTI) is a widely used psychological self-report instrument used to assess people's orientation toward the Jungian types (Myers, 1962). Correlations between individuals' scores on the MBTI and the LSI should give some empirical indication of validity of relationships between Jung's personality types and the learning styles proposed above. Some caution in using such data is appropriate, however. First, both the LSI and the MBTI instruments are based on self-analysis and report. Thus, we are testing whether those who take the two tests agree with our predictions of the similarity between Jung's concepts and those of experiential learning theory; we are not testing, except by inference, their actual behavior. Second, it is not clear how adequately the MBTI reflects Jung's theory. In particular, the items in the MBTI introversion/extraversion scale seem to be heavily weighted in favor of the American conception of the dimension mentioned earlier—extraversion as social and interpersonal ease, and introversion as shyness and social awkwardness.

Table 4.3 reports data from three studies by different investigators of three populations: Kent State undergraduates (Taylor, 1973), University of Wisconsin M.B.A.s (Wynne, 1975), and education administrators (McBer and Company, personal communication). The data in Table 4.3 tend to support our hypotheses, but not consistently in all groups: The strongest and most consistent relationships appear to be between concrete/abstract and feeling/ thinking and between active/reflective and extravert/introvert.

In a more systematic study of 220 managers and M.B.A. students, Margerison and Lewis (1979) investigated the relations between LSI and MBTI scores using the technique of canonical correlation. They found a significant canonical correlation of .45 ($p < .01$) between the two sets of test scores. When the resulting pattern of psychological types is plotted on the two-dimensional LSI learning-space, relationships between the Jungian types and learning styles become clear and consistent with our predictions (see Figure 4.3). The sensing type is associated with the accommodative learning style, and the intuitive type

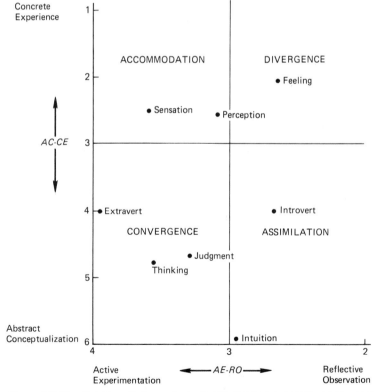

Figure 4.3 The Relations Between Learning Styles and Jung's Psychological Types [*Source:* Adapted from C.J. Margerison and R.G. Lewis, *How Work Preferences Relate to Learning Styles* (Bedfordshire, England: Cranfield School of Management, 1979)]

Table 4.3 Correlations Between Learning Style Inventory Scores and The Myers-Briggs Type Indicator

		Learning Style Inventory Scores					
Group	n	CE	RO	AC	AE	AC-CE	AE-RO
MYERS-BRIGGS TYPE INDICATOR[a]							
Extraversion/Introversion							
Kent State undergrads	135	.06	.06	.03	$-.18^c$	-.01	-.13
U. of Wisc. M.B.A.s	74	.08	$.34^d$	.03	$-.27^c$	—	—
Sensation/Intuition							
Undergrads	135	$-.25^d$	-.07	$.23^d$	$-.20^c$	$.29^d$	.09
M.B.A.s	74	-.02	-.15	.19	-.12	—	—
Thinking/Feeling							
Undergrads	135	$.34^d$	-.02	$-.25^d$	.05	$-.35^d$	.04
M.B.A.s	74	.08	-.17	.00	-.01	—	—
Judging/Perceiving							
Undergrads	135	-.06	.11	-.11	-.13	-.02	-.16
M.B.A.s	74	.01	-.12	.06	-.05	—	—
MYERS-BRIGGS TYPE INDICATOR[b]							
Extraversion administr.	46	-.13	-.27	.28	—	.25	-.16
Introversion administr.	46	.18	$.36^c$	$-.35^c$	—	-.20	$-.33^c$
Sensation administr.	46	—	.12	-.26	-.11	-.19	-.13
Intuition administr.	46	$-.31^c$	—	.20	—	.14	—
Thinking administr.	46	$.39^d$	—	.22	-.16	$.30^c$	-.16
Feeling administr.	46	-.22	—	$-.34^c$	.12	$-.42^d$	.11
Judging administr.	46	.19	—	—	—	.14	—
Perceiving administr.	46						

[a] High scores on MBTI variables indicate that the mode listed second is dominant (e.g., a high score on thinking/feeling indicates the dominance of feeling orientation). Missing correlations are due to missing data.

[b] Scores on these MBTI variables are limited to the single modes and are not comparable to paired modes. Missing correlations are due to missing data.

[c] $p < .05$

[d] $p < .01$, 2-tailed test

Data sources: Kent State; Taylor, 1973; U. of Wisc., Wynne, 1976; education administrators, McBer and Company personal communication.

falls in the assimilative quadrant; the feeling personality type is divergent in learning style, and thinking types are convergent.

Regarding introversion and extraversion, Margerison and Lewis conclude:

> It is clear that extroverts describe themselves as very active in learning situations. This is to be expected, in that extroverts use their energy to go out into their environment and enjoy contact with people and things. In contrast, introverts are far more reflective as would be expected. However, it is noticeable that both extroverts and introverts prefer involvement in learning situations which are neither excessively detached nor concrete. Clearly, while there is a fair degree of variance, the evidence from our sample illustrates that there is little difference between introverts and extroverts overall in this aspect. The real difference is in their emphasis on a preference for active as against reflective types of role. [Margerison and Lewis, 1979, p. 13]

They also find judgment related to the abstract-conceptualization mode and perception related to concrete experience, but unrelated to action or reflection.

Taken together, these studies suggest that the Jungian personality type associated with the accommodative learning style is extraverted sensing.[1] This personality type as described by Myers is remarkably similar to our description of the accommodative learning orientation:

> This combination makes the adaptable realist, who good-naturedly accepts and uses the facts around him, whatever they are. He knows what they are, since he notices and remembers more than any other type. He knows what goes on, who wants what, who doesn't, and usually why. And he does not fight those facts. There is a sort of effortless economy in the way he goes at a situation, never uselessly bucking the line.
>
> Often he can get other people to adapt, too. Being a perceptive type, he looks for the satisfying solution, instead of trying to impose any "should" or "must" of his own, and people generally like him well enough to consider any compromise that he thinks "might work." He is unprejudiced, open-minded, and usually patient, easygoing and tolerant of everyone (including himself). He enjoys life. He doesn't get wrought up. Thus he may be very good at easing a tense situation and pulling conflicting factions together. . . .
>
> Being a realist, he gets far more from first-hand experience than from books, is more effective on the job than on written tests, and is doubly effective when he is on familiar ground. Seeing the value of new ideas, theories and possibilities may well come a bit hard, because intuition is his least developed process. [Myers, 1962, pp. A5]

The divergent learning style is associated with the personality type having introversion and feeling as the dominant process. Here again, Myers's description of this type fits ours:

[1] The procedure for determining types and dominant and auxiliary processes is complicated (see Myers, 1962, pp. 51-62 and Appendix A1-A8). Basically, the choice of introversion or extraversion plus the choice of a single perceiving or judgment mode determines a dominant process.

An introverted feeling type has as much wealth of feeling as an extraverted feeling type, but uses it differently. He cares more deeply about fewer things. He has his warm side inside (like a fur-lined coat). It is quite as warm but not as obvious; it may hardly show till you get past his reserve. He has, too, a great faithfulness to duty and obligations. He chooses his final values without reference to the judgment of outsiders, and sticks to them with passionate conviction. He finds these inner loyalties and ideals hard to talk about, but they govern his life.

His outer personality is mostly due to his auxiliary process, either S or N, and so is perceptive. He is tolerant, open-minded, understanding, flexible and adaptable (though when one of his inner loyalties is threatened, he will not give an inch). Except for his work's sake, he has little wish to impress or dominate. The contacts he prizes are with people who understand his values and the goals he is working toward.

He is twice as good when working at a job he believes in, since his feeling for it puts added energy behind his efforts. He wants his work to contribute to something that matters to him, perhaps to human understanding or happiness or health, or perhaps to the perfecting of some product or undertaking. He wants to have a purpose beyond his paycheck, no matter how big the check. He is a perfectionist wherever his feeling is engaged, and is usually happiest at some individual work involving personal values. With high ability, he may be good in literature, art, science or psychology. [Myers, 1962, p. A4]

The assimilative learning style is characterized by the introverted intuitive type. Myers's description of this type is similar to the description of the assimilative conceptual orientation but suggests a slightly more practical orientation than we indicate:

The introverted intuitive is the outstanding innovator in the field of ideas, principles and systems of thought. He trusts his own intuitive insight as to the true relationships and meanings of things, regardless of established authority or popularly accepted beliefs. His faith in his inner vision of the possibilities is such that he can remove mountains—and often does. In the process he may drive others, or oppose them, as hard as his own inspirations drive him. Problems only stimulate him; the impossible takes a little longer, but not much.

His outer personality is judging, being mainly due to his auxiliary, either T or F. Thus he backs up his original insight with the determination, perseverance and enduring purpose of a judging type. He wants his ideas worked out in practice, applied and accepted, and spends any time and effort necessary to that end. [Myers, 1962, p. A8]

The convergent learning style is characterized by the extraverted thinking type. Here, Myers's description is very consistent with the learning orientation of convergence:

The extraverted thinker uses his thinking to run as much of the world as may be his to run. He has great respect for impersonal truth, thought-out plans and orderly efficiency. He is analytic, impersonal, objectively critical, and not likely to be convinced by anything but reasoning. He organizes facts, situations and operations well in advance, and makes a systematic effort to reach his carefully planned objectives on schedule. He believes everybody's conduct should be governed by logic, and governs his own that way so far as he can.

He lives his life according to a definite set of rules that embody his basic judgments about the world. Any change in his ways requires a conscious change in the rules.

He enjoys being an executive, and puts a great deal of himself into such a job. He likes to decide what ought to be done and to give the requisite orders. He abhors confusion, inefficiency, halfway measures, and anything aimless and ineffective. He can be a crisp disciplinarian, and can fire a person who ought to be fired. [Myers, 1962, p. A1]

Educational Specialization

A major function of education is to shape students' attitudes and orientations toward learning—to instill positive attitudes toward learning and a thirst for knowledge, and to develop effective learning skills. Early educational experiences shape individual learning styles; we are taught how to learn. Although the early years of education are for the most part generalized, there is an increasing process of specialization that develops beginning in earnest in high school and, for those who continue to college, developing into greater depth in the undergraduate years. This is a specialization in particular realms of social knowledge; thus, we would expect to see relations between people's learning styles and the early training they received in an educational specialty or discipline.

These differences in learning styles can be illustrated graphically by the correspondence between people's LSI scores and their undergraduate majors. This is done by plotting the average LSI scores for managers in our sample who reported their undergraduate college major; only those majors with more than ten people responding are included (see Figure 4.4). When we examine these people who share a common professional commitment to management, we see that some of the differences in their learning orientations are explained by their early educational specializations in college. Undergraduate business majors tend to have accommodative learning styles; engineers on the average fall in the convergent quadrant; history, English, political science, and psychology majors all have divergent learning styles; mathematics, economics, sociology, and chemistry majors have assimilative learning styles; physics majors are very abstract, falling between the convergent and assimilative quadrants.

Some cautions are in order in interpreting these data. First, it should be remembered that all the people in the sample are managers or managers-to-be. In addition, most of them have completed or are in graduate school. These two facts should produce learning styles that are somewhat more active and abstract than those of the population at large (as indicated by total sample mean scores on *AC-CE* and *AE-RO* of +4.5 and +2.9 respectively). The interaction among career, high level of education, and undergraduate major may produce distinctive learning styles. For example, physicists who are not in industry may

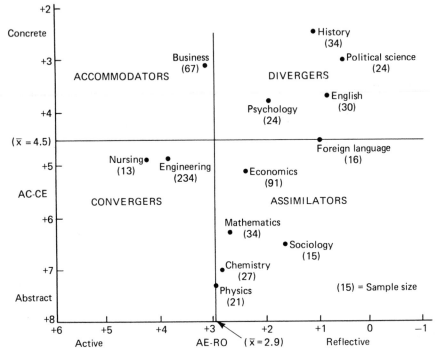

Figure 4.4 Average LSI Scores on Active Reflective (*AE-RO*) and Abstract/Concrete (*AC-CE*) by Undergraduate College Major

be somewhat more reflective than those in this sample. Second, undergraduate majors are described only in the most gross terms. There are many forms of engineering or psychology. A business major at one school can be quite different from one at another.

Liam Hudson's (1966) work on convergent and divergent learning styles predicts that people with undergraduate majors in the arts would be divergers and that those who major in the physical sciences would be convergers. Social-science majors should fall between these two groups. In order to test Hudson's predictions about the academic specialities of convergers and divergers, the data on undergraduate majors were grouped into three categories: the arts (English, foreign language, education/liberal arts, philosophy, history, and other miscellaneous majors such as music, not recorded in Figure 4.4, total $n = 137$); social science (psychology, sociology/anthropology, business, economics, political science, $n = 169$); and physical science (engineering, physics, chemistry, mathematics, and other sciences, such as geology, $n = 277$). The prediction was that the arts should be concrete and reflective and the physical sciences should be abstract and active, with the social sciences falling in between. The mean scores for these three groups of the six LSI scales are shown in Table 4.4. All these differences are highly significant and

Table 4.4 Learning-Style Inventory Scores for People Whose Undergraduate College Majors Were in the Arts, Social Sciences, and Physical Sciences

	Concrete Experience (CE)		Reflective Observation (RO)		Abstract Conceptualization (AC)		Active Experimentation (AE)		Abstract/ Concrete (AC-CE)		Active/ Reflective (AE-RO)	
	$\bar{X}$	SD	$\bar{X}$	SD	$\bar{X}$	SD	$\bar{X}$	SD	$\bar{X}$	SD	$\bar{X}$	SD
A. Arts n = 137	15.41	3.26	14.20	3.35	16.69	3.68	15.11	3.37	+1.31	6.18	+0.96	5.95
B. Social Science n = 169	14.26	3.35	12.75	3.68	18.05	3.67	16.09	3.43	+3.86	6.23	+3.31	6.37
C. Physical Science n = 277	13.32	3.16	12.70	3.17	18.98	3.57	16.53	3.35	+5.64	5.83	+3.83	5.69

T-tests for significance between groups (1-tail, only probabilities < .10 are shown)
Arts vs. physical sciences, all differences are significant; $p < .005$.
Arts vs. social sciences, CE, $p < .005$; RO, $p < .0005$; AC, $p < .0005$; AE, $p < .01$; $AC-CE$, $p < .0005$; $AE-RO$, $p < .0005$.
Physical sciences vs. social sciences, CE, $p < .005$; RO, n.s.; AC, $p < .005$; RO, $p < .10$; $AC-CE$, $p < .005$; $AE-RO$, n.s.

in the predicted direction, with the exception that the social sciences and physical sciences do not differ significantly on the active/reflective dimension.

Another pattern of significance in the data portrayed in Figure 4.4 is the fact that managers who majored in basic academic disciplines are far more reflective in their learning styles than are the managers who made early professional career commitments in either business or engineering. As we will discuss in greater depth later (see Chapter 7), the traditional nonprofessional collegiate learning environment is highly reflective and develops this orientation in its students. As a result, the transition from education to work involves for many a transition from a reflective learning orientation to an active one.

What these data show is that one's undergraduate education is a major factor in the development of his or her learning style. Whether this is because people are shaped by the fields they enter or because of the selection processes that put people into and out of disciplines is an open question at this point. Most probably, both factors are operating—people choose fields that are consistent with their learning styles and are further shaped to fit the learning norms of their field once they are in it. When there is a mismatch between the field's learning norms and the individual's learning style, people will either change or leave the field.

Professional Career

A third set of forces that shape learning style stems from professional career choice. One's professional career choice not only exposes one to a specialized learning environment; it also involves a commitment to a generic professional problem, such as social service, that requires a specialized adaptive orientation. In addition, one becomes a member of a reference group of peers who share a *professional mentality,* a common set of values and beliefs about how one should behave professionally. This professional orientation shapes learning style through habits acquired in professional training and through the more immediate normative pressures involved in being a competent professional (see Chapter 7, p. 182). In engineering, for example, this involves adapting a rigorous scientific and objective stance toward problems. In nursing, it may involve compassion and caring for the sick. In management, much of the professional orientation centers on decisiveness and a pragmatic orientation.

Learning Style Inventory scores have been collected for a number of different professional groups, allowing a comparison between them. The studies are not representative samples of the professions and hence cannot with certainty be said to describe each profession as a whole. They do, however, offer reasonable indications of the learning-style orientations that characterize the different professions. The results of these studies are shown in Figure 4.5. The first conclusion to be drawn from this figure is that the professions in general have an active as opposed to a reflective learning orientation. The social professions—education, nursing, social work, and agricultural extension— comprise people who are heavily or primarily accommodative in their learning

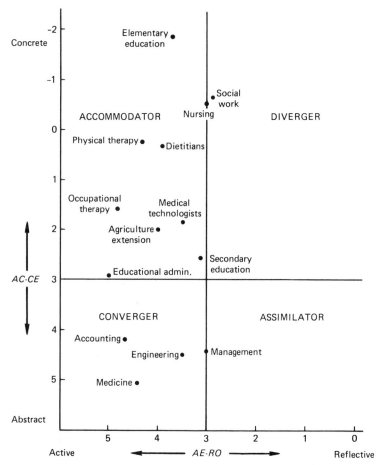

Figure 4.5 Learning-Style Scores for Various Professional Groups (*Data Sources:* Medicine: Practitioners, 46% of sample convergers, Wunderlich & Gjerde, 1978. Students, 56% of sample convergers, Plovnick, 1974. Nursing: 70% of sample diverger or accommodator, Christensen & Bugg, 1979. 62% of sample diverger or accommodator, Bennet, 1978. Social work and engineering, Sims, 1980. Agricultural extension, 44% accommodators, Pigg, 1978. Accounting, Clark et al., 1977. Management, educ. admin., second educ., elementary educ., Kolb, 1976. Occup. ther., phys. ther., dietitions, and med. tech., Bennet, 1978.)

style. Professions with a technical or scientific base—accounting, engineering, medicine, and, to a lesser degree, management—have people with primarily convergent learning styles. There is considerable variation around these professional averages, however. In medicine, for example, about half of practitioners and students are convergers (Plovnick, 1974; Wunderlich and Gjerde, 1978), but some medical specialties, such as occupational therapy, are accommodative in their orientation. In social work and nursing, practitioners are clearly concrete as opposed to abstract but fall heavily in the diverger as well as accommodator quadrant (Sims, 1980; Christensen and Bugg, 1979). As will be seen in the next section, some of this variation can be accounted for by the professional's specific job role.

Current Job Role

The fourth level of factors influencing learning style is the person's current job role. The task demands and pressures of a job tend to shape a person's adaptive orientation. *Executive jobs,* such as general management, that require a strong orientation to task accomplishment and decision making in uncertain emergent circumstances require an accommodative learning style. *Personal jobs,* such as counseling or personnel administrator, that require the establishment of personal relationships and effective communication with other people demand a divergent learning style. *Information jobs,* such as planning and research, that require data gathering and analysis and conceptual modeling have an assimilative learning-style requirement. *Technical jobs,* such as bench engineering and production, that require technical and problem-solving skills require a convergent learning orientation.

These differences in the demands of jobs can be illustrated by an examination of variations among the learning styles of managers in different jobs in a single industrial firm. (For a more detailed analysis of this data, see Weisner, 1971.) We studied about 20 managers from each of five functional groups in a midwestern division of a large American industrial corporation. The five functional groups are described below, followed by our hypothesis about the learning style that should characterize each group given the nature of the work.

1 *Marketing* ($n = 20$). This group is made up primarily of former salesmen. They have a nonquantitative, "intuitive" approach to their work. Because of their practical sales orientation in meeting customer demand, they should have accommodative learning styles.

2 *Research* ($n = 22$). The work of this group is split about 50/50 between pioneer research and applied research projects. The emphasis is on basic research. Researchers should be the most assimilative group.

3 *Personnel/Labor Relations* ($n = 20$). In this company, men from this department serve two primary functions, interpreting personnel policy and promoting interaction among groups to reduce conflict and disagreement. Because of their "people orientation," these men should be predominantly divergers.

4 *Engineering* ($n = 18$). This group is made up primarily of design engineers who are quite production-oriented. They should be the most convergent subgroup, although they should be less abstract than the research group. They represent a bridge between thought and action.

5 *Finance* ($n = 20$). This group has a strong computer, information-system bias. Finance men, given their orientation toward the mathematical task of information-

system design, should be highly abstract. Their crucial role in organizational survival should produce an active orientation. Thus, finance-group members should have convergent learning styles.

Figure 4.6 shows the average scores on the active/reflective (*AE-RO*) and abstract/concrete (*AC-CE*) learning dimensions for the five functional groups. These results are consistent with the predictions above, with the exception of the finance group, whose scores are less active than predicted and thus fall between the assimilative and the convergent quadrants. The LSI clearly differentiates the learning styles that characterize managers with different jobs in a single company.

Further evidence for the proposed relationship between job demands and learning style comes from the medical profession. Plovnick (1974, 1975) studied the relationship between learning style and the job specialty choices of senior medical students. He hypothesized that academic jobs stressing research and teaching would attract assimilators more than other learning-style types, and practice-oriented specialties requiring frequent patient interaction would attract the more active types. In addition, he expected that subspecialty practices (such as cardiology), having a more "scientific" orientation, would attract convergers more, whereas practices in family medicine or primary care involving more concern for the socioemotional aspects of patient care would attract accommodators more. Psychiatry was expected to attract divergers,

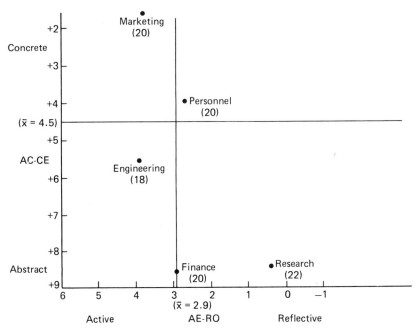

Figure 4.6 Average LSI Scores on Active/Reflective *(AE-RO)* and Abstract/Concrete *(AC-CE)* by Organizational Function

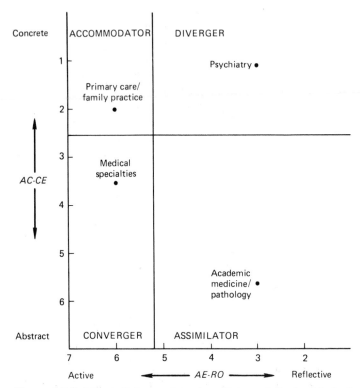

Figure 4.7 Relations Between Learning Style and Senior Medical Student's Choice of Specialty (*Source:* Adapted from Mark Plovnick, "Primary Career Choices and Medical Student Learning Styles," *J Med Education, 50,* Sept 1975)

because of its humanistic orientation and because of the more reserved, reflective nature of the practitioner role in psychiatry. As can be seen in Figure 4.7, these predictions were borne out.[2]

Sims (1981), in his study of job role demands in the social-work and engineering professions, found that social-work administrators were primarily accommodative in their learning style, whereas those in direct service had divergent learning styles. However, he found no differences among the three major job roles of professional engineers—bench engineer, technical manager, and general manager—even though he did identify significant differences in the actual learning-style demands of these three job roles.

---

[2] A follow-up study by Wunderlich and Gjerde (1978) failed to replicate these findings with active medical practitioners. This may be due to a difference in data analysis procedures between the two studies. Plovnick created types by dividing *AE-RO* and *AC-CE* scores at the sample median, whereas Wunderlich and Gjerde used the zero point on the scales to create types.

Adaptive Competencies

The fifth most specific and immediate level of forces that shapes learning style is the specific task or problem the person is currently working on. Each task we face requires a corresponding set of skills for effective performance. The effective matching of task demands and personal skills results in an *adaptive competence.* The concept of competence represents a new approach to the improvement of performance by matching persons with jobs. The previous approach, that of measurement and selection of personnel by generalized aptitudes, has proved a dismal failure in spite of heroic efforts to make it succeed (see Tyler, 1978, Chapter 6 for a review). The basic problem of the aptitude-testing approach was that aptitudes were too generalized and thus did not relate to the specific tasks in a given job, producing low correlations between the aptitude measure and performance. In addition, the aptitude and task measures often were not commensurate; that is, they did not measure the person and the task demand in the same terms. The competency-assessment approach focuses on the person's repertoire of skills as they relate to the specific demands of a job.

We have conceived of the elementary learning styles as *generic adaptive competencies;* that is, as higher-level learning heuristics that facilitate the development of a generic class of more specific skills that are required for effective performance on different tasks (compare Chapter 6, p. 151). To study the relations between learning styles as generic adaptive competencies and the specific competencies associated with each of the four styles, the self-rated competencies of professional engineers and social workers were correlated with LSI *AC-CE* and *AE-RO* scales. Although this self-rating methodology is of limited usefulness in assessing with great accuracy a person's level of competence in a given situation, it can be used to assess the patterns of interrelationship among competencies, which was the objective of this research study. The correlations between LSI scores and competence self-ratings were plotted on the two-dimensional learning space (see Figure 4.8). For example, the skill of "being personally involved" correlated $-.25$ with *AC-CE* and $+.10$ with *AE-RO,* placing it in the accommodative quadrant of the learning-style space. As a result of this study, the list of competencies was revised and expanded and a second study was conducted with a sample of social-work and engineering graduates (see Figure 4.9). These data were subjected to further factor analysis and refinement, resulting in what can be called a "competency circle" describing specific competencies arranged in a two-dimensional space by their association with the generic adaptive competence of learning style (see Figure 4.10).

The accommodative learning style encompasses a set of competencies that can best be termed *acting skills:* committing oneself to objectives, seeking and exploiting opportunities, influencing and leading others, being personally involved, and dealing with people. The divergent learning style is associated

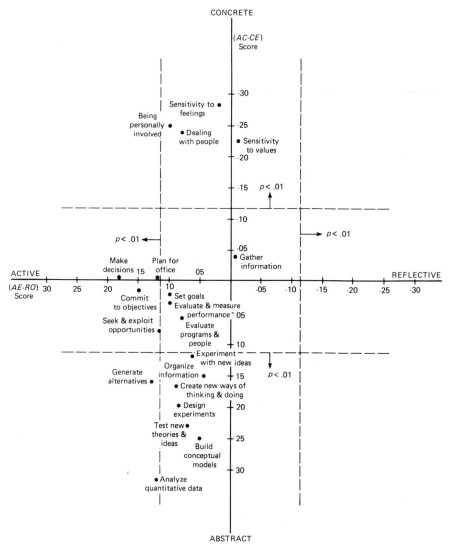

Figure 4.8 Correlations Among Work Abilities and Learning Styles (Social-Work and Engineering Graduates; N = 420)

with *valuing skills:* being sensitive to people's feelings and to values, listening with an open mind, gathering information, and imagining implications of ambiguous situations. Assimilation is related to *thinking competencies:* organizing information, building conceptual models, testing theories and ideas, designing experiments, and analyzing quantitative data. The convergent learning style is associated with *decision skills:* creating new ways of thinking and doing, experimenting with new ideas, choosing the best solution to

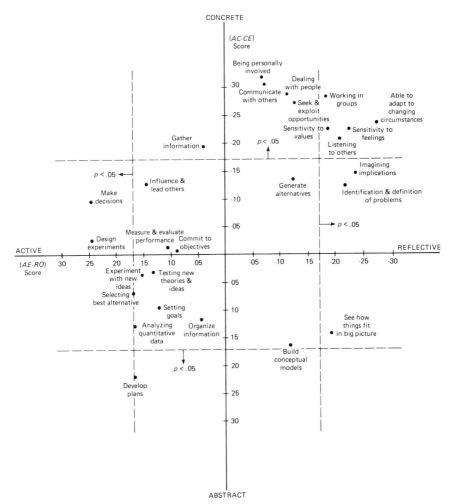

Figure 4.9 Correlations Among Work Abilities and Learning Styles (Social-Work and Engineering Graduates; $N = 59$)

problems, setting goals, and making decisions. Since these adaptive competencies are defined as congruences between personal skills and task demands, it seems reasonable to conclude that tasks requiring given specific skills will to some degree influence the expression of the learning style associated with those skills.

SUMMARY AND CONCLUSION

This chapter has described individual differences in learning by introducing the concept of learning styles. Learning styles are conceived not as fixed

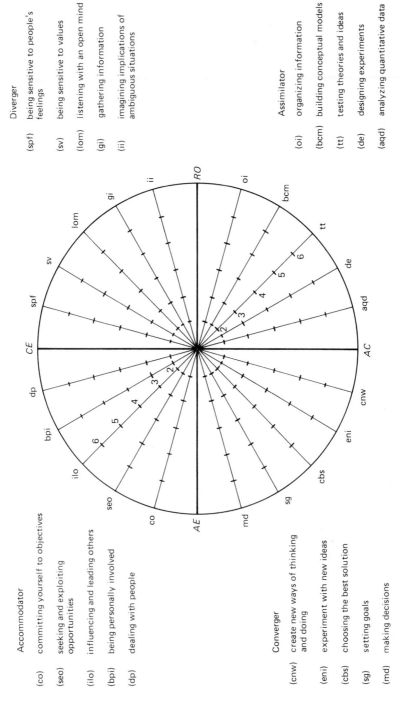

Diverger

(spf) being sensitive to people's feelings

(sv) being sensitive to values

(lom) listening with an open mind

(gi) gathering information

(ii) imagining implications of ambiguous situations

Assimilator

(oi) organizing information

(bcm) building conceptual models

(tt) testing theories and ideas

(de) designing experiments

(aqd) analyzing quantitative data

Accommodator

(co) committing yourself to objectives

(seo) seeking and exploiting opportunities

(ilo) influencing and leading others

(bpi) being personally involved

(dp) dealing with people

Converger

(cnw) create new ways of thinking and doing

(eni) experiment with new ideas

(cbs) choosing the best solution

(sg) setting goals

(md) making decisions

Figure 4.10 The Competency Circle, Showing Adaptive Competencies as They Relate to Learning Styles

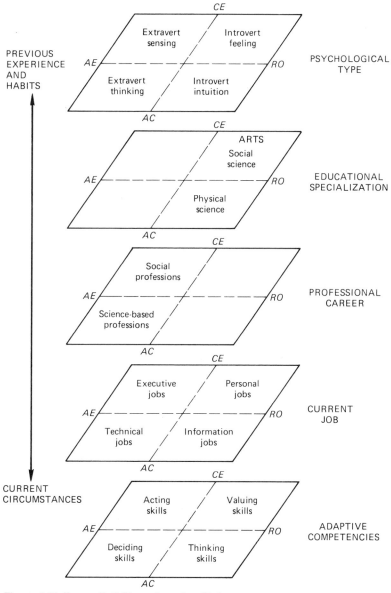

Figure 4.11 Forces that Shape Learning Styles

personality traits but as possibility-processing structures resulting from unique individual programming of the basic but flexible structure of human learning. These possibility-processing structures are best thought of as adaptive states or orientations that achieve stability through consistent patterns of transaction with the world; for example, my active orientation helps me perform well in active tasks, and since I am rewarded for this performance, I choose more active tasks, which further improves my active skills, and so on.

We have examined five levels at which these transactions between people and the world around them shape the basic learning styles—accommodation, divergence, assimilation, and convergence. For example, my own learning style at this moment is shaped by my *personality disposition* toward introversion and feeling, my *undergraduate specializations* in psychology, philosophy, and religion, my *professional academic career* commitment, the *demands of my current job* as a professor, and the *specific task* I am working on now—this book. Thus, my learning style is clearly reflective and, at the moment, tipped toward assimilation, although other tasks in my professional role, such as teaching and counseling students, may shift me toward divergence. The forces that shape learning styles at these four levels are summarized in Figure 4.11. At one extreme there are those basic past experiences and habits of thought and action, our basic personality orientation and education, that exert a moderate but pervasive influence on our behavior in nearly all situations. At the other end of the continuum are those increasingly specific environmental demands stemming from our career choice, our current job, and the specific tasks that face us. These forces exert a somewhat stronger but more situation-specific influence on the learning style we adopt.

When learning style is viewed from the two-dimensional perspective proposed here, we can represent the current state of a person's learning style as a single point on the abstract/concrete and active/reflective learning space. The position of this point—for example, in the center of the grid or at one of the extreme corners—is determined by the summative influence of the forces described above. But this representation summarizes only qualitative differences in elementary learning orientations. To fully appreciate a person's approach to learning, we need to understand his or her position on a third dimension, that of development. An explanation of this dimension is yet to come, in Chapter 6. But before describing the experiential learning theory of development, we turn first to an examination of the nature of knowledge and how it is created by learning from experience, since individual approaches to learning and development, as we have seen, are determined by one's transactions with the various systems of social knowledge.

five

The Structure
of Knowledge

Experience is not a veil that shuts off man from nature, it is a means of penetrating continually further into the heart of nature. **John Dewey**

No account of human learning could be considered complete without an examination of culturally accumulated knowledge, its nature and organization, and the processes whereby individual learners contribute to and partake of that knowledge. Individual learning styles are shaped by the structure of social knowledge and through individual creative acts; knowledge is formed by individuals. To understand learning fully, we must understand the nature and forms of human knowledge and the processes whereby this knowledge is created and recreated. Piaget, in the conclusion to his 1970 book, *Genetic Epistemology*, describes three approaches to learning and knowledge creation and their relation to learning from experience:

> *These few examples may clarify why I consider the main problem of genetic epistemology to be the explanation of the construction of novelties in the development of knowledge. From the empiricist point of view, a "discovery" is new for the person who makes it, but what is discovered was already in existence in external reality and there is therefore no construction of new realities. The nativist or apriorist maintains that the forms of knowledge are predetermined inside the subject and thus again, strictly speaking, there can be no novelty. By contrast, for the genetic epistemologist, knowledge results from continuous construction, since in each act of understanding, some degree of invention is involved; in development, the passage from one stage to the next is always characterized by the formation of new structures which did not exist before, either in the external world or in the subject's mind. [Piaget, 1970a, p. 77]*

The empiricist, apriorist (rationalist), and genetic-epistemology (interactionist) perspectives on the acquisition of knowledge have defined epistemological debates in Western philosophy since the classical Greek philosophers. In the seventeenth century came the first challenge to the dogma of religious and political authority. The unitary world view of medieval scholasticism that had dominated the Christian world up until that time gave way to the development of rational and, later, empirical concepts that made possible control and mastery of the material world. In the seventeenth century, knowledge was thought to be accessible to the mind alone through rational analysis and introspection. The rationalist philosophers—most notably Descartes, Spinoza, and Libnetz—posed the thesis that truth was to be discovered by use of the tools of logic and reason. Ideas were real and *a priori* to the empirical world. Since experiences were merely reflections of ideal forms, it was the ideal forms in the mind that gave meaning to experiences in the world. As Descartes put it:

> [God] laid down these laws in nature just as a king lays down laws in his kingdom. There is no single one that we cannot understand if our minds turn to consider it. They are all inborn in our minds just as a king would imprint his laws on the hearts of his subjects if he had enough power to do so. [Cited in Frankfurt, 1977, p. 36]

The eighteenth century gave rise to the antithesis of rationalism—empiricism. According to the empiricist philosophers—Locke, Hobbes, and others—knowledge was to be found in the accumulated associations of our sense impressions of the world around us. The mind was a *tabula rasa,* recording these accumulated sense impressions but making no contribution of its own save its capacity to recognize "substance." Truth was to be found in careful observation of the world, a notion that gave rise to a burgeoning of scientific investigation in the eighteenth century.

The nineteenth century saw a synthesis of the rationalist and empiricist positions in the critical idealism of Kant, the first of the interactionist epistemologists. For Kant, the mind possessed *a priori* equipment that enabled it to interpret experience—specifically, equipment to locate forms in time and space and equipment to understand order and uniformity. Thus, the laws of geometry and logic were considered to be beyond experience and essential for interpreting it. Truth in critical idealism was the product of the interaction between the mind's forms and the material facts of sense experience.

APPREHENSION VS. COMPREHENSION— A DUAL-KNOWLEDGE THEORY

This brief overview of the history of epistemological philosophy is perhaps sufficient to frame the contribution of experiential learning theory to the question of how knowledge is acquired. A moment's reflection on the experiential learning cycle (see Figure 3.1) will suffice to illustrate the limitations of either the rationalist or the empiricist philosophies alone as an epistemological foundation for experiential learning. As we have seen in Chapter 3, experiential learning is based on a dual-knowledge theory: the empiricists' concrete experience, grasping reality by the process of direct apprehension, and the rationalists' abstract conceptualization, grasping reality via the mediating process of abstract conceptualization. We are thus left with Piaget in the interactionist position.

The interactionist epistemology of experiential learning theory, however, is different in some significant ways from the Piagetian interactionism of genetic epistemology. As has been suggested (Chapter 2, p. 25, Chapter 3, pp. 40, 50, and 52, and Chapter 6), Piaget's interactionism is decidedly rationalist in spirit. Consider, for example, his explanation of how it is that mathematical formulations have consistently anticipated subsequent empirical findings:

> This harmony between mathematics and physical reality cannot in positivist fashion be written off as simply the correspondence of a language with the object it designates. . . . Rather it is a correspondence of human operations with those of object operators, a harmony, then, between this particular operator—the human being as body and mind—and the innumerable operators in nature—physical objects at their several levels. Here we have remarkable proof of that preestablished harmony among windowless monads of which Liebnitz dreamt . . . the most beautiful example of biological adaptation that we know of. [Piaget, 1970, pp. 40-41]

Substitute the processes of "biological adaptation" for "imprinting of his laws on our hearts," and the "human operations" of the mind according to Piaget are nearly identical with the "inborn laws" of Descartes in the quote just cited. For both men, the powers of the mind are directly connected with the structure of reality. This rationalist orientation is reflected in the predominant position of action in Piaget's theory about how knowledge is created. For him, sensations and perceptions are only the starting point of knowing; it is the organization and transformation of these sensations through action, most particularly internalized actions or thoughts, that creates knowledge. Knowledge then, for Piaget, is the progressive internalization of the action transformations through which we construct reality—a decidedly rationalist interactionism in which sensation (or knowing by apprehension) is secondary.

The interactionism of experiential learning theory places knowing by apprehension on an equal footing with knowing by comprehension, resulting in a stronger interactionist position, really a transactionalism, in which knowledge emerges from the dialectic relationship between the two forms of knowing.[1]

---

[1] We focus in this chapter on the prehension dimension of apprehension and comprehension rather than the transformation dimension of intention and extension, because the prehension dimension describes the current state of our knowledge of the world—the content of knowledge, if you will—whereas the transformation dimension describes the rates or processes by which that

This dialectic relationship is not the Kantian dialectic, in which thesis and antithesis stand only in logical contradiction, but the Hegelian dialectic, in which contradictions and conflicts are borne out of both logic and emotion in a thesis and antithesis of mutually antagonistic convictions.

To better understand the nature of this dialectic, let us examine the nature of the two knowing processes whose opposition fuels it. To begin with, knowing by apprehension is here-and-now. It exists only in a continuously unfolding present movement of apparently limitless depth wherein events are related via synchronicity—that is, a patterned interrelationship in the moment (compare Jung, 1960). It is thus timeless—at once instantaneous and eternal, the dynamic form of perceiving that Werner calls physiognomic (see Chapter 6, p. 139). Comprehension, on the other hand, is by its very nature a record of the past that seeks to define the future; the concept of linear time is perhaps its most fundamental foundation, underlying all concept of causality. As Hume pointed out, the mind cannot learn causal connections between events by experience alone (apprehension). All we learn through apprehension is that event B follows event A. There is nothing in the sense impression to indicate that A causes B. This judgment of causality is based on inferences from our comprehension of A and B.

The interplay between these two forms of knowing in the creation of knowledge is illustrated in what has been a difficult circular-argument problem in physics—the fact that speed is defined by using time and time is measured by speed. In classical mechanics, speed and time are coequal, since speed is defined as the relation between traveled space and duration. In relativistic mechanics, however, speed is more elementary, since it has a maximum velocity (the speed of light). This formulation led Einstein to ask Piaget, when they met in 1928, to investigate from the psychological viewpoint questions as to whether there was a sense of speed that was independent of time and that was more fundamental (acquired earlier). What Piaget and his associates found (Piaget, 1971) was that speed is the more basic notion, based on perception (apprehension), whereas time is a more inferential, complex construct (based on comprehension). Their experiments involved asking children to describe a moving object that passed behind nine vertical bars. Seventy to 80 percent of the subjects reported movement acceleration when the object passed behind the bars. Piaget's conclusion was that following the moving object with one's eyes was handicapped in the barred sections by momentary fixations on the bars, causing an impression of greater speed in the moving object. The apprehension of speed thus seems to be based on the muscular effort expended in attending to a moving object. The comprehension of time, however, occurs

---

knowledge is changed. Although both content and process are legitimate aspects of structure, it is the content of knowledge and its form that have been the primary concern of epistemology, Piaget's emphasis on behavioral transformation not withstanding. This is in a sense a convenience of exposition, since enduring effects of transformation processes will be represented in the content of knowledge just as the rate of water flowing into a tub is reflected in the level of water in the tub.

later developmentally and is much more complex. The apparent circularity of space/time equations in physics therefore appears to be psychologically rooted in the dialectic relationships of knowing speed by apprehension and time by comprehension.

A second difference between knowing by apprehension and knowing by comprehension is that apprehension is a registrative process transformed intentionally and extensionally by appreciation, whereas comprehension is an interpretive process transformed intentionally and extensionally by criticism. Michael Polanyi describes this difference in his comparison of articulate form (comprehension-based knowledge) and tacit knowledge (based on apprehension):

> Where there is criticism, what is being criticized is, every time, the assertion of an articulate form. . . . The process of logical inference is the strictest form of human thought, and it can be subjected to severe criticism by going over it stepwise any number of times. Factual assertations and denotations can also be examined critically, although their testing cannot be formalized to the same extent.
>
> In this sense just specified, tacit knowing cannot be critical . . . systematic forms of criticism can be applied only to articulate forms which you can try out afresh again and again. We should not apply, therefore, the terms critical or uncritical to any process of tacit thought by itself any more than we would speak of the critical or uncritical performance of a high jump or a dance. Tacit acts are judged by other standards and are to be regarded accordingly as a-critical. [Polanyi, 1958, p. 264]

The enduring nature of the articulate forms of comprehensive knowledge makes it possible to analyze, criticize, and rearrange these forms in different times and contexts. It is through such critical activity that the network of comprehensive knowledge is refined, elaborated, and integrated. Any attempt to be critical of knowledge gained through apprehension, however, only destroys that knowledge. Criticism requires a reflective, analytic, objective posture that distances one from here-and-now experience; the here-and-now experience in fact becomes criticizing, replacing the previous immediate apprehension. Since I am an avid golfer, this fact has been illustrated in my experience too many times. In approaching a green to putt the ball, I note the distance of the ball from the hole, the slope of the green, the length and bend of the grass, how wet or dry it is, and other relevant factors. I attempt to attend to these factors without analyzing them, for when my mind is dominated by an analytic formula for hitting the ball (for instance, hit it harder because it's wet), the putt invariably goes awry. What seems to work better is an appreciation of the total situation (the situation being defined by my previous comprehension of relevant aspects to attend to) in which I, the putter, ball, green, and hole are experienced holistically (no pun intended; compare Polanyi, 1966, pp. 18-19).

Much can be said about the process and method of criticism, indeed, most scholarly method is based on it. The process of appreciation is less recognized and understood. Thus, it is worth describing in some detail the character of appreciation. First, appreciation is intimately associated with perceptual attention processes. Appreciation is largely the process of attending to and being interested in aspects of one's experience. We notice only those aspects of reality that interest us and thereby "capture our attention." Interest is the basic fact of mental life and the most elementary act of valuing. It is the selector of our experience. Appreciation involves attending to and being interested in our apprehensions of the world around us. Such attention deepens and extends the apprehended experience. Vickers, along with Zajonc (see Chapter 3), suggests that such appreciative apprehensions precede judgments of fact; in other words, that preferences preceded inferences:

> For even that basic discriminatory judgment "this" is a "that" is no mere finding of fact, it is a decision to assimilate some object of attention, carved out of the tissue of all that is available to some category to which we have learned, rightly or wrongly, that it is convenient to assimilate such things. [Vickers, 1968, pp. 139-40]

A second characteristic of appreciation, already alluded to, is that it is a process of valuing. Appreciation of an apprehended moment is a judgment of both value and fact:

> Appreciative behavior involves making judgments of value no less than judgements of reality. . . . Interests and standards . . . are systematically organized, a value system, distinguishable from the reality system yet inseparable from it. For facts are relevant only by reference to some judgment of value and judgments of value are meaningful only in regard to some configuration of fact. Hence the need for a word to embrace the two, for which I propose the word appreciation, a word not yet appropriated by science which in its ordinary use (as in "appreciation of a situation") implies a combined judgment of value and fact. [Vickers, 1968, pp. 164-98]

Appreciation of apprehended reality is the source of values. Most mature value judgments are combinations of value and fact. Yet it is the affective core of values that fuel them, giving values the power to select and direct behavior.

Finally, appreciation is a process of affirmation. Unlike criticism, which is based on skepticism and doubt (compare Polanyi, 1958, pp. 269ff.), appreciation is based on belief, trust, and conviction. To appreciate apprehended reality is to embrace it. And from this affirmative embrace flows a deeper fullness and richness of experience. This act of affirmation forms the foundation from which critical comprehension can develop. In Polanyi's words:

> We must now recognize belief once more as the source of all knowledge. Tacit assent and intellectual passions, the sharing of an idiom and of a cultural heritage, affiliation to a like-minded community; such are the impulses which shape our vision of the nature of things on which we rely for our mastery of things. No intelligence, however critical or original, can operate outside such a fiduciary framework. [Polanyi, 1958, p. 266]

Appreciative apprehension and critical comprehension are thus fundamentally different processes of knowing. Appreciation of immediate experience is an act of attention, valuing and affirmation, whereas critical comprehension of symbols is based on objectivity (which involves *a priori* control of attention, as in double blind controlled experiments), dispassionate analysis, and skepticism. As we will see, knowledge and truth result not from the preeminence of one of these knowing modes over the other but from the intense coequal confrontation of both modes.

A third difference between knowing by apprehension and by comprehension is perhaps the most critical for our understanding of the nature of knowledge in its relationship to learning from experience. Apprehension of experience is a personal subjective process that cannot be known by others except by the communication to them of the comprehensions that we use to describe our immediate experience. Comprehension, on the other hand, is an objective social process, a tool of culture, as Engels would call it. From this it follows that there are two kinds of knowledge: *personal knowledge,* the combination of my direct apprehensions of experience and the socially acquired comprehensions I use to explain this experience and guide my actions; and *social knowledge,* the independent, socially and culturally transmitted network of words, symbols, and images that is based solely on comprehension. The latter, as Dewey noted (Chapter 2, pp. 35-36), is the civilized objective accumulation of the individual person's subjective life experience.

It is commonly assumed that what we are calling social knowledge stands alone from the personal experience of the user. When we think of knowledge, we think of books, computer programs, diagrams, and the like, organized into a coherent system or library. Social knowledge, however, cannot exist independently of the knower but must be continuously recreated in the knower's personal experience, whether that experience be through concrete interaction with the physical and social world or through the media of symbols and language. With symbols and words in particular, we are often led into the illusion that knowledge exists independently in the written work or mathematical notation. But to understand these words and symbols requires a knower who understands and employs a transformational process in order to yield personal knowledge and meaning. If, for example, I read that a "black hole" in astronomy is like a gigantic spiral of water draining from a bathtub, I can create for myself some knowledge of what a black hole is like (such as the force of gravity drawing things into it) based on my concrete experiences in the bath. This, however, is quite a different knowledge of black holes from that of the scientists who understand the special theory of relativity, the idea that gravity curves space, and so on. Personal knowledge is thus the result of the transaction between the form or structure of its external representational and transformational grammar (social knowledge, such as the bathtub image or the formal theory of relativity) and the internal representational and transformation processes that the person has developed in his or her personal knowledge system.

THE DIALECTICS OF APPREHENSION
AND COMPREHENSION

Thoughts without content are empty
Intuitions without concepts are blind.

Immanuel Kant

The dynamic relation between apprehension and comprehension lies at the core of knowledge creation. The mind, to use Sir Charles Sharrington's famous phrase, is "an enchanted loom where millions of flashing shuttles weave a dissolving pattern, always a meaningful pattern though never an abiding one. . . ." Normal human consciousness is a combination of two modes of grasping experiences, forming a continuous experiential fabric, the warp of which represents apprehended experiences woven tightly by the weft of comprehended representations. Just as the patterns in a fabric are governed by the interrelations among warp and weft, so too, personal knowledge is shaped by the interrelations between apprehension and comprehension. The essence of the interrelationship is expressed in Kant's analysis of their interdependence: Apprehensions are the source of validation for comprehensions ("thoughts without content are empty"), and comprehensions are the source of guidance in the selection of apprehensions ("intuitions without concepts are blind").

Immediate apprehended experience is the ultimate source of the validity of comprehensions in both fact and value. The factual basis of a comprehension is ultimately judged in terms of its connection with sense experience. Its value is similarly judged ultimately by its immediate affective utility. Albert Einstein describes the relation between apprehension and comprehension thus:

> For me it is not dubious that our thinking goes on for the most part without use of signs (words) and beyond that to a considerable degree unconsciously. For how otherwise should it happen that sometimes we "wonder" quite spontaneously about some experience? This "wondering" seems to occur when an experience comes into conflict with a world of concepts which is already sufficiently fixed in us. Whenever such a conflict is experienced hard and intensively, it reacts back upon our thought world in a decisive way. The development of this thought world is in a certain sense a continuous flight from "wonder." . . .
>
> I see on the one side the totality of sense experiences and, on the other, the totality of the concepts and propositions which are laid down in books. The relations between the concepts and propositions among themselves and each other are of a logical nature, and the business of logical thinking is strictly limited to the achievement of the connection between concepts and propositions among each other according to firmly laid down rules which are the concern of logic. The concepts and propositions get "meaning," viz. "content," only through their connection with sense-experiences. The connection of the latter with the former is purely intuitive, not itself of a logical nature. The degree of certainty with which this relation, viz. intuitive connection, can be undertaken, and nothing else differentiates empty phantasy from scientific "truth." [Schilpp, 1949]

More directly, the physicist David Bohm says, "All knowledge is a structure of abstractions, the ultimate test of the validity of which is, however, in the process of coming into contact with the world that takes place in immediate perception" (1965, p. 220).

Comprehensions, on the other hand, guide our choices of experiences and direct our attention to those aspects of apprehended experience to be considered relevant. Comprehension is more than a secondary process of representing selected aspects of apprehended reality. The process of critical comprehension is capable of selecting and reshaping apprehended experience in ways that are more powerful and profound. The power of comprehension has led to the discovery of ever-new ways of seeing the world, the very connection between mind and physical reality that Piaget noted earlier (compare Dewey, 1958, pp. 67-68). Dewey describes the powers of comprehension over the immediacy of apprehension in his reference to William James:

> Genuine science is impossible as long as the object esteemed for its own intrinsic qualities is taken as the object of knowledge. Its completeness, its immanent meaning, defeats its use as indicating and implying.
>   Said William James, "Many were the ideal prototypes of rational order: teleological and esthetic ties between things . . . as well as logical and mathematical relations. The most promising of these things at first were of course the richer ones, the more sentimental ones. The baldest and least promising were mathematical ones; but the history of the latter's application is a history of steadily advancing successes, while that of the sentimentally richer ones is one of relative sterility and failure. Take those aspects of phenomena which interest you as a human being most . . . and barren are all your results. Call the things of nature as much as you like by sentimental moral and esthetic names, no natural consequences follow from the naming. . . . But when you give the things mathematical and mechanical names and call them so many solids in just such positions, describing just such paths with just such velocities, all is changed. . . . Your "things" realize the consequences of the names by which you classed them."
>   A fair interpretation of these pregnant sentences is that as long as objects are viewed telically, as long as the objects of the truest knowledge, the most real forms of being, are thought of as ends, science does not advance. Objects are possessed and appreciated, but they are not known. To know means that men have become willing to turn away from precious possessions; willing to let drop what they own, however precious, in behalf of a grasp of objects which they do not as yet own. Multiplied and secure ends depend upon letting go existent ends, reducing them to indicative and implying means. [John Dewey quoting William James, 1958, pp. 130-31]

Dialectics, Doubt, and Certainty

The relationship between apprehension and comprehension is dialectic in the Hegelian sense that although the results of either process cannot be entirely explained in terms of the other, these opposite processes merge toward a higher truth that encompasses and transcends them. The process whereby this synthesis is achieved, however, is somewhat mysterious; that is, it cannot be explained by logical comprehension alone. Thus the development of knowledge, our sense of progress in the refinement of ideas about ourselves and the world around us, proceeds by a dynamic that in prospect is filled with surprising, unanticipated experiences and insights, and in retrospect makes our earlier earnest convictions about the nature of reality seem simplistic and dogmatic. As learners, engaged in this process of knowledge creation, we are alternatively enticed into a dogmatic embrace of our current convictions and threatened with utter skepticism as what we thought were adamantine crystals of truth dissolve like fine sand between our grasping fingers. The posture of partial skepticism, of what Perry (1970) calls commitment within relativism, that is needed to openly confront the conflict inherent in the dialectic process is difficult to maintain. The greatest challenge to the development of knowledge is the comfort of dogmatism—the security provided by unquestioned confidence in a statement of truth, or in a method for achieving truth—or even the shadow dogmatism of utter skepticism (for to be utterly skeptical is to dogmatically affirm that nothing can be known).

Our primitive ancestors leaned toward a dogmatic affirmation of apprehension and a tenacious reliance on immediate sensation and feelings, a concrete approach to knowledge that was manifest in the formulation of animistic world views and a "science of the concrete" (Levi-Strauss, 1969). In Plato's *Phaedrus*, the ancients' mistrust of comprehension is nicely portrayed in the mythical conversation between the Egyptian god Thoth, who invented writing, and Thamus, a god-king who chastises Thoth for his invention:

> This discovery of yours will create forgetfulness in the learner's souls because they will not use their memories; they will trust to the external written characters and not remember of themselves. The specific which you have discovered is an aid not to memory, but to reminiscence; and you give your disciples not truth, but only the semblance of truth; they will be hearers of many things and will have learned nothing; they will appear to be omniscient and will generally know nothing; they will be tiresome company, having the show of wisdom without its reality. [From Sagan, 1977, pp. 222-23]

The modern tendency, however, is to embrace the comprehension pole of the knowledge dialectic and to view with suspicion the intuitions of subjective experience. The clearest and most extreme intellectual expressions of modern reliance on comprehension are manifest in the domination of American psychology by behaviorist theories and methodologies and in the epistemological philosophy that spawned behaviorism—logical positivism. In a zeal born out of the upending of the tidy system of classical physics before the discoveries of modern twentieth century physics, positivism sought to affirm that all knowledge must ultimately be based on empirical or logical data. In this way, the most dogmatic of the positivists denied the existence of subjective experience (apprehensions) except insofar as these were verifiable by a

community of observers following logical and scientific conventions (comprehensions).

In response to the positivists' dogmatic embrace of comprehension,
Polanyi proposes an equally dogmatic embrace of apprehension to confront the
modern supremacy of analytic powers:

> As I surveyed the operations of the tacit coefficient in the act of knowing, I
> pointed out how everywhere the mind follows its own self-set standards, and I
> gave my tacit or explicit endorsement to this manner of establishing truth. Such
> an endorsement is an action of the same kind as that which it accredits and is to
> be classed therefore as a consciously a-critical statement.
>
> This invitation to dogmatism may appear shocking; yet it is but the
> corollary to the greatly increased critical powers of man. These have enhanced
> our mind with a capacity for self-transcendence of which we can never divest
> ourselves. We have plucked from the Tree a second apple which has forever
> emperiled our knowledge of Good and Evil, and we must learn to know these
> qualities henceforth in the blinding light of our new analytical powers. Humanity
> has been deprived a second time of its innocence, and driven out of another
> garden which was, at any rate, a Fool's Paradise. Innocently, we had trusted that
> we could be relieved of all personal responsibility for our beliefs by objective
> criteria of validity—and our own critical powers have shattered this hope. Struck
> by our sudden nakedness, we may try to brazen it out by flaunting it in a
> profession of nihilism. But modern man's immorality is unstable. Presently his
> moral passions reassert themselves in objectivist disguise and the scientistic
> Minotaur is born. [Polanyi, 1958, p. 268]

We are thus led to the conclusion that the proper attitude for the creation
of knowledge is neither a dogmatism of apprehension *or* comprehension nor an
utter skepticism, but an attitude of partial skepticism in which the knowledge of
comprehension is held provisionally to be tested against apprehensions, and
vice versa. The critical difference between personal and social knowledge is the
presence of apprehension as a way of knowing in personal knowledge. It should
be clear that the apprehensional portion of personal knowledge is all that
prevents us from losing our identity as unique human beings, to be swallowed
up in the command feedback loops of the increasingly computerized social-
knowledge system. Because we can still learn from our *own experience*,
because we can subject the abstract symbols of the social-knowledge system to
the rigors of our own inquiry about these symbols and our personal experience
with them, we are free. This process of choosing to believe is what we feel when
we know that we are free to chart the course of our own destiny.

THE STRUCTURE OF SOCIAL KNOWLEDGE:
WORLD HYPOTHESES

Since all social knowledge is learned, it is reasonable to suspect that there is
some isomorphism between the structure of social knowledge and the structure
of the learning process. Thus it seems likely that some systems of knowledge

will rely heavily on comprehension and others will rely on apprehension; some will be oriented to extension and practical application and others will be oriented toward intention and basic understanding. The philosopher Stephen Pepper, in his seminal work, *World Hypotheses*, proposes just such a framework for describing the structure of knowledge based on the fundamental metaphysical assumptions or "root metaphors" of systems for developing refined knowledge from common sense:

> *This tension between common sense and expert knowledge, between cognitive security without responsibility and cognitive responsibility without full security, is the interior dynamics of the knowledge situation. The indefiniteness of much detail in common sense, its contradictions, its lack of established grounds, drive thought to seek definiteness, consistency, and reasons. Thought finds these in the criticized and refined knowledge of mathematics, science, and philosophy, only to discover that these tend to thin out into arbitrary definitions, pointer readings, and tentative hypotheses. Astounded at the thinness and hollowness of these culminating achievements of conscientiously responsible cognition, thought seeks matter for its definitions, significance for its pointer readings, and support for its wobbling hypotheses. Responsible cognition finds itself insecure as a result of the very earnestness of its virtues. But where shall it turn? It does, in fact, turn back to common sense, that indefinite and irresponsible source which it so lately scorned. But it does so, generally, with a bad grace. After filling its empty definitions and pointer readings and hypotheses with meaning out of the rich confusion of common sense, it generally turns its head away, shuts its eyes to what it has been doing, and affirms dogmatically the self-evidence and certainty of the common-sense significance it has drawn into its concepts. Then it pretends to be securely based on self-evident principles or indubitable facts. If our recent criticism of dogmatism is correct, however, this security in self-evidence and indubitability has proved questionable. And critical knowledge hangs over a vacuum unless it acknowledges openly the actual, though strange, source of its significance and security in the uncriticized material of common sense. Thus the circle is completed. Common sense continually demands the responsible criticism of refined knowledge, and refined knowledge sooner or later requires the security of common-sense support. [Pepper, 1942, pp. 44-46]* *

Root metaphors are drawn from experiences of common sense and are used by philosophers to interpret the world. Each of the major philosophies has cognitively refined one of these root metaphors into a set of categories that hang together and claim validity by all evidence of every kind. From the seven or eight such clues or root metaphors in the epistemological literature, Pepper argues that there are only four that are relatively adequate in precision (how accurately they fit the facts) and scope (the extent to which all known facts are covered) and can thus claim the status of a world hypothesis.

---

*Reprinted from *World Hypotheses* by Stephen C. Pepper by permission of the University of California Press, Berkeley, California.

The first of these, Pepper calls *formism* (also known as realism), whose root metaphor is the observed similarity between objects and events. The second is *mechanism* (also called naturalism or materialism), whose root metaphor is the machine. The third is *contextualism* (better known as pragmatism), with the root metaphor of the changing historical event. The final relatively adequate world hypothesis is *organicism* (absolute idealism), whose root metaphor is achievement of harmonious unity. None of these world hypotheses is reflected in pure form in the work of any single philosopher, since most philosophers tend to be somewhat eclectic in their use of world hypotheses. For purposes of understanding, however, we can say that formism originated in the classical works of Socrates, Plato, and Aristotle, and mechanism in the works of Democritus, Lucretius, and Galileo. Contextualism is more modern, originating in the works of Dewey, James, Peirce, and Mead, as is organicism, developed primarily in the work of Hegel and Royce.

The isormorphism between Pepper's system of world hypotheses and the structure of the learning process becomes apparent in his analysis of the interrelationships among the four world hypotheses. Formism and mechanism, the two world hypotheses underlying modern science, are primarily analytic in nature, wherein elements and factors are the basic facts from which any synthesis is a derivative. Contextualism and organicism, on the other hand, are synthetic, wherein the basic facts are contexts and complexes such that analysis of components is a derivative of the synthetic whole. Within both the analytic and synthetic world hypotheses there is a further polarity between dispersive and integrative strategies of inquiry. Formism and contextualism are both dispersive in their plan, explaining facts one by one without systematic relationship to one another. Indeed, both formism and contextualism see the world as indeterminate and unpredictable. Organicism and mechanism are integrative in their plan, believing in an integrated world order where indeterminance is simply a reflection of inadequate knowledge. Because they seek integrative determinant explanations, the strength of the integrative world hypotheses (organicism and mechanism) is precision and predictability; their weakness is lack of scope, their inability to achieve an integrated explanation of all things. The dispersive world hypotheses, on the other hand, are weak in precision, offering several possible interpretations for many events, but strong in scope, since their explanatory range is not restricted by any integrative principle.

Figure 5.1 shows Pepper's system of world hypotheses overlaid on the structural dimensions of the learning process. The analytic world views emphasize knowing by comprehension, and the synthetic world views give primary emphasis to knowing by apprehension. The dispersive philosophies emphasize transformation by extension, the discovery and explanation of laws and events in the external world; the integrative philosophies emphasize transformation by intention, the search for underlying principles and integrated meaning.

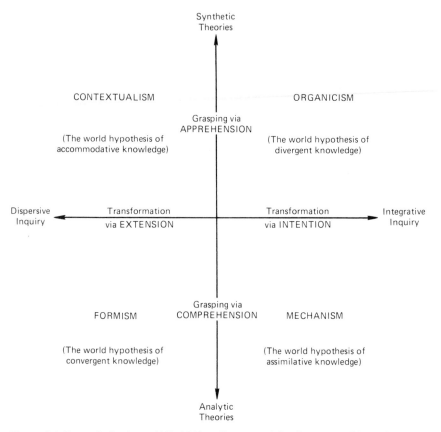

Figure 5.1 Pepper's System of World Hypotheses and the Structure of Learning

Formism and Mechanism—The Analytic World Hypotheses Based on Comprehension

Inquiry in modern science rests primarily on the metaphysical foundations of formism and mechanism. The modern version of formism, realism, incorporates many of the characteristics of mechanism, such as an emphasis on space/time location, so that the two root metaphors are often indistinguishable. E.A. Burtt describes this interrelationship between the two analytic world hypotheses by illustrating how both are central to the concept of law:

> *In its very essence this concept [law] preserves something vital in the formistic conception of "form" as well as something vital in the mechanistic conception of "regular interrelationship" among the parts of a machine. And I can think of no statement of either formism or mechanism as a metaphysical view, calculated to appear at all persuasive to any modern mind, which has not somewhere drawn upon those features of modern science which synthesize earlier formism and mechanism in precisely this fashion. [Burtt, 1943, p. 600]*

There is, however, an important sense in which the two analytic world hypotheses support different modes of inquiry based on the dispersive nature of formism and the integrative nature of mechanism. Mechanism as an integrative strategy is better suited as a foundation for basic research in the physical sciences and mathematics, whereas formism's dispersive plan is more attuned to inquiry in the applied sciences and the science-based professions, where the dictates of practical circumstance often take precedence over the achievement of integrative frameworks. Even though the dispersive nature of formism creates constant difficulties of precision because of the many interpretations to which a single fact is amenable, from a practical standpoint this variety offers flexibility in problem solving.

Formism's root metaphor of similarity is based on the commonsense perception of similar things. It is reliance on this root metaphor that allows the creation of systems of classifications based on similarity, such as the periodic table of elements or biological phyla. It is also the basis by which the validity of models, maps, and mathematical relationships is judged—that is, by similarity of these symbolic comprehensions to the reality being studied. Thus, the formist theory of truth is correspondence; the truth of a description lies in its degree of correspondence to the object of reference.

The modern formist inquiry strategy, sometimes called scientific empiricism, places great emphasis on the judgments of concrete existence through reports of sense experience controlled by the conventions of logic and scientific method. In this sense, even logical positivism, which adamantly denies any metaphysical foundation, is based on formism, since *similar* judgments by scientists of their sense experience are the basis for confidence in positivistic statements. Knowledge in modern formist inquiry is created when the community of scientists is able to agree on the reliable and accurate location of phenomena in time and space—to answer the inquiry questions, "When?" and "Where?" Singer (1959) traces the Platonic origins of such space/time individuation and compares this empirical approach to the rationalist Leibnitzian approach:

> As for the tradition, it goes back at least as far as to Plato, who in his Timaeus *makes space the "pure matter" that individuates general qualities (i.e., takes care of the distinction between* this thing and *that other precisely like thing). And from Plato's time down, it would be possible to trace an imposing history of space-time individuation. As for practical sanctions, our courts of justice recognize the all-important difference between the evidence established by "identification by minute description" and the evidence established by "individuation by space-time coordinates." The former, Leibnitizian, method of identification is exactly the one underlying our present method of "police identification." With sufficient refinement of detail, Bertillon measurements may be made to constitute an indefinitely minute description of the kind of man a certain individual is. But suppose the accused "identified" with the culprit to the limit of available description; how long would he remain in the dock could he establish an "alibi"? In insisting that the same individual cannot be in two places at the same time, in*

admitting that two individuals, however like, can be, the law throws the whole weight of its authority on the side of Kant and against Leibnitz. [Singer, 1959, p. 43]

The basic units of knowledge in formism are empirical uniformities and natural laws. The emphasis is on the analysis, measurement, and categorization of observable experience and the establishment of empirical uniformities defining relationships between observed categories—that is, natural laws—with a minimum of reliance on inferred structures or processes that are not directly accessible to public experience.

Mechanism as a world hypothesis is less trusting of the appearances of sense experience and relies more on rationalist principles to analytically separate appearances from reality. The root metaphor of mechanism is the machine, and knowledge in mechanism is refined by analyzing the world as if it were a machine. Central to this analysis is the distinction between primary and secondary qualities. Primary qualities are those features and characteristics that are essential to describing the functioning of the machine. The traditional primary qualities have been size, shape, motion, solidity, mass, and number. In the case of a lever, for example, the primary qualities would be the length of the lever, the location of the fulcrum, and the weights applied at either end. Secondary qualities would be all other characteristics of the lever, such as its color and the material the weights are made of, that are not essential to explaining its functioning. As Democritus, one of the classical founders of mechanism, put it, "By convention colored, by convention sweet, by convention bitter; in reality only atoms and the void." There are six steps or categories in mechanistic analysis:

1 Specification of the field of location in time and space. (In mechanism, everything that exists exists somewhere, unlike classical formism, where form exists independently of particulars in time and space.)
2 Identification of primary qualities.
3 Description of laws governing primary qualities.
4 Description of secondary qualities.
5 Principles for connecting secondary qualities and primary qualities.
6 Laws for regularities among secondary qualities.

The theory of truth in mechanism is somewhat problematic, since, as Pepper points out, primary qualities can be known only by inference from secondary qualities; in other words, they are comprehensions:

> . . . *all immediate evidence seems to be of the nature of secondary qualities (all ultimate primary qualities such as the properties of electrons and the cosmic field being far from the range of immediate perceptions); moreover, this evidence seems to be correlated with the activities of organisms, specifically with each individual organism that is said to be immediately aware of evidence. All immediate evidence is, therefore, private to each individual organism. It follows*

that knowledge of the external world must be symbolic and inferential. . . . So that in a mature mechanism, the primary qualities and all the primary categories are not evidence but inference, or if you will, speculation. [Pepper, 1942, pp. 221 and 224]

The proper theory of truth for mechanism thus lies in the correlation of primary qualities with secondary qualities in what Pepper calls the causal adjustment theory of truth: Does knowledge of the machine in question allow the person to make causal adjustments with predictable consequences for secondary qualities?

The basic units of knowledge in mechanism are the primary qualities or structures that make up the world. Structuralism is thus a modern variant of mechanism. Model building is a typical inquiry method of mechanism that seeks to answer the basic inquiry question, "What is real? What are the basic structures of reality?"—as, for example, in the discovery of the structure of the DNA molecule.

We must stand in awe of the achievements of modern science and thereby give great credibility to the scientific inquiry methods based on formism and mechanism. These represent the highest refinement of human powers of comprehension. Yet ironically, the greatest achievement of scientific inquiry may be the discovery of its own limitations. The history of science is marked by the successive overthrow of widely accepted views of the nature of reality in favor of new, more all-encompassing but more question-provoking views. Today there is little dogma in enlightened scientific inquiry, for the assumptions on which scientific systems of comprehension are based have been challenged by scientific discoveries at the forefront of knowledge. The invention and later validation of non-Euclidian geometry in Einstein's theory of space and time brought down the principles of nineteenth-century science and the "self-evident" Kantian *a priori* forms on which they were based. A number of subsequent discoveries brought into question the very notion of permanent external objects independent of the observer. Whether light is a wave or particle depends on how it is measured. The so-called "bootstrap" theory of the nucleus suggests that subatomic particles inside the nucleus of the atom have no self-sufficient existence, since their properties are determined by their neighbors, and vice versa. Thus, particles in the nucleus gain existence only when they are knocked out of the nucleus by a scientist. The well-known Heisenberg principle of indeterminacy showed that one cannot measure both the location and the momentum of a particle with certainty. In Heisenberg's words, "What we observe is not nature itself, but nature exposed to our methods of questioning."

There are corresponding limitations and indeterminacies in formal systems of logic. In 1931, Kurt Gödel showed that no consistent formal system sufficiently rich to contain elementary arithmetic can by its own principles of reasoning demonstrate its own consistency, a theorem that defined the limits of comprehension as a way of knowing. From Gödel's theorem we are led to the conclusion that to judge the logical consistency of any complex formal system, we must go outside it. Commenting on this indeterminate characteristic of formal systems, a characteristic that he calls tacit meaning, Polanyi says:

> Thus to speak a language is to commit ourselves to the double indeterminacy due to our reliance both on its formalism and on our own continued reconsideration of this formalism in its bearing on our experience. For just as, owing to the ultimately tacit character of all our knowledge, we remain ever unable to say all that we know, so also in view of the tacit character of meaning, we can never quite know what is implied in what we say. [Polanyi, 1958, p. 95]

Contextualism and Organicism—The Synthetic World Hypotheses Based on Apprehension

The recently recognized limitations of comprehension-based knowledge structures have undoubtedly given sustenance to the development of the synthetic world hypotheses based on apprehension. John Dewey, in *Experience and Nature*, argued that the earlier dogmatic intellectualism of science created an unnatural separation of primary experience from nature in which nature became indifferent and dead and human beings were alienated from their own subjective experience, their hopes and dreams, fears and sorrows:

> The assumption of intellectualism goes contrary to the facts of what is primarily experienced. For things are objects to be treated, used, acted upon and with, enjoyed and endured, even more than things to be known. They are things had before they are things cognized. . . . When intellectual experience and its material are taken to be primary, the cord that binds experience and nature is cut. [Dewey, 1958, pp. 21 and 23]

The systems of social knowledge based on the synthetic world hypotheses operate under something of a handicap, since they must express understandings stemming from apprehension in the social language of comprehension. When the linear, digital descriptions of language and mathematics are used to describe the holistic, analogic context of apprehended experience, the result often seems exceedingly complex and abstract. Yet organicism and contextualism have proven themselves strong in the field of human values and practical affairs—areas where the analytic world theories are weak. Pepper states, for example:

> It may be pointed out that the mechanistic root metaphor springs out of the commonsense field of uncriticized physical fact, so that there would be no analogical stretch, so to speak, in the mechanistic interpretations of this field, while the stretch might be considerable in the mechanistic interpretation of the commonsense field of value; and somewhat the same, in the reverse order, with

respect to organistic interpretations. Moreover, mechanism has for several generations been particularly congenial to scientists and organicism to artists and to persons of religious bent. Also, the internal difficulties which appear from a critical study of the mechanistic theory seem to be particularly acute in the neighborhood of values, and counterwise the internal difficulties of organicism seem to be particularly acute in the neighborhood of physical fact. [Pepper, 1942, p. 110]

Like mechanism and formism, the synthetic world theories contextualism and organicism tend to combine and:

. . . are so nearly allied that they may almost be called the same theory, the one with a dispersive, the other with an integrative plan. Pragmatism has often been called an absolute idealism without an absolute; and, as a first approximate description, this is acceptable. So a little more emphasis on integration, as Dewey for instance shows in his Art as Experience, *produces a contextualistic-organistic eclecticism; as likewise a little less emphasis on final integration in organicism, as is characteristic of Royce. Royce even called himself somewhere a pragmatic idealist. [Pepper, 1942, p. 147]*

The contextualist approach, however, has a certain affinity to the world of practical affairs in business, politics, and the social professions, whereas the organistic approach, with its emphasis on absolute values and ideals, is more attuned to the humanities, arts, and social sciences.

The root metaphor of organicism is what Burtt calls harmonious unity. The metaphor stems from the biological organism growing to its fulfillment. The central concern of organismic world views is growth and development, with a focus on the processes whereby the ideal is realized from the actual. These processes are most often conceived as some process of differentiation and higher-order integration. This process is teleological toward the absolute, not evolutionary as in the biological principles of natural selection, which are closer to contextualism's open-ended developmental processes. The organismic view of development is the basis of modern humanistic developmental psychology—most notably, Abraham Maslow's theory of self-actualization—and in somewhat more dispersive, contextual, evolutionary forms, organicism is the basis for research in cognitive and adult development. Much historical analysis is loosely based on the organistic world hypothesis, although Hegel's teleological progression to the Absolute is widely questioned. To modern organicists, Hegel's view of development was a dogmatic and unnecessarily narrow progression from maximum fragmentation to his ultimate integration via the dialectic process:

Hegel was right, say these later organicists, in the inevitability of the trend of cognition toward a final organization in which all contradictions vanish. He was right in his observation that the nexes of fragments lead out toward other fragments which develop contradictions and demand coherent resolution. He was right in his idea that these nexes have a particular attraction for those relevant traits which are peculiarly recalcitrant to harmonization with the facts already gathered. It was the aberrations in the orbit of Uranus, those recalcitrant data which refused to harmonize with the Newtonian laws, that particularly attracted the attention of astronomers and led to the discovery of Neptune. In all these things Hegel was right. But he was wrong and invited undeserved ridicule for the organistic program by his fantastic, arbitrary, and rigid picture of the path of progress. [Pepper, 1942, pp. 294-95]

The theory of truth in organicism is coherence and is derived from the endpoint of development, the Absolute—an organic whole that includes everything in a totally determinant order. Thus, the truth of a proposition is the degree to which it is inclusive, determinant, and organized in an organic whole where every element relates to every other in an interdependent system. There is a certain similarity in this description of organismic truth to the primary quality structures of mechanism, but in mechanism, the emphasis is on structures, whereas in organicism, it is on the *processes* by which progress is made to the determinant orderliness of the whole.

The basic inquiry question of organicism is one of ultimate values—why things are as they are. Whereas mechanism relies on symbols and the denotative functions of language, there is a tendency in organicism to rely on images and the connotative aspects of language to describe the apprehensions (appearances) from which reality emerges. Dewitt identifies five characteristics of organic concepts: They are holistic, visually apprehended, organized aesthetically and neatly, and functionally based:

In sum [these characteristics] emphasize the relation of organic concepts to ordinary experience; that is, experience in a universe where straight parallel lines meet at infinity, where the sun visibly rises and sets, where the earth is flat (at least its curvature is of no practical importance), where cause and effect have a direct sequential relationship, where action does not take place without an immediate objective as the motive of the action, where objects are visibly finite. This is the universe which accounts for almost all our everyday experiences but represents a very limited range of experience—involving, if you will, the statistical fallacy that frequency of occurrence is an index of importance. [Dewitt, 1957, p. 182]

The final world hypothesis is contextualism. Although Pepper treats each of the four systems evenhandedly in his 1942 book, later, in *Concept and Quality* (1966), he embraces a modified version of contextualism (he calls his new world hypothesis "selectivism") as the most adequate of the existing world hypotheses. The advantage of contextualism (selectivism) over the other three world hypotheses is that it integrates fact and value in an open-minded and open-eyed way—a way that is emergent and slightly optimistic, with no dogma of method or tool save a commitment to humanity. The root metaphor of contextualism is the historical event—not the past historical event, but the immediate event, alive in the present—actions in their context evolving and creating the future. Contextualism as a synthetic world hypothesis is concerned with the concrete event as experienced in all its complexity. The one constant in contextualism is change. Reality is constantly being created and recreated. Thus, the permanent forms of formism or structures of mechanism cannot exist in the contextualist world view. Whitehead (1933, p. 255) puts it this way: "Thus the future of the universe, though conditioned by the immanence of its past, awaits for its complete determination the spontaneity of the novel individual occasions as in their season they come into being."

Inquiry in contextualism is focused on the quality and texture of the immediate event as experienced; hence its association with phenomenology. Lewin's (1951) conception of the person's life space as a field of forces in which behavior is determined by ahistorical causation (only forces existing in the moment, such as a memory, determine behavior) is a primary example of contextually based theory. In this theory of truth, the contextualist works from the present event outward in what is called the operational theory of truth. The basic inquiry question is how to act or think. Actions are true if they are workable; that is, if they lead to desired end states in experience. Hypotheses are true when they give insight into—are verified by—the quality and texture of the event they refer to. Hypotheses thus achieve qualitative confirmation by the experiences they refer to. In pure contextualism, however, the truth of a hypothesis gives no insight into the qualities of nature; for nature is constantly emerging and changing. A hypothesis is only a tool for controlling nature. "It does not mirror nature in the way supposed by the correspondence theory, nor is it a genuine partial integration of nature in the way supposed by the coherence theory of organicism" (Pepper, 1942, p. 275).

Summary

Table 5.1 summarizes the characteristics of the four world hypotheses—contextualism, organicism, formism, and mechanism—relating them to the fields of inquiry in which they seem to flourish best: respectively, the social professions, the humanities and social science, the science-based professions, and natural science and mathematics. The significance of Pepper's metaphysical analysis lies in the identification of the basic inquiry structures for refining knowledge. These are derived from simple metaphors of common sense, which lay bare the root assumptions on which knowledge in each system is based. His typology introduces some order to the tangled, fast-growing thicket of social knowledge. The system is perhaps best treated in the framework of contextualism—as a set of hypotheses to be verified, as useful tools for examining knowledge structures in specific contexts. It is to just such an analysis that we now turn.

Table 5.1 A Typology of Knowledge Structures (World Hypotheses) and Their Respective Fields of Inquiry

	Contextualism	Formism	Mechanism	Organicism
World hypothesis	Contextualism	Formism	Mechanism	Organicism
Root metaphor	Changing historical event	Similarity	The machine	Harmonious unity
Inquiry strategy	Discrete synthesis	Discrete analysis	Integrative analysis	Integrative synthesis
Modern philosophical forms	Pragmatism, phenomenology	Realism, scientific empiricism (positivism)	Materialism, naturalism, structuralism	Idealism, absolute idealism
Theory of truth	Operationalism—workability, verification, qualitative confirmation	Correspondence	Causal adjustment—correlation of structure with secondary qualities	Coherence—inclusiveness, determinacy, organicity
Basic inquiry question	How	When, where	What	Why
Basic units of knowledge	Events	Natural laws; empirical uniformities	Structures: the locations and laws governing primary qualities	Processes
Dominant method of portraying knowledge	Actions	Things	Symbols	Images
Field of inquiry where it dominates	Social professions	Science-based professions	Natural science and mathematics	Humanities and social sciences

SOCIAL KNOWLEDGE AS LIVING SYSTEMS OF INQUIRY—THE RELATION BETWEEN THE STRUCTURE OF KNOWLEDGE AND FIELDS OF INQUIRY AND ENDEAVOR

Knowledge does not exist solely in books, mathematical formulas, or philosophical systems; it requires active learners to interact with, interpret, and elaborate these symbols. The complete structure of social knowledge must therefore include living systems of inquiry, learning subcultures sharing similar norms and values about how to create valid social knowledge. Academic disciplines, professions, and occupations are homogeneous cultures that differ on nearly every dimension associated with the term. There are different languages (or at least dialects). There are strong boundaries defining membership and corresponding initiation rites. There are different norms and values, particularly about the nature of truth and how it is to be sought. There are different patterns of power and authority and differing criteria for attaining status. There are differing standards of intimacy and modes for its expression. Cultural variation is expressed in style of dress (lab coats and uniforms, business suits, beards and blue jeans), furnishings (wooden or steel desks, interior decoration, functional rigor, or "creative disorder"), architecture, and use of space and time. Most important, these patterns of variation are not random but have a meaning and integrity for the members. There is in each discipline or profession a sense of historical continuity and, in most cases, historical mission.

If the central mission of the university is learning in the broadest sense, encompassing the student in the introductory lecture course and the advanced researcher in the laboratory, library, or studio, then it seems reasonable to hypothesize that different styles of learning, thinking, and knowledge creation are the focal points for cultural variation among disciplines. Different styles of learning manifest themselves in variations among the primary tasks, technologies, and products of disciplines—criteria for academic excellence and productivity, teaching methods, research methods, methods for recording and portraying knowledge—and in other patterns of cultural variation—differences in faculty and student demographics, personality and aptitudes, values and group norms. For example, Anthony Biglan (1973b) has found significant variations in departmental concerns and organization. In the soft areas (social professions and humanities/social science), there is less faculty interaction than in the hard areas (science-based professions and natural science/mathematics); and in the hard areas, this interaction is strongly associated with research productivity. Hard-area scholars produce fewer manuscripts but more journal articles. The emphasis in soft areas is on teaching, and in hard areas on research. Applied areas (social and science-based professions) show more faculty social connectedness than do basic areas (humanities/social science, natural science/mathematics). Their research goals are influenced more by others, including outside agencies, although they are less interested in research than are their basic area colleagues. They publish more technical reports than their basic area colleagues, whose interest in research is not reflected in the time they spend on it.

In reviewing other research on differences among academic disciplines, one is struck by the fact that relatively little comparative research has been done on academic disciplines and departments. The reason for this lies in the same difficulties that characterize all cross-cultural research—the problem of access and the problem of perspective. The relatively closed nature of academic subcultures makes access to data difficult, and it is equally difficult to choose an unbiased perspective for interpreting data. To analyze one system of inquiry according to the ground rules of another is to invite misunderstanding and conflict and further restrict access to data.

To study disciplines from the perspective of learning offers some promise for overcoming these difficulties, particularly if learning is defined not in the narrow psychological sense of modification of behavior but in the broader sense of acquisition of knowledge. The access problem is eased, because every discipline has a prime commitment to learning and inquiry and has developed a learning style that is at least moderately effective. Viewing the acquisition of knowledge in academic disciplines from the perspective of the learning process promises a dual reward—a more refined epistemology that defines the varieties of truth and their interrelationships, and a greater psychological understanding of how people acquire knowledge in its different forms. Twenty years ago, Carl Bereiter and Mervin Freedman envisioned these rewards:

> There is every reason to suppose that studies applying tests of these sorts to students in different fields could rapidly get beyond the point of demonstrating the obvious. We should, for instance, be able to find out empirically whether the biological taxonomist has special aptitudes similar to his logical counterpart in the field of linguistics. And there are many comparisons whose outcomes it would be hard to foresee. In what fields do the various memory abilities flourish? Is adaptive flexibility more common in some fields than in others? Because, on the psychological end, these ability measures are tied to theories of the structure or functioning of higher mental processes, and because, on the philosophical end, the academic disciplines are tied to theories of logic and cognition, empirical data linking the two should be in little danger of remaining for long in the limbo where so many correlational data stay. [Bereiter and Freedman, 1962, pp. 567-68]

It is surprising that with the significant exception of Piaget's pioneering work on genetic epistemology, few have sought to reap these rewards.

The research that has been done has instead focused primarily on what from the perspective above are the peripheral norms of academic disciplines rather than the pivotal norms governing learning and inquiry. Thus, studies have examined political/social attitudes and values (Bereiter and Freedman, 1962;), personality patterns (Roe, 1956), aspirations and goals (Davis, 1965), sex distribution and other demographic variables (Feldman, 1974), and social interaction (Biglan, 1973b; Hall, 1969). The bias of these studies is no doubt a reflection of the fact that psychological research has until quite recently been predominantly concerned with the social/emotional aspects of human behavior and development. Concern with cognitive/intellectual factors has been neatly wrapped into concepts of general intelligence. Thus, most early studies of intellectual differences among disciplines were interested only in which discipline has the smarter students (for example, Wolfle, 1954; Terman and Oden, 1947).

The hypothesis to be explored in this section is that since learning, broadly conceived as adaptation, is the central mission of every discipline and profession, the cultural variations among fields of inquiry and endeavor will be organized in a way that is congruent with the structure of the learning process and the structure of knowledge. When one examines academic disciplines in the four major groupings we have identified—the social professions, the science-based professions, humanities/social science, and natural science/ mathematics—it becomes apparent that what constitutes valid knowledge in these four groupings differs widely. This is easily observed in differences in how knowledge is reported (for instance, numerical or logical symbols, words or images), in inquiry method (such as case studies, experiments, logical analysis), and in criteria for evaluation (say, practical vs. statistical significance). Figure 5.2 illustrates the specific relationship predicted among fields of inquiry, the structure of knowledge, and the structure of the learning process. We have in the preceding section elaborated on the relation between knowledge structures and the learning process and seen in this analysis suggestions concerning the relation of knowledge and learning to living systems of inquiry. Synthetic knowledge structures learned via apprehension are associated with qualitative, humanistic fields, whereas analytic knowledge structures learned via comprehension are related to the quantitative scientific fields, dispersive knowledge structures learned via extension are related to the professions and applied sciences, and integrative knowledge structures learned via intention are related to the basic academic disciplines.

The Structure of Academic Fields

The first suggestion that experiential learning theory might provide a useful framework for describing variations in the inquiry norms of academic disciplines came in Chapter 4, when we examined the undergraduate majors of practicing managers and graduate students in management (see Figure 4.4.) Although these people shared a common occupation, variations in their learning styles were strongly associated with their undergraduate educational experience. There was a good fit with the predictions outlined in Figure 5.2, showing a relation between the structure of learning as measured by individual learning style and one's chosen field of specialization in college. Undergraduate business majors tended to have accommodative learning styles; engineers, on the average, fell in the convergent quadrant; history, English, political science, and psychology majors all had divergent learning styles; mathematics and chemistry

124

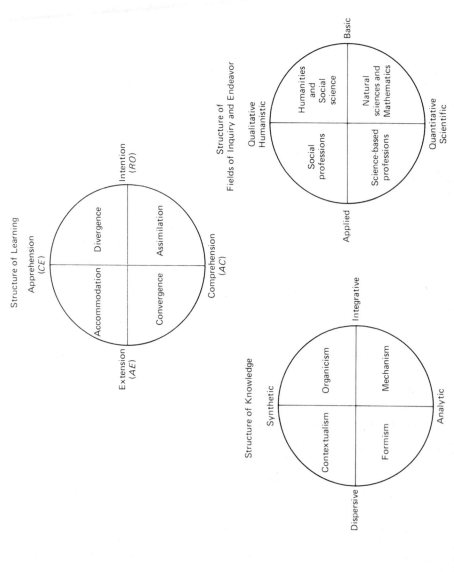

Figure 5.2 Relationships Among the Structure of the Learning Process, the Structure of Knowledge, and Fields of Inquiry and Endeavor

majors had assimilative learning styles, as did economics and sociology majors; and physics majors were very abstract, falling between the convergent and assimilative quadrants. These data suggested that undergraduate education was a major factor in shaping individual learning style, either by the process of selection into a discipline or socialization while learning in that discipline, or, as is most likely the case, both.

We now examine how others perceive the differences between academic disciplines and whether these perceptions are congruent with the structure of knowledge and learning. Anthony Biglan (1973a) used a method well suited to answer these questions in his studies of faculty members at the University of Illinois and a small western college. Using the technique of multidimensional scaling, he analyzed the underlying structures of scholars' judgments about the similarities of subject matter in different academic disciplines. The procedure required faculty members to group subject areas on the basis of similarity without any labeling of the groupings. Through a kind of factor analysis, the similarity groupings are then mapped onto an n-dimensional space where n is determined by goodness of fit and interpretability of the dimensions. The two dimensions accounting for the most variance in the University of Illinois data were interpreted by Biglan to be hard-soft and pure-applied. When academic areas at Illinois are mapped on this two-dimensional space (Figure 5.3), we see a great similarity between the pattern of Biglan's data and the structure of knowledge and learning described in Figure 5.2. Business (assumed equivalent to accounting and finance) is accommodative in learning style and contextualist in knowledge structure. Engineering fits with convergent learning and formist knowledge. Physics, mathematics, and chemistry are related to assimilative learning and mechanistic knowledge, and the humanistic fields—history, political science, English, and psychology—fall in the divergent, organistic quadrant. Foreign languages, economics, and sociology were divergent in Biglan's study rather than assimilative as in Figure 4.4. Biglan also reported that the pattern of academic-area relationships in the small-college data was very similar to that in the Illinois data.

These two studies suggest that the two basic dimensions of experiential learning theory, abstract/concrete and active/reflective, are major dimensions of differentiation among academic disciplines. A more extensive data base is needed, however. The learning-style data came from a single occupation, and in the case of some academic areas, sample sizes were small. Biglan's study, on the other hand, was limited to two universities, and differences here could be attributed to the specific characteristics of these academic departments.

In search of a more extensive and representative sample, data collected in the Carnegie Commission on Higher Education's 1969 study of representative American colleges and universities were examined. These data consisted of 32,963 questionnaires from graduate students in 158 institutions and 60,028 questionnaires from faculty in 303 institutions. Using tabulations of these data reported in Feldman (1974), ad hoc indices were created of the abstract/concrete and active/reflective dimensions for the 45 academic fields identified in

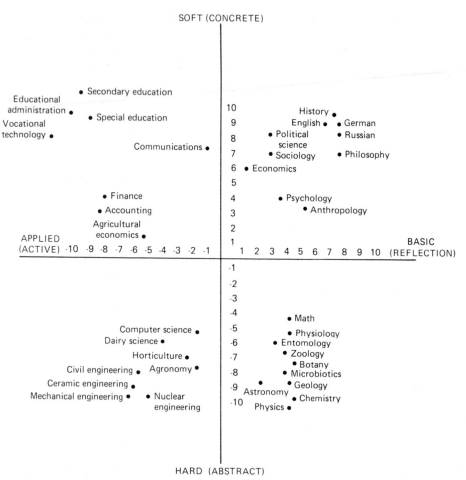

Figure 5.3 Similarities Among 36 Academic Specialties at the University of Illinois [*Source:* Adapted from A. Biglan, "The Characteristics of Subject Matter in Different Academic Areas," *Journal of Applied Psychology,* 57 (1973).]

the study. The abstract/concrete index was based on graduate student responses to two questions asking how important an undergraduate background in mathematics or humanities was for their fields. The mathematics and humanities questions were highly negatively correlated (-.78). The index was computed using the percentage of graduate-student respondents who strongly agreed that either humanities or mathematics was very important:

$$\frac{\% \text{ Math important} + (100 - \% \text{ Humanities important})}{2}$$

Thus, high index scores indicated a field where a mathematics background was important and humanities was not important.

The active/reflective index used faculty data on the percentage of faculty in a given field who were engaged in paid consultation to business, government, and so on. This seemed to be the best indicator on the questionnaire of the active, applied orientation of the field. As Feldman observed, "Consulting may be looked upon not only as a source of added income but also as an indirect measure of the 'power' of a discipline; that is, as a chance to exert the influence and knowledge of a discipline outside the academic setting" (1974, p. 52). The groupings of academic fields based on these indices are shown in Figure 5.4.

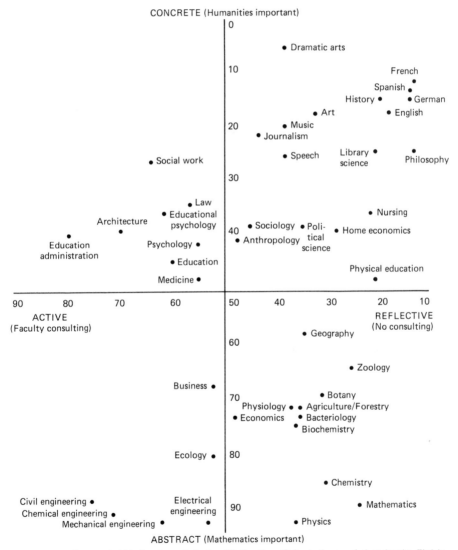

Figure 5.4 Concrete/Abstract and Active/Reflective Orientations of Academic Fields Derived from the Carnegie Commission Study of American Colleges and Universities

The indices produce a pattern of relationships among academic fields that is highly consistent with Biglan's study and the managerial learning-style data. The results suggest that the widely shared view that cultural variation in academic fields is predominantly unidimensional, dividing the academic community into two camps—the scientific and the artistic (for example, Snow, 1963; Hudson, 1966)—is usefully enriched by the addition of a second dimension of action/reflection or applied/basic. When academic fields are mapped on this two-dimensional space, a fourfold typology of disciplines emerges. In the abstract/reflective quadrant, the *natural sciences and mathematics* are clustered; the abstract/active quadrant includes the *science-based professions,* most notably the engineering fields; the concrete/active quadrant encompasses what might be called the *social professions,* such as education, social work, and law; the concrete/reflective quadrant includes the *humanities and social sciences.*

Some fields seem to include within their boundaries considerable variation on these two dimensions of experiential learning theory. Several of the professions (particularly management, medicine, and architecture) are themselves multidisciplinary, encompassing specialties that emphasize different learning styles. Medicine requires both a concern for human service and scientific knowledge. Architecture has requirements for artistic and engineering excellence. Management involves integration of both quantitative and qualitative analysis in active decision making. Several of the social sciences, particularly psychology, sociology, and economics, can vary greatly in their basic inquiry paradigm. Clinical psychology emphasizes divergent learning skills, experimental psychology emphasizes convergent skills, and industrial and educational psychology emphasize practical, accommodative skills. Sociology can be highly abstract and theoretical (as in Parsonian structural functionalism) or concrete and active (as in phenomenology or ethnomethodology). Some economics departments may be very convergent, emphasizing the use of econometric models in public policy, and others are divergent, emphasizing economic history and philosophy. Indeed, every field will show variation on these dimensions within a given department, between departments, from undergraduate to graduate levels, and so on. The purpose of this analysis is not to "pigeonhole" fields but to identify a common structural model for learning, knowledge, and field of inquiry that is useful for describing variations in the learning/inquiry process in any specific educational or work setting.

The Structure of Careers and Career Development

Since learning is a lifelong process and knowledge is created at work as well as at the university, there is reason to suspect a similar isomorphism between knowledge/learning structures and the structure of career paths. The data presented in Chapter 4, showing the relationships with learning style of professional careers (Figure 4.5) and jobs (Figures 4.6 and 4.7), support this contention. More systematic relationships, however, can be seen in the occupational classification scheme developed by Anne Roe. In her book, *The Psychology of Occupations,* she develops a two-dimensional scheme that defines eight general categories of occupations with six developmental levels in each category. The eight occupational categories and paths of career development are these:

1 Service (from chambermaid to therapist)

2 Business contact (from peddler to promoter)

3 Organization (from messenger to president)

4 Technology (from laborer to inventor)

5 Outdoor (from laborer to specialist)

6 Science (from helper to scientist)

7 General culture (from clerk to scholar)

8 Arts and entertainment (from stagehand to artist)

Reviewing studies of the characteristics of persons in these fields, she states:

> *Groups are so arranged that, with one exception, contiguous ones are more closely related than noncontiguous ones. Each of groups IV, V and VI is related to the other two to about the same degree. Group V placed between IV and VI, observing the close relationship between these two. The groups are arranged in this way because IV is also related to III and VI to VII, whereas V is less closely related to any of the others. The arrangement should be thought of as circular, that is, Group VIII is related to Group I as well as to Group VII. [Roe, 1956, pp. 144-45]*

In her later work she suggests that in the circle arrangement, Groups I, II, III, VII, and VIII are classified as people-oriented career areas, whereas Groups IV, V, and VI are non-people-oriented, and thus "an ordered, counterclockwise arrangement of these groups is not untenable" (1957, p. 217). These remarks serve to orient her career classifications on the two-dimensional framework of experiential learning theory.[2] Figure 5.5 shows the correspondence between Roe's circle of careers and the structures of learning, knowledge, and fields of inquiry postulated by experiential learning theory. (Categories IV and V are reversed here, since I share Roe's concern about the misplacement of the outdoor category, and in experiential learning-theory terms, category IV (technology) should be more abstract.)

In addition, Figure 5.5 represents the developmental levels within each career path as six-level pyramids rising from each category. These levels,

---

[2] Other schemes show a similar isomorphism, such as that of Holland (Osipow, 1973, p. 60); compare Samuelson (1982) for the suggested link between experiential learning and Roe's work.

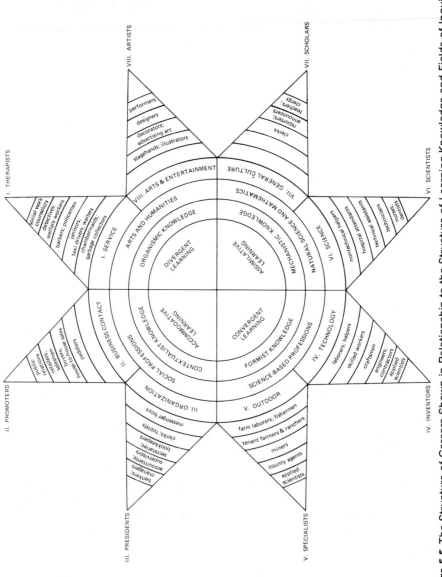

Figure 5.5 The Structure of Careers Shown in Relationship to the Structure of Learning Knowledge and Fields of Inquiry

according to Roe, are defined by increasing levels of responsibility, capacity, and skill.[3] In this framework, higher-level jobs require greater integrative complexity and adaptive flexibility (see Chapter 8, p. 213) in order to deal with the greater extension of their responsibilities in time and space. Jacques has suggested that this extension can be measured with great reliability in jobs by what he calls the time span of discretion. As he defines it:

> The higher a person goes in an executive system the longer is the time framework within which he or she works. . . . A job's size can be directly and simply measured by completion times targeted for the longest tasks that are required to be carried out in that role, namely the time span of discretion. [Jacques, 1979, pp. 126-27]

Thus, the highest-level jobs in the eight career paths, such as scientist, inventor, and artist, have time spans of discretion that transcend even lifetimes, whereas jobs at the lower levels are increasingly constrained in their time (and space) limits.

Figure 5.5 may serve as a focal point for a review of the very lengthy progress of argument in this chapter. It shows the relationships among the structure of learning, the structure of social knowledge, and living systems of inquiry (academic fields) and endeavor (careers). It has been argued here that the isomorphism among these structures is rooted in the structure of learning and, in particular, in the integration of the apprehensive and comprehensive way of knowing the world. Social knowledge is a cultural tool that comes alive only in the personal knowledge of the user. In the unique individuality of apprehended experience lies the creative force for expanding, shaping, and validating social knowledge. This social knowledge, in turn, is invaluable in guiding people in their choices of experiences in a field of personal life space and physical reality that is expanding continuously, often by the proactive human tendency to choose experiences that explore and expand these boundaries. We have seen that the success of this learning venture is highly dependent on the proper attitude—an attitude of partial skepticism requiring that each act of knowing be steadily steered between the Scylla of appreciative apprehension and the Charybdis of critical comprehension. The course thus steered is the path to development.

[3]In experiential learning theory terms, these levels can be seen as stages of development toward integrative complexity. Referring to the cone model of development to be described in Chapter 6 (Figure 6.3), the reader can imagine viewing the cone from the bottom with the facing slopes of the cone peeled back to display the six levels of development described in each of the eight pyramids. These six levels roughly correspond to the six levels of consciousness described in Chapter 6 (Figure 6.2).

six

The Experiential Learning Theory of Development

The course of nature is to divide what is united and to unite what is divided.
Goethe

There is a quality of learning that cannot be ignored. It is assertive, forward-moving, and proactive. Learning is driven by curiosity about the here-and-now and anticipation of the future. It was John Dewey who saw that the experiential learning cycle was not a circle but a spiral, filling each episode of experience with the potential for movement, from blind impulse to a life of choice and purpose (see Chapter 2, "Dewey's Model of Learning"). He compared this progression in learning from experience to the advance of an army:

> *Each resting place in experience is an undergoing in which is absorbed and taken home the consequences of prior doing, and unless the doing is that of utter caprice or sheer routine, each doing carries in itself meaning that has been extracted and conserved. As with the advance of an army, all gains from what has been already effected are periodically consolidated, and always with a view to what is to be done next. If we move too rapidly, we get away from the base of supplies—of accrued meanings—and the experience is flustered, thin, and confused. If we dawdle too long after having extracted a net value, experience perishes of inanition.* [Dewey, 1934, p. 56]

Learning is thus the process whereby development occurs. This view of the relation between learning and development differs from some traditional conceptions that suggest that the two processes are relatively independent. This latter perspective, which is shared by the intelligence-testing movement and classical Piagetians, suggests that learning is a subordinate process not actively involved in development: To learn, one uses the achievements of development, but this learning does not modify the course of development. In intelligence testing, for example, development is seen as a prerequisite for learning—it is necessary for a child's mental functions to mature before more complex subject matter can be taught. Similarly, for Piaget, development forms the superstructure within which learning occurs. His research has been guided by the implicit assumption that the sequence of cognitive-developmental stages evolves from an internal momentum and logic, with little influence from environmental circumstance. Recent research by those who might be called neo-Piagetians (such as Bruner et al., 1966) have called this assumption into question by showing in cross-culture studies that the child's level of cognitive development at a given age is strongly influenced by access to Western-type schooling.

LEARNING AND DEVELOPMENT AS TRANSACTIONS BETWEEN PERSON AND ENVIRONMENT

Without denying the reality of biological maturation and developmental achievements (that is, enduring cognitive structures that organize thought and action), the experiential learning theory of development focuses on the transaction between internal characteristics and external circumstances, between personal knowledge and social knowledge. It is the process of learning from experience that shapes and actualizes developmental potentialities. This learning is a social process; and thus, the course of individual development is shaped by the cultural system of social knowledge.

This position has been best articulated by the Soviet cognitive theorist, L.S. Vygotsky. He used the concept of the zone of proximal development to explain how learning shapes the course of development. The zone of proximal development is defined as "the distance between the actual developmental level as determined by independent problem solving and the level of potential development as determined through problem solving under adult guidance or in collaboration with more capable peers" (Cole et al., 1978, p. 86). The zone of proximal development is where learning occurs. Through experiences of imitation and communication with others and interaction with the physical environment, internal developmental potentialities are enacted and practiced until they are internalized as an independent development achievement. Thus, learning becomes the vehicle for human development via interactions between individuals with their biologic potentialities and the society with its symbols, tools, and other cultural artifacts. Human beings create culture with all its artificial stimuli to further their own development. Vygotsky's ideas about how the tools of culture shape development were greatly influenced by Friedrich Engels, who saw culturally created tools as the specific symbol of man's transformation of nature—that is, production. As Vygotsky himself put it:

> *The keystone of our method . . . follows directly from the contrast Engels drew between naturalistic and dialectical approaches to the understanding of human history. Naturalism in historical analysis, according to Engels, manifests itself in the assumption that only nature affects human beings and only natural conditions determine historical development. The dialectical approach, while admitting the influence of nature on men, asserts that man in turn affects nature and creates, through his changes in nature, new natural conditions for his existence. . . .*
>
> *All stimulus response methods share the inadequacy that Engels ascribes to the naturalistic approach to history. Both see the relation between human behavior and history as unidirectionally reactive. My collaborators and I, however, believe that human behavior comes to have that "transforming reaction on nature" which Engels attributed to tools. [Cole et al., 1978, pp. 60-61]*

It is this proactive adaptation that is the distinctive characteristic of human learning, a proactive adaptation that is made possible by the use of auxiliary cultural stimuli, social knowledge, to actively transform personal knowledge. For example, the symbolic tools acquired through the internalization of language allow us to anticipate, plan for, and practice reactions to upcoming situations in our life. As the tools of culture change, so too will the course of human development be altered (as with the widespread use of home computers; compare Papaert, 1980). In this sense, the laws and limitations of human development can never be known, since human nature is constantly emerging in the transaction between individuals and their culture.

The process of learning that actualizes development requires a confrontation and resolution of the dialectic conflicts inherent in experiential learning. The process is one that Paulo Freire describes as praxis—using dialogue to stimulate reflection and action on the world in order to transform it. Denis Goulet, in the introduction to Freire's *Education for Critical Consciousness*, describes it this way:

> *Paulo Freire's central message is that one can know only to the extent that one "problematizes" the natural, cultural and historical reality in which s/he is immersed . . . to "problematize" in his sense is to associate an entire populace to the task of codifying total reality into symbols which can generate critical consciousness and empower them to alter their relations with nature and social forces. This reflective group exercise . . . thrusts all participants into dialogue with others whose historical "vocation" is to become transforming agents of their social reality. Only thus do people become subjects, instead of objects, of their own history. [Freire, 1973, p. ix]*

DIFFERENTIATION AND INTEGRATION IN DEVELOPMENT

From the dialectics of learning comes a human developmental progression marked by increasing differentiation and hierarchic integration of functioning. The concepts of differentiation and hierarchic integration are fundamental to virtually all theories of cognitive development and adult development. This principle of psychological development was borrowed from biological observations of evolution and development that show increasing physical differentiation and integration as one moves up the phylogenetic scale, particularly in the evolution of the nervous system.

Differentiation has two aspects, an increasing complexity of units and a decreasing interdependence of parts. The course of learning and development is to refine, discriminate, and elaborate the categories of experience and the variety of behavior while at the same time increasing the independence of functioning among these separate parts. An example of differentiation can be seen in the development of the infant's emotional life. In an early observational study of young children, Katherine Bridges (1932) described the increasing differentiation of the growing infant's emotions from undifferentiated excitement to the basic distinction between distress and delight, to a refined spectrum of emotions encompassing fear, disgust, anxiety, jealousy, joy, parental affection, and so on (see Figure 6.1).

Hierarchic integration is the organism's organizing response to the complexity and diffusion caused by increasing differentiation. Hierarchic integration is multilevel. At the first level are simple fixed rules for organizing differentiated dimensions of experience in an absolutistic way. For example, experience may be classified as either good or bad. At a somewhat higher level, alternative interpretive rules emerge, allowing for alternative interpretations of situations. The absolutistic right-wrong view of the world becomes somewhat more flexible by the use of simple contingency thinking; for instance, in situation A, this rule is true, but in situation B, another rule holds. At a still higher level, more complex rules than simple contingency thinking are developed for determining the perspective taken on experience. These rules are more "internalized," free from fixed application based on past experience or the external stimulus. The highest level of integration adds still another system of

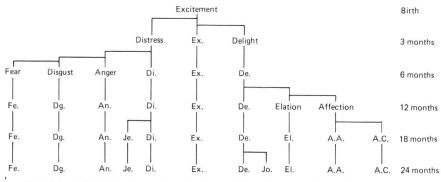

Key: A.A. = Affection for Adults; A.C. = Affection for Children; An. = Anger; De. = Delight; Dg. = Disgust; Di. = Distress; El. = Elation; Ex. = Excitement; Fe. = Fear; Je. = Jealousy; Jo. = Joy

Figure 6.1 Differentiation of Infant's Emotional Life [*Source:* Katherine Bridges, "Emotional Development in Early Infancy," *Child Development*, 3 (1932)]

rules that forms a structure for generating very complex relationships. This highest level allows great flexibility in the integration and organization of experience, making it possible to cope with change and environmental uncertainty by developing complex alternative constructions of reality. These four levels of hierarchic integration, as they are described by Schroder, Driver, and Streufert (1967), are shown graphically in Figure 6.2.

Through hierarchic integration, the individual maintains integrity and wholeness through the creation of superordinate schema, including concepts, sentiments, acts, and observations. These schema organize and control the deployment of subordinate, differentiated concepts, sentiments, acts, and observations. In the example above of differentiation of the infant's emotional life, the growing child develops progressively higher-order sentiments to control the application of these refined emotions to different settings and persons, introducing continuity and meaning to his or her experience. The unity and consistency of experience that at birth was the benefit of an undifferentiated view of the world must increasingly be purchased by integrative organizational efforts. Yet the dividends of these developmental processes are great—an increasingly conscious awareness and sophisticated control of ourselves in the world around us. In Lewin's conception, integration was presumed to lag behind differentiation, producing cyclic patterns of development alternating between stages dominated by the diffusion of differentiation and stages dominated by the unity of hierarchic integration—a description not unlike Dewey's advancing-army metaphor quoted earlier.

UNILINEAR VS. MULTILINEAR DEVELOPMENT

The experiential learning theory of development differs significantly from most Piaget-inspired theories of adult development in its emphasis on development as a multilinear process. The Piagetian theories of cognitive and adult development portray the course of development as unilinear, as some form of movement toward increasing differentiation and hierarchic integration of the structures that govern behavior. This is true of Piaget's theory of cognitive development (Flavell, 1963), Loevinger's theory of ego development (1976), Kohlberg's theory of moral development (1969), Perry's theory of moral and intellectual development (1970), the conceptual systems approach of Harvey, Hunt, and Schroeder (1961) and its derivatives by Hunt in education (1974), by Schroeder et al. in information processing (1967), and by Harvey in personality theory (1966). Although experiential learning theory recognizes the overall linear trend in development from a state of globality and lack of differentiation to a state of increasing differentiation, articulation, and hierarchic integration, it takes issue with the exclusive linearity of the Piagetian approach in three respects.

First, it recognizes individual differences in the developmental process. In Piagetian schemes, individuality is manifest only in differential progression along

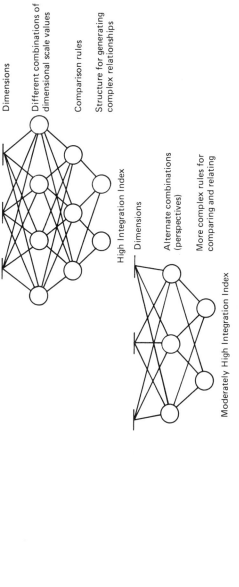

Dimensions

Different combinations of
dimensional scale values

Comparison rules

Structure for generating
complex relationships

High Integration Index

Dimensions

Alternate combinations
(perspectives)

More complex rules for
comparing and relating

Moderately High Integration Index

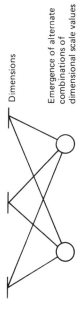

Dimensions

Emergence of alternate
combinations of
dimensional scale values

Moderately Low Integration Index

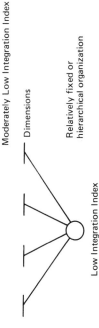

Dimensions

Relatively fixed or
hierarchical organization

Low Integration Index

Figure 6.2 Levels of Hierarchic Integration [*Source:* H.M. Schroeder, M.J. Driver, and S. Streufert, *Human Information Processing* (New York: Holt, Rinehart & Winston, 1967)]

the single yardstick of development—progression toward the internalized logic of scientific rationality. Individuals are different only insofar as they are at different stages of development. In experiential learning theory, however, individuality is manifest not only in the stage of development but also in the course of development—in the particular learning style the person develops. In this respect, the theory follows the Gestalt development approach of Heinz Werner:

> The orthogenetic law, by its very nature, is an expression of unilinearity of development. But, as is true of the other polarities discussed here, the ideal unilinear sequence signified by the universal developmental law does not conflict with the multiplicity of actual developmental forms . . . coexistence of unilinearity and multiplicity of individual developments must be recognized for psychological just as it is for biological evolution. In regard to human behavior in particular, this polarity opens the way for a developmental study of behavior not only in terms of universal sequence, but also in terms of individual variations, that is, in terms of growth viewed as a branching-out process of specialization. . . . [Werner, 1948, p. 137]

A second difference arises from the transactional perspective of experiential learning that conceptualizes development as the product of personal knowledge and social knowledge. Since a person's state of development is the product of the transaction between personal experience and the particular system of social knowledge interacted with, it is unreasonable to conceive of this state as solely a characteristic of the person, the view held by Piaget.[1] The developmental structures observed in human thought are just as likely to be characteristics of the social knowledge system; thus the findings that children with Western schooling display Piaget's developmental progressions more consistently than those whose schooling is embedded in other cultural knowledge systems (Bruner et al., 1966). This is an important proposition, for it argues that the paths of development can be as varied as the many systems of social knowledge. David Feldman has developed the ramifications of this view most thoroughly, suggesting a continuum of developmental regions ranging from the *universals* of intellect studied by Piaget (such as object permanence) through cognitive skills that are specific to a given *culture*, to a *discipline-based* knowledge system, and finally to *idiosyncratic* and *unique* capabilities that are developed by individuals through interactions with specialized or unique environments. Some of these unique accomplishments are judged to be creative, Feldman argues, and are fed back into the system of social knowledge, perhaps ultimately achieving disciplinary, cultural, or even universal status.

Emphasis on the specialized paths of development leads to the third difference with Piagetian theories. For Piaget, all development is *cognitive*

---

[1] "We have seen that there exist structures that belong only to the subject, that they are built, and that this is a step-by-step process. We must therefore conclude that there exist stages of development" (Piaget, 1970a, p. 710).

development. Experiential learning theory describes four development dimensions—affective complexity, perceptual complexity, symbolic complexity, and behavioral complexity—all interrelated in the holistic adaptive process of learning. The recognition of separate developmental paths helps to explain certain developmental phenomena that are anomalous in the Piagetian scheme. Werner gives one such example, the case of physiognomic perception. This affective mode of perceiving, in which perception and feeling are fused (for example, a gloomy landscape), is characteristic of young children but also seems to be highly developed in the adult artist:

> To illustrate, "physiognomic" perception appears to be a developmentally early form of viewing the world, based on the relative lack of distinction between properties of persons and properties of inanimate things. But the fact that in our culture physiognomic perception, developmentally, is superseded by logical, realistic, and technical conceptualization poses some paradoxical problems, such as, What genetic standing has adult aesthetic experience? Is it to be considered a "primitive" experience left behind in a continuous process of advancing logification, and allowed to emerge only in sporadic hours of regressive relaxation? Such an inference seems unsound; it probably errs in conceiving human growth in terms of a simple developmental series rather than as a diversity of individual formations, all conforming to the abstract and general developmental conceptualization. Though physiognomic experience is a primordial manner of perceiving, it grows, in certain individuals such as artists, to a level not below but on a par with that of "geometric-technical" perception and logical discourse. [Werner, 1948, p. 138]

Similar questions can be raised about the highly developed intuitive and behavioral skill of the executive (Mintzberg, 1973), which resembles in structure the child's trial-and-error enactive learning process.

   Another example is what Turner (1973) calls recentered thinking, in which the relationship of social knowledge to the specific knowing individual must be established in order for people to particularize general cognitive principles. This particularization requires the synthesis of affective and cognitive components. Although Piaget's developmental theory specifies how concepts gain independence from concrete experience, it does not specify the processes by which concepts are revisited with personal experience. In Piaget's terms, assimilation ultimately takes priority over accommodation in his theory of development.

   The final point of difference lies in the practical implications of the issues above. As was indicated in the first chapter, Piagetian theories have had a profound influence on American education, primarily through Jerome Bruner's introduction of Piaget's work at the prestigious Woods Hole conference on education in 1958. This conference, which framed our nation's educational response to the Sputnik challenge, found in Piaget's developmental theory the ideal framework for emphasizing and rationalizing the technoscientific dominance of education. In the race to regain the lead over the Soviets in technological supremacy, the educational system embraced scientific thinking as *the* way of knowing. Nurtured by federal largesse, educational institutions were transformed into technological institutions where scientific inquiry prospered and other approaches to knowing—the affective expression of the arts, the metaphysical reflection of philosophy and religion, and the integrative ideals of liberal education—all atrophied. Without in any way denigrating the intrinsic value or achievements of scientific inquiry, the multilinear developmental perspective of experiential learning suggests that science and technology alone are not enough. It rejects the view that other forms of inquiry must be subjected to science; that what ought to be is discovered in empirical investigation of what is; that the role of the humanities is to help us understand and cope with technological change rather than shape its directions. The true path toward individual and cultural development is to be found in equal inquiry among affective, symbolic, perceptual, and behavioral knowledge systems. Its intelligent direction requires integrated judgments about the future of humanity born from conflict and dialogue among these perspectives. (Compare Chapter 8, pp. 224-230.

THE EXPERIENTIAL LEARNING THEORY OF DEVELOPMENT

The way learning shapes the course of development can be described by the level of integrative complexity in the four learning modes—affective complexity in concrete experience results in higher-order sentiments, perceptual complexity in reflective observation results in higher-order observations, symbolic complexity in abstract conceptualization results in higher-order concepts, and behavioral complexity in active experimentation results in higher-order actions. Figure 6.3 illustrates this experiential learning model of development. The four dimensions of growth are depicted in the shape of a cone, the base of which represents the lower stages of development and the apex of which represents the peak of development—representing the fact that the four dimensions become more highly integrated at higher stages of development. Development on each dimension proceeds from a state of embeddedness, defensiveness, dependence, and reaction to a state of self-actualization, independence, proaction and self-direction. This process is marked by increasing complexity and relativism in dealing with the world and one's experience and by higher-level integrations of the dialectic conflicts among the four primary learning modes. In the early stages of development, progress along one of these four dimensions can occur with relative independence from the others. The child and young adult, for example, can develop highly sophisticated symbolic proficiencies and remain naive emotionally. At the highest stages of development, however, the adaptive commitment to learning and creativity produces a strong need for integration of the four adaptive modes. Development in one mode precipitates development in the others. Increases in symbolic complexity, for example, refine and sharpen both perceptual and behavioral possibilities. Thus,

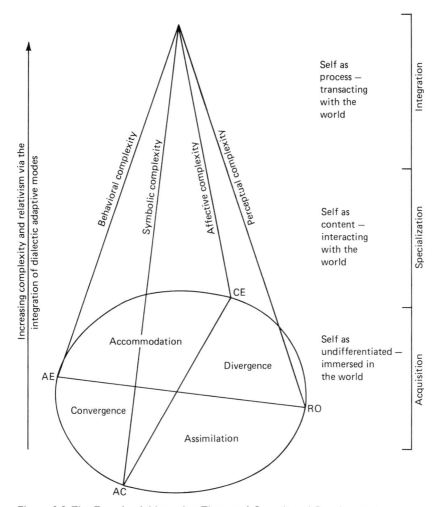

Figure 6.3 The Experiential Learning Theory of Growth and Development

complexity and the integration of dialectic conflicts among the adaptive modes are the hallmarks of true creativity and growth.

The human developmental process is divided into three broad development stages of maturation: acquisition, specialization, and integration. By maturational stages we refer to the rough chronological ordering of ages at which developmental achievements become possible in the general conditions of contemporary Western culture. Actual developmental progress will vary depending on the individual and his or her particular cultural experience. Even though the stages of the developmental growth process are depicted in the form of a simple three-layer cone, the actual process of growth in any single life history probably proceeds through successive oscillations from one stage to another. Thus, a person may move from stage 2 to stage 3 in several separate subphases of integrative advances, followed by consolidation or regression into specialization.

Stage One: Acquisition

This stage extends from birth to adolescence and marks the acquisition of basic learning abilities and cognitive structures. This, the most intensively studied period of human development, is described by Piaget as having four major substages (Chapter 2, p. 23). The first stage, from birth until about 2 years, is called the sensorimotor stage, because learning is primarily *enactive;* that is, knowledge is externalized in actions and the feel of the environment. Thus, accommodative learning, apprehension transformed by extension, is the dominant mode of adaptation. The second stage, from 2 to 6 years is called the *iconic* stage, because at this point, internalized images begin to have independent status from the objects they represent. It is at this stage that early forms of divergent learning, apprehension transformed by intention, are acquired. The third stage, from 7 to 11 years, marks the beginning of symbolic development in what Piaget calls the stage of concrete operations. Here the child begins development of the logic of classes and relations and inductive powers—in other words, assimilative learning via the transformation of comprehension by intention. The final stage of development in Piaget's scheme occurs in adolescence (12 to 15 years). Here, symbolic powers achieve total independence from concrete reality in the development of representational logic and the process of hypothetical deductive reasoning. These powers enable the child to imagine or hypothesize implications of purely symbolic systems and test them out in reality—convergent learning via transformation of comprehensions by extension. Development in the acquisition phase is marked by the gradual emergence of internalized structures that allow the child to gain a sense of self that is separate and distinct from the surrounding environment. This increasing freedom from undifferentiated immersion in the world begins with basic discrimination between internal and external stimuli and ends with that delineation of the boundaries of selfhood that Erikson (1959) has called the identity crisis.

Stage Two: Specialization

This stage extends through formal education and/or career training and the early experiences of adulthood in work and personal life. People shaped by cultural, educational, and organizational socialization forces develop increased competence in a specialized mode of adaptation that enables them to master the particular life tasks they encounter in their chosen career (in the broadest sense of the word) paths. Although children in their early experiences in family and school may already have begun to develop specialized preferences and abilities in their learning orientations (see Hudson, 1966), in secondary school and beyond they begin to make choices that will significantly shape the course of their development. The choice of college versus trade apprenticeship, the choice of academic specialization, and even such cultural factors as the choice of where to live begin to selectively determine the socialization experiences people will have and thereby influence and shape their mode of adaptation to the world. The choices a person makes in this process tend to have an accentuating, self-fulfilling quality that promotes specialization.

In the experiential learning theory of adult development, stability and change in life paths are seen as resulting from the interaction between internal personality dynamics and external social forces in a manner much like that described by Super (Super et al., 1963). The most powerful developmental dynamic that emerges from this interaction is the tendency for there to be a closer and closer match between self characteristics and environmental demands. This match comes about in two ways: (1) Environments tend to change personal characteristics to fit them (socialization), and (2) people tend to select themselves into environments that are consistent with their personal characteristics. Thus, development in general tends to follow a path toward accentuation of personal characteristics and skills (Feldman and Newcomb, 1969; Kolb and Goldman, 1973), in that development is a product of the interaction between choices and socialization experiences that match these choice dispositions such that resulting experiences further reinforce the same choice disposition for later experience. This process is inherent in the concept of learning styles as possibility-processing structures that govern transactions with the environment and thereby define and stabilize individuality.

Thus, in the specialization stage of development, the person achieves a sense of individuality through the acquisition of a specialized adaptive competence in dealing with the demands of a chosen "career." One's sense of self-worth is based on the rewards and recognition received for doing "work" well. The self in this stage is defined primarily in terms of *content*—things I can do, experiences I have had, goods and qualities I possess. The primary mode of relating to the world is *interaction*—I act on the world (build the bridge, raise the family) and the world acts on me (pays me money, fills me with bits of knowledge), but neither is fundamentally changed by the other. Paulo Freire describes this stage-2 sense of self and the "banking" concept of education that serves to reinforce it:

> *Implicit in the banking concept is the assumption of a dichotomy between man and the world: Man is merely in the world, not with the world or with others; man is spectator, not re-creator. In this view, man is not a conscious being; he is rather the possessor of a consciousness; an empty "mind" passively open to the reception of deposits of reality from the world outside. . . . This view makes no distinction between being accessible to consciousness and entering consciousness. The distinction, however, is essential: The objects which surround me are simply accessible to my consciousness not located within it.*
>
> *It follows logically from the banking notion of consciousness that the educator's role is to regulate the way the world "enters into" the students. His task is to organize a process which already occurs spontaneously, to "fill" the*

students by making deposits of information which he considers to constitute true knowledge. And since men "receive" the world as passive entities, education should make them more passive still, and adapt them to the world. The educated man is the adapted man, because he is better "fit" for the world. [Freire, 1974, p. 62]

Stage Three: Integration

The specialized developmental accomplishments of stage 2 bring social security and achievement, often paid for by the subjugation of personal fulfillment needs. The restrictive effects that society's socializing institutions have on personal fulfillment has been a continuing theme of Western thought, particularly since the Enlightenment. Freud and his followers in psychoanalysis developed the socioemotional dimensions of this conflict between individual and society—libidinous instincts clashing with repressive social demands. In modern organization theory, this conflict has been most clearly articulated by Argyris (1962). Yet it is Carl Jung's formulation of this conflict and the dimensions of its resolution in his theory of psychological types that is most relevant here. The Jungian theory of types, like the experiential learning model, is based on a dialectic model of adaptation to the world. Fulfillment, or individuation, as Jung calls it, is accomplished by higher-level integration and expression of nondominant modes of dealing with the world. This drive for fulfillment, however, is thwarted by the needs of civilization for specialized role performance.

The needs of Western specialized society have long stood in conflict with individuals in their drive for integrative development. In 1826, the German poet and historian, Friedrich Schiller, wrote:

> *When the commonwealth makes the office or function the measure of the man; when of its citizens it does homage only to the memory in one, to a tabulating intelligence in another, and to a mechanical capacity in a third; when here, regardless of character, it urges only towards knowledge while there it encourages a spirit of order and law-abiding behavior with the profoundest intellectual obscurantism—when, at the same time, it wishes these single accomplishments of the subject to be carried to just as great an intensity as it absolves him of extensity—is it to be wondered at that the remaining faculties of the mind are neglected, in order to bestow every care upon the special one which it honors and rewards? [Schiller, 1826, p. 23]*

Commenting on this passage by Schiller, Jung says:

> *The favoritism of the superior function is just as serviceable to society as it is prejudicial to the individuality. This prejudicial effect has reached such a pitch that the great organizations of our present day civilization actually strive for the complete disintegration of the individual, since their very existence depends upon a mechanical application of the preferred individual functions of men. It is not man that counts but his one differentiated function. Man no longer appears as man in*

collective civilization; he is merely represented by a function—nay, further, he is even exclusively identified with this function and denied any responsible member- ship to the level of a mere function, because this it is what represents a collective value and alone affords a possibility of livelihood. But as Schiller clearly discerns, differentiation of function could have come about in no other way: "There was no other means to develop man's manifold capacities than to set them one against the other. This antagonism of human qualities is the great instrument of culture; it is only the instrument, however, for so long as it endures man is only upon the way to culture." [Jung, 1923, p. 94]

The transition from stage 2 to stage 3 of development is marked by the individual's personal, existential confrontation of this conflict. The personal experience of the conflict between social demands and personal fulfillment needs and the corresponding recognition of self-as-object precipitates the individual's transition into the integrative stage of development. The experience can develop as a gradual process of awakening that parallels specialized development in stage 2, or it can occur dramatically as a result of a life crisis such as divorce or losing one's job. Some may never have this experience, so immersed are they in the societal reward system for performing their differentiated specialized function.

With this new awareness, the person experiences a shift in the frame of reference used to experience life, evaluate activities, and make choices. The nature of this shift depends upon the specifics of the person's dominant and nonexpressed adaptive modes. For the reflective person, the awakening of the active mode brings a new sense of risk to life. Rather than being influenced, one now sees opportunities to influence. The challenge becomes to shape one's own experience rather than observing and accepting experiences as they happen. For the person who has specialized in the active mode, the emergence of the reflective side broadens the range of choice and deepens the ability to sense implications of actions. For the specialist in the concrete mode, the abstract perspective gives new continuity and direction to experience. The abstract specialist with a new sense of immediate experience finds new life and meaning in abstract constructions of reality. The net effect of these shifts in perspective is an increasing experience of self as *process*. A learning process that has pre- viously been blocked by the repression of the nonspecialized adaptive modes is now experienced deeply to be the essence of self.

CONSCIOUSNESS, LEARNING, AND DEVELOPMENT

In the experiential learning model of development, there are three distinct levels of adaptation, representing successively higher-order forms of learning. These forms of learning are governed by three qualitatively different forms of consciousness. We will refer to these three levels of adaptation as performance, learning, and development.

In the acquisition phase of development, adaptation takes the form of performance governed by a simple registrative consciousness. In the specialization phase of development, adaptation occurs via a learning process governed by a consciousness that is increasingly interpretative. The integrative phase of development marks the achievement of a holistic developmental adaptive process governed by a consciousness that is integrative in its structure. Thus, each developmental stage of maturation is characterized by acquisition of a higher-level structure of consciousness than the stage preceding it, although earlier levels of consciousness remain; that is, adults can display all three levels of consciousness: registrative, interpretative, and integrative. These consciousness structures govern the process of learning from experience through the selection and definition of that experience.

How Learning Shapes Consciousness

To understand the role of consciousness in learning and development requires further examination of the structural learning model proposed earlier. Previous chapters have described four elementary forms of learning—accommodation, assimilation, convergence, and divergence—and alluded to higher-order forms of learning that emerge from combinations of these elementary forms. In the developmental terms of differentiation and integration, the elementary learning processes are the primary means for differentiation of experience; the higher-order combinations of the elementary forms represent the integrative thrust of the learning process. The conscious focus of experience that is selected and shaped by one's actual developmental level is refined and differentiated in the zone of proximal development by grasping and transforming it.

To illustrate, take the example of my recent trip to the auto museum. Preoccupied as I was with explaining how learning from experience is developmental, I found myself during the visit focusing on how I was developing my concept of automobile. First, I walked around and found many forms and variations of cars to refine and elaborate the concept; here I was learning via convergence, differentiating my concept through extension. Later I began learning about automobiles via assimilation, intensively transforming the concept to search for its precise meaning and critical attributes: How is an auto different from a bicycle? Must an automobile have an engine? In both cases, I was differentiating my conscious experience of the automobile concept.

Integrative learning occurs when two or more elementary forms of learning combine to produce a higher-order integration of the elementary differentiations around their common learning mode(s). In the automobile example, if I use the assimilative and convergent forms of learning together, I search the museum for cars without engines and find none, although I do find a tricycle-like contraption with a small motor. The result is an incremental increase in the symbolic integrative complexity of my concept of automobile. Not only do I have a more extensive population of cars in my concept (acquired via convergence) and a more refined elaboration of the essential and nonessential attributes of the concept (acquired via assimilation), but in their combination, my comprehension of automobiles is increased. In determining that automobiles have some form of self-propulsion as an essential attribute and that "looking like a bicycle" is a nonessential attribute, my automobile concept has become more complex and integrated—an increase in actual developmental level. As such, it now asserts a greater measure of control over the choice and definition of my future focal experiences; for example, I now begin to see motorcycles as a special subcategory of automobiles.

In serving as the integrative link between dialectically opposed learning orientations, the common learning mode of any pair of elementary learning forms becomes more hierarchically integrated, thereby giving that common learning orientation a greater measure of organization and control over the person's experience. This process is depicted in Figure 6.4 using the automobile example. Here, in the classic confrontation of the dialectic between intention and extension of a concept, we find a unique resolution via the refinement of the concept to encompass greater differentiation via hierarchic integration—that is, an increase in *symbolic* integrative complexity.

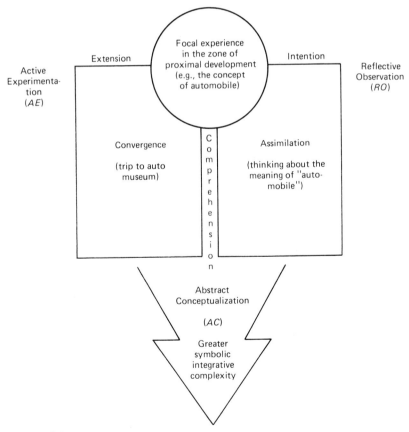

Figure 6.4

Similar increases in hierarchic integration of the common learning mode occur with other pairs of elementary learning forms. When convergence and accommodation combine, the result is an increase in *behavioral* integrative complexity via the resolution of the dialectic between comprehension and apprehension. In the pool-playing example cited in Chapter 4, convergent problem solving suggesting that the angle of incidence equals the angle of reflection, combined with the accommodative feel of the table, the cue stick, and the position of the balls produces refined behavioral skills in controlling the course of the cue ball. This refinement results from the comprehension of the basic laws of physics and the apprehension of the internal body cues and external physical circumstances integrated through extension—behavioral acts that operationalize the abstract concept in the concrete physical setting. The behavioral acts are guided and refined by a negative feedback loop between the goal defined by comprehension and the actual circumstance experience by apprehension; I keep practicing until I can hit the ball to the position I predict.

When the elementary learning forms of accommodation and divergence combine, the result is an increase in *affective* integrative complexity via the resolution of the dialectic between intention and extension. The artist stands before the canvas, brush in hand, experiencing a flow of images and feelings (divergence). The stroke of color applied (accommodation) externalizes the internal flow of experience, creating a frozen record of a dynamic process. The extent to which the stroke is successful in capturing that internal process is measured by its ability to recreate the internal gestalt of the moment of its birth, thus allowing the wholeness of that recreated experience to carry forward into the second stroke . . . and the third. It is from this cycle of action and reaction that sentiments are crystalized and refined, sentiments whose level of development is measured by their ability to sustain and carry forward experience (Gendlin, 1964).

The combination of the divergent and assimilative learning forms produces increases in *perceptual* integrative complexity via the resolution of the dialectic between apprehension and comprehension. The inductive model building of assimilation in combination with the apprehended observations of divergence produces more integratively complex categories of perception. Detective stories offer numerous examples of the synthesis of these two elementary learning forms, wherein the investigator is simultaneously inducing scenarios of how the crime was committed from the clues gathered and creating new clues and observations by juxtaposing scenarios with actual events. The creative synthesis of the comprehended scenario and apprehended events is illustrated by the fact that these new observations are not only about what happened but also about what did not happen but should have happened if a given scenario or alibi were correct. Thus, higher-order perceptual observations are not carbon copies of reality but integrations of what "is" and what "ought to be."

Registrative, Interpretative, and Integrative Consciousness

To illustrate further the levels of consciousness in learning, let us return to my automobile museum trip. The focal experience in this case was my concept of automobile. In my learning from that experience using the elementary convergent form of learning, my comprehension of the automobile concept was extended by my examination of the array of cars in the local auto museum. In this process, the concept of automobile was elaborated via a consciousness that was basically registrative. Each car I examined was "filed away" as another instance of an automobile. The focal experience "concept of automobile" did not change but was elaborated through grasping it via comprehension and transforming it via extension. When this convergent learning process was combined with assimilation (thinking about the meaning and critical attributes of the concept of automobile), my consciousness took on an interpretive quality that began to alter the focal experience itself; that is, the combination of these two learning forms produced an increase in the symbolic complexity of my concept "automobile," which in turn modified the focal experience to include bicycle-like self-propelled vehicles.

This second-level interpretative consciousness has two important characteristics that are lacking in the first-level registrative consciousness associated with the elementary learning forms. First, the combination of the two elementary learning modes creates an evaluative process that selectively interprets the focal experience. This is accomplished in the dialectic resolution of opposing learning modes (intention and extension, in the auto example). Second, this interpretation of the focal experience alters it selectively, redefining it and carrying it forward in terms of the hierarchically integrated learning mode. The combination of assimilative and convergent learning about the concept automobile refined the concept and enhanced the abstract/symbolic focus of the experience.

Thus the (second) interpretative level of consciousness associated with pairwise combinations of the elementary learning forms serves to define and shape the flow of experience, channeling it into more highly integrated forms of affective, perceptual, symbolic, and behavioral complexity. This level of consciousness gives direction and structure to the unfocused elaboration of registrative consciousness. But how then is the direction of the interpretative level of consciousness determined? How does one choose what experience to attend to and how to define it, either affectively, perceptually, symbolically, or behaviorally? In the absence of third-order integrative consciousness, the process is the one or random accentuation described in the specialization phase of development. An experience is chosen (concept of automobile) that "pulls for" a particular orientation (comprehension), and the refinement of the orientation (via increases in symbolic complexity) further increases the "pull" for that orientation, creating a positive feedback loop that serves to channel experience more and more in that direction.

Integrative consciousness introduces purpose and focus to this random process via integration of the opposition between the grasping dialectic of apprehension and comprehension and the transformation dialectic of intention and extension. This "centering" of experience, although not easily achieved, serves to answer the more strategic questions of life, such as, Why think about automobiles anyway? And why focus on the concept of automobile as opposed to the apprehension and aesthetic appreciation of particular cars? In this particular case, I choose automobiles more or less randomly to illustrate a point about the learning process. I choose to focus on the "concept" of automobile because the example of the dialectic between intention and extension is clearest for abstract concepts (see Chapter 3, p. 51). As I now try to push the example to explain integrative consciousness, I experience a kind of "stuckness." The example seems academic, trivial, and unrelated to me personally; I am lacking any apprehension about the focal experience, "concept of automobile." In searching for this personal relevance, I recall thinking, at the museum, that I would like to own a classic car, and further, that I often pause in airports to admire and get literature about those classic-car kits one builds on a Volks-wagen chassis. On impulse, I have even bought a set of mechanic's tools with this idea vaguely in mind. By my bringing these accommodative learning experiences to bear on my conscious focal experience, its nature changes to include apprehensions of my personal feelings and desires about cars. The focal experience changes from *concept* of car to include specific cars and my relation to them, including the attractive fantasy of building one from a classic-car kit. Suddenly I begin to experience questions, and a fourth perspective on the experiences emerges—divergence, the transformation of these apprehensions by intention. How much of my self-image, money, and time do I really want to invest in a car? There is something vaguely decadent and ostentatious about fancy cars. And come to think of it, the whole concept of a self-propelled vehicle makes little sense in my life, where most things are close by and I need the exercise.

Even though this example may be a bit strained, it serves to illustrate the nature of integrative consciousness. To interpretative consciousness, integrative consciousness adds a holistic perspective. Interpretative consciousness is primarily analytic; experiences can be treated singly and in isolation. Integrative consciousness is primarily synthetic, placing isolated experiences in a context that serves to redefine them by the resulting figureground contrasts. Another feature of integrative consciousness is its scope. Its concern is more strategic than tactical, and as a result, issues in integrative consciousness are defined broadly in time and space. Finally, integrative consciousness creates integrity by centering and carrying forward the flow of experience. This centering of experience is created by a continuous learning process fueled by successive resolutions of the dialectic between apprehension and comprehension and intention and extension.

ADAPTATION, CONSCIOUSNESS, AND DEVELOPMENT

With this example as a starting point, let us now turn to a more systematic formulation of the interrelationships among the stages of developmental maturation, the levels of adaptation, and the structure of consciousness as summarized in Table 6.1. It was Kurt Lewin who first articulated how consciousness increases in time/space extension with developmental maturation:

> The three-month-old child living in a crib knows few geographical areas around him, and the areas of possible activities are comparatively few. The child of one year is familiar with a much wider geographical area and a wider field of activities. He is likely to know a number of rooms in the house, the garden, and certain streets. . . .
> During development, both the space of free movement and the life space usually increase. The area of activity accessible to the growing child is extended because his own ability increases, and it is probable that social restrictions are removed more rapidly than they are erected as age increases, at least beyond the infant period. . . . The widening of the scope of the life space occurs sometimes gradually, sometimes in rather abrupt steps. The latter is characteristic for so-called crises in development. This process continues well into adulthood.
> A similar extension of the life space during development occurs in what may be called the "psychological time dimension." During development, the scope of the psychological time dimension of the life space increases from hours to days, months, and years. In other words, the young child lives in the immediate present; with increasing age, an increasingly more distant psychological past and future affect present behavior. [Lewin, 1951, pp. 103-4]

As the extension of consciousness increases, the same behavioral action is imbued with broader significance, representing an adaptation that takes account of factors beyond the immediate time and space situation. The infant will instinctively grasp the shiny toy before it; the young child may hesitate before picking up her brother's toy gun, knowing it will make him angry; an adult may ponder the purchase of that same toy gun, considering the moral implications of letting her child play with guns. Thus, what is considered the correct or appropriate response will vary depending on the conscious perspective used to judge it. When we judge performance, our concern is usually limited to relatively current and immediate circumstances. When we judge learning, the time frame is extended to evaluate successful adaptation in the future, and the situational circumstance is enlarged to include generically similar situations. When we evaluate development, the adaptive achievement is presumed to apply in all life situations throughout one's lifetime; and if the achievement is recorded as a cultural "tool," the developmental scope may extend even beyond one's lifetime.

Table 6.1 Experiential Learning Theory of Development: Levels of Adaptation and the Structure of Consciousness

Developmental stage of maturation	Acquisition	Specialization	Integration
Level of adaptation	Performance	Learning	Development
Structure of consciousness:	Registrative	Interpretative	Integrative
Extension in time	seconds minutes hours	days weeks months	years decades lifetimes
Extension in life space	responses acts tasks	projects jobs occupations	careers lives generations
Feedback structure	Goal-directed first-order feedback to achieve goals	Learning how to learn; 2nd-order feedback to change goals & strategies	Consciousness/Integrity; 3rd-order feedback to link goals to life purpose
Hierarchic integration of learning modes:	Many differentiated structures with low integration between them	Fewer but larger specialized structures; high integration within structures; low integration between structures	Development of complementary specialized structures; high integration between structures
Concrete experience—affective complexity via apprehension	Direct sensing and feeling Continuity of sensation and feeling—emergence of enduring sentiments	Self-aware system of sentiments and values Differentiating self's & others' sentiments and values	Relativistic appreciation of value systems Value commitment within relativism

Reflective observation—Perceptual complexity via intention	Attention	Watching—development of continuous images	Reflection; giving observations personal meaning	Creating alternative meaning and observation schemes	Relativistic appreciation of different meaning schemes & points of view	Intuition; choosing meaningful perspectives
Abstract conceptualization—Symbolic complexity via comprehension	Recognizing; enactive thought	Object constancy; "ikonic" thought	Concrete symbolic operations	Formal hypothetico-deductive reasoning	Attaching concrete meanings to symbol systems	Finding and solving meaningful problems
Active experimentation—Behavioral complexity via extension	Responding to circumstance	Doing; short-range intentional acts toward goals	Achieving; development of clear goals and longer-range	Risk taking; making goal & strategy tradeoffs	Experimental hypothesis testing; change goals & strategies based on results	Responsible action; accepting unknown emergent reality

Along with this relatively continuous expansion of the scope of consciousness, there are also discontinuous qualitative shifts in the organization of consciousness as growth occurs. These shifts represent the hierarchic addition of more complex information-processing structures, giving consciousness an interpretative and integrative capability to supplement the simple registrative consciousness of infancy. William Torbert, in his seminal book, *Learning from Experience: Toward Consciousness,* has described the hierarchic structure of consciousness as a three-tiered system of higher-order feedback loops. As in our approach, he uses this three-level structure of consciousness to solve problems that arise in explaining how the focus of experience (what constitutes feedback, in his terms) is determined. He explains his model as follows:

> Recognition of these problems [of what constitutes feedback] has led social systems theorists to attempt to deal with them by postulating two orders of feedback over and above goal-directed feedback (Deutsch, 1966; Mills, 1965). Goal-directed feedback is referred to as first-order feedback. Its function is to redirect a system as it negotiates its outer environment towards a specific goal. The goals and boundaries of the system are assumed to be defined, so feedback is also defined. . . . The two higher orders of feedback can be viewed as explaining how goals and boundaries come to be defined. Second-order feedback has been named "learning" by Deutsch. Its function is to alert the system to changes it needs to make within its own structure to achieve its goal. The change in structure may lead to a redefinition of what the goal is and always leads to a redefinition of the units of feedback (Buckley, 1967). Third-order feedback is called "consciousness" by Deutsch. Its function is to scan all system-environment interactions immediately in order to maintain a sense of the overall, lifetime, autonomous purpose and integrity of the system.
>
> The terms "purpose" and "integrity," critical to the meaning of "consciousness," can be elaborated as follows: The "inner" conscious purpose can be contrasted to the "external" behavioral goal. Goals are subordinate to one's purpose. Goals are related to particular items and places, whereas purpose relates to one's life as a whole, one's life as act. Purpose has also been termed "intention" (Husserl, 1962; Miller, Galanter, and Pribram, 1960) and can be related to the literary term "personal destiny."
>
> The concept of integrity can be related to Erikson's (1959) life-stage that has the same name. A sense of integrity embraces all aspects of a person, whereas the earlier life-stage in Erikson's sequence, named "identity," represents the glorification of certain elements of the personality and the repudiation of others (Erikson, 1958, p. 54). The distinction between a system's identity and a system's integrity can be sharpened by regarding identity as the particular quality of a system's structure, whereas integrity reflects the operation of consciousness. In this sense, consciousness provides a system with "ultrastability" (Cadwallader, 1968). Ultrastability gives the system the possibility of making changes in its structure because the system's essential coherence and integrity are not dependent upon any given structure. [Torbert, 1972, pp. 14-15]

A simple example will illustrate these three levels of feedback and their interrelationship in determining behavior. The classic example of first-order feedback is the household thermostat. The setting of the thermostat represents the goal, and the built-in thermometer is the sensory receptor that starts the furnace when the reading is below the setting and stops it when the set temperature is reached. A similar thermostat inside the human body performed this same registrative function of consciousness in our earlier time, when feeling cold led our ancestors to throw another log on the fire. Second-order feedback is created by the structure that governs how we set the thermostat. One person may set the thermostat at 70. His decision is based on a structure designed to maximize personal comfort. Another person may set the thermostat at 65. Her decision is based on a structure designed to save money. The units of feedback here are dollars. Thus, second-order feedback structures are interpretive, governing both goals and the meaning (units) of feedback. Most of us share in some degree both these personal-comfort and economic structures, as well as others based on patriotic energy conservation, concern for one's health, and so on. Third-order feedback provides the integrative perspective or integrity that allows for consistent choice about which structure or combination of structures to apply to this particular problem. It governs the process whereby we trade off the values and units of feedback defined by noncompatible structures and answer such questions as, How much will I pay to avoid feeling chilly at times? and, How much personal comfort will I sacrifice for the good of the country?

The thermostat is a good model for registrative consciousness. Events are registered in consciousness on the basis of a structure that defines goals and units of feedback, but at this first level of consciousness we have no awareness of the higher-level structure that governs the process of registering experience. We respond automatically in terms of that structure, just as a thermostat would respond by turning on the furnace when it got dark if we replaced the thermometer with a light sensor. We undoubtedly share this first level of consciousness with the higher animals, whose second-order interpretive structures are largely instinctively determined. At this level of consciousness, the hierarchic integration of the four learning modes is low. Concrete experience is limited to stimulus-bound sensations and feelings. The emergence of enduring sentiments that exist in the absence of their referent sets the stage for the beginning of interpretive consciousness. Similarly, reflective observation, abstract conceptualization, and active experimentation are all immediate and bound up in the stimulus situation in the first stage of registrative consciousness, and they move toward a constancy of images, concepts, and actions as interpretative consciousness begins.

With the hierarchic integration of the four learning modes and increasing affective, perceptual, symbolic, and behavioral complexity comes the emergence of interpretative consciousness and second-order "learning" feedback.[2] This is the distinctively human consciousness that most of us associate with the

[2] The reason that other animals do not develop the higher levels of consciousness may lie in the fact that they lack the symbolic comprehension powers associated with the left brain and thus cannot participate in the triangulation of experience that results from the dialectic between apprehension and comprehension producing hierarchic integration of experience.

term. In addition to the simple registration of experience, there is an awareness of an "I" who is doing the registering and guiding the choice and definition of a focal experience. As we have seen, this control of the choice and definition of our experiences is achieved by the development of higher-order sentiments, observations, concepts, and actions that interpret experience selectively. These highest-order structures can be seen as learning heuristics that control the definition and elaboration of experience by giving a priori preference to some interpretations over others.

An example of how learning heuristics operate to interpret consciousness is found in Adriaan de Groot's (1965) research on how chess masters and novices perceive game situations and formulate chess strategy. It was originally thought that chess masters were more skilled than novices because they thought further ahead and examined more possible moves. It turns out that masters do not think further ahead and, in fact, examine only a few possible moves. Instead, they think about the game at a higher level than novices do, perceiving grouped patterns of pieces that act as a kind of filter to ignore "bad" moves, much as an amateur might use similar but simpler patterns in order not to perceive illegal moves, such as moving the rook diagonally. These higher-level learning heuristics serve to simplify and refine moves in the game by eliminating from consideration a vast array of potential moves that are of little value in viewing the game. Harry Harlow (1959) has argued that all learning is based on this process of inhibiting incorrect responses, creating internalized programs or learning sets that selectively interpret new experiences.

With specialized development, each learning mode organizes clusters of learning heuristics based upon that particular learning orientation. With increased affective complexity comes a self-aware system of sentiments and values to guide one's life, a system that at higher levels becomes differentiated from a growing awareness of the values and sentiments of others. Increasing perceptual complexity is reflected in the development of perspectives on experience that have personal meaning and coherence. At higher levels of interpretative consciousness, one develops the ability to observe experience from multiple perspectives. Increasing symbolic complexity results first in Piaget's stage of concrete symbolic operations and later in formal hypothetico-deductive reasoning. Increased behavioral complexity results in achievement/action schemes—longer-term goals with complex action strategies to reach them. At higher levels of behavioral complexity, these action schemes are combined and traded off in a process that recognizes the necessity of risk taking.

Integrative consciousness based on third-order feedback represents the highest level of hierarchic integration of experience. In Torbert's view, it is a level of consciousness that few achieve in their lifetime. The reason that integrative consciousness is so difficult to achieve is that interpretative consciousness has a self-sealing, self-fulfilling character that deceives us with the illusion of a holistic view of an experience when it is fact fragmented and specialized (see Argyris and Schon, 1978). Precisely because interpretative consciousness selects and defines the flow of experience by excluding aspects of the experience that do not fit its structure, interpretative consciousness contains no contradictions that would challenge the validity of the interpretation. The person highly trained in, say, the symbolic interpretation of her experience rests at the center of that interpretative consciousness confident of the certainty and sufficiency of her view of the world. It is only at the margins that this view seems shaky, as with logical analysis of personal relationships; and only the most advanced forms of symbolic inquiry, such as Gödel's theorem in logic, call its comprehensive application into question.

To achieve integrative consciousness, one must first free oneself from the domination of specialized interpretative consciousness. Jung called this transition to integrative consciousness the process of individuation, whereby the adaptive orientations of the conscious social self are integrated with their complementary nonconsciousness orientations. In *Psychological Types*, he gives numerous examples of the power of the dominant conscious orientation (interpretative consciousness, in our terms) in thwarting this integration and of the strong measures needed to overcome it:

> For there must be a reason why there are different ways of psychological adaptation; evidently one alone is not sufficient, since the object seems to be only partly comprehended when, for example, it is either merely thought or felt. Through a one-sided (typical) attitude there remains a deficit in the resulting psychological adaptation, which accumulates during the course of life; from this deficiency a derangement of adaptation develops which forces the subject towards a compensation. But the compensation can be obtained only by means of amputation (sacrifice) of the hitherto one-sided attitude. Thereby a temporary heaping up of energy results and an overflow into channels hitherto not consciously used though already existing unconsciously. [Jung, 1923, p. 28]

Jung's prescription for the amputation of the dominant function is dramatized by his illustrative example of Origin, a third-century Christian convert from Alexandria, who marked his conversion by castration so that, in Origin's words, "all material things" could be "recast through spiritual interpretation into a cosmos of ideas." Betty Edwards, in her system for learning to draw by using the right side of the brain, suggests a less drastic approach for getting around the dominance of the specialized left-brain interpretative consciousness.

> Since drawing a perceived form is largely a right brain function, we must keep the left brain out of it. Our problem is that the left brain is dominant and speedy and is very prone to rush in with words and symbols, even taking over jobs which it is not good at. The split brain studies indicated that the left brain likes to be boss, so to speak, and prefers not to relinquish tasks to its dumb partner unless it really dislikes the job—either because the job takes too much time, is too detailed or slow or because the left brain is simply unable to accomplish the task. That's exactly what we need—tasks that the dominant left brain will turn down. [Edwards, 1979, p. 42]

Because we are ensnared by our particular specialized interpretative consciousness and reinforced for this entrapment through the specialized structure of social institutions, we know little of the nature of integrative consciousness. Most descriptions of this state have come from the mystical or transcendental religious literature, descriptions that fall on deaf ears for those at the interpretative level of consciousness who find the rapturous prose about "golden flowers" and the "Clear Light" to be so much baloney. The problem, of course, is that *integrative* consciousness by its very nature cannot be described by any single *interpretation*. Thus, all these descriptions have an elusive and even contradictory quality, such as that which characterizes Zen Koans. For example:

> *Jōshū asked the teacher, Nansen, "What is the true Way?"*
> *Nansen answered, "Everyday way is the true Way."*
> *Jōshū asked, "Can I study it?"*
> *Nansen answered, "The more you study, the further from the Way."*
> *Jōshū asked, "If I don't study it, how can I know it?"*
> *Nansen answered, "The Way does not belong to things seen: Nor to things unseen. It does not belong to things known: Nor to things unknown. Do not seek it, study it, or name it. To find yourself and it, open yourself wide as the sky. [Zen Buddhism, 1959, p. 22]*

The transcendent quality of integrative consciousness is precisely that, a "climbing out of" the specialized adaptive orientations of our worldly social roles. With that escape comes the flood of contradictions and paradoxes that interpretative consciousness serves to stifle. It is through accepting these paradoxes and experiencing their dialectical nature fully that we achieve integrative consciousness in its full creative force. This state of consciousness is not reserved for the monastery but is a necessary ingredient for creativity in any field. Albert Einstein once said, "The most beautiful and profound emotion one can feel is a sense of the mystical. . . . It is the dower of all true science."

In accepting and experiencing fully the dialectic contradictions of experience, one's self becomes identified with the process whereby the interpretative structures of consciousness are created, rather than being identified with the structures themselves. The key to this sense of self-as-process lies in the reestablishment of a symbiosis or reciprocity between the dialectic modes of adaptation such that one both restricts and establishes the other, and such that each in its own separate sphere can reach its highest level of development by the activity of the other. Carl Rogers, in his description of the peak of human functioning, describes as well as anyone the process-centered nature of integrative consciousness:

> *There is a growing and continuing sense of acceptant ownership of these changing feelings, a basic trust in his own process. . . . Experiencing has lost almost completely its structure bound aspects and becomes process experiencing—that is, the situation is experienced and interpreted in its newness, not as the*

past. . . . The self becomes increasingly simply the subjective and reflexive awareness of experiencing. The self is much less frequently a perceived object, and much more frequently something confidently felt in process. . . . Personal constructs are tentatively reformulated, to be validated against further experience, but even then to be held loosely. . . . Internal communication is clear, with feelings and symbols well matched, and fresh terms for new feelings. There is the experiencing of effective choice of new ways of doing. [Rogers, 1961, pp. 151-52]

The development of integrative consciousness begins with the transcendence of one's specialized interpretative consciousness and continues with, first, the exploration of the previously nonexpressed adaptive orientations and, later, the full acceptance of the dialectic relationship between the dominant and nondominant orientation. This embrace of the dialectic nature of experience leads to a self-identification with the *process* of learning. As can be seen in the description of the highest levels of hierarchic integration in the four learning modes (Figure 6.5), this process orientation is reflected in the incorporation of

Figure 6.5 *Liberation,* by M.C. Escher (lithograph, 1955)

dialectic opposites in each of the modal descriptions. The integrative levels of affective complexity begin with the relativistic appreciation (in the fullest sense of the term) of value systems and conclude with an active value commitment in the context of that relativism (compare Perry, 1970). Integration in perceptual complexity begins with a similar relativistic appreciation of observational schemes and perspectives and concludes with intuition—the capacity for choosing meaningful perspectives and frameworks for interpreting experience. With integrative consciousness, symbolic complexity achieves first the ability to match creatively symbol systems and concrete objects and finally the capacity for finding and solving meaningful problems. Behavioral complexity at the integrative level begins with the development of an experimental, hypothesis-testing approach to action that introduces new tentativeness and flexibility to goal-oriented behavior—a tentativeness that is tempered in the final stage by the active commitment to responsible action in a world that can never be fully known because it is continually being created.

In his 1955 lithograph entitled, "Liberation," M.C. Escher captures the essence of the three developmental stages of experiential learning. The bottom third of the figure (Figure 6.5) shows the emergence of figures from an undifferentiated background, as in the acquisition stage of development. The middle third of the figure shows the articulation of form in tightly locked interaction between figure and ground, much as development in the specialization stage is achieved by finding one's "niche" in society. The top of the figure shows the birds in free flight, emphasizing the process of flying over the content of their form, symbolizing the freedom and self-direction of integrative development.

seven

Learning and Development in Higher Education

. . . the ways in which we believe and expect have a tremendous effect on what we believe and expect. We have discovered at last that these ways are set, almost abjectly so, by social factors, by tradition and the influence of education. Thus we discover that we believe many things not because the things are so but because we have become habituated through the weight of authority, by imitation, prestige, institution, and unconscious effect of language, etc. We learn, in short, that qualities which we attribute to objects ought to be imputed to our ways of experiencing them, and that these in turn are due to the force of intercourse and custom. This discovery marks an emancipation; it purifies and remakes the objects of our direct or primary experience. **John Dewey,** Experience and Nature

From the perspective of experiential learning theory, educational institutions are the curators of social knowledge. Chief among the responsibilities of their curatorship is the creation of conditions whereby social knowledge is made accessible to individual learners for their development. Jerome Bruner has underscored the importance of this task:

Perhaps the task of converting knowledge into a form fit for transmission is, after all, the final step in our codification of knowledge. Perhaps the task is to go beyond the learned scholarship, scientific research, and the exercise of disciplined sensibility in the arts to the transmission of what we have discovered. Surely no culture will reach its full potential unless it invents ever better means for doing so. [Bruner, 1971, p. 19]

This responsibility includes the individual development of participants in these institutions in all three developmental stages of experiential learning: (1) acquisition, the preparation of individual learners in basic skills so that they can access and utilize the tools of social knowledge; (2) specialization, the selection and socialization of learners into specialized areas of knowledge that suit their talents and meet societal needs; and (3) integration, the development of the unique capabilities of the whole person toward creativity, wisdom, and integrity. The first of these responsibilities has traditionally been the province of primary and secondary education, although the increased knowledge necessary to function effectively in modern society, coupled with the general decline in the public educational system, has caused considerable overflow of this responsibility into the system of higher education.

The third educational responsibility of integrative fulfillment has for many years been suffering at the expense of the second, specialized occupational training. The selection of Charles Eliot as president of Harvard in 1869 marked the end of classical education in American colleges whereby all students took the same courses in Greek, Latin, and mathematics. By introducing electives and "majors" in the Harvard curriculum, he began what, considering the rapid growth of knowledge, was the inevitable specialization and fragmentation that characterizes the modern university. In the system that has emerged in the last 100 years, students have been increasingly free to select their courses and to define programs suited to their needs, interests, and abilities. Academic disciplines have enjoyed a corresponding freedom to choose those students who best fit their requirements. This trend toward specialization and vocationalism in higher education has recently gained momentum from post-"baby-boom" demographics, a tight job market, and the multifaceted financial crises of institutions of higher learning. College and universities are thus increasingly specialized and fragmented, held together by little more than Robert Hutchins's central heating system, Warren Bennis's parking authority, and a few distribution requirements. In a highly complex and specialized society, the pressures toward specialization in education feed on themselves. Higher education is increasingly called upon to deliver the specialized knowledge, skills, and attitudes needed for students to find their niche in society, and to service that niche as well. Institutions, in turn, become increasingly dependent on these "social niches" for their own survival, and lend further support to the forces of knowledge specialization, usually at the expense of integrative education. Speaking of the specialized formal educational requirements required for entry in occupations, Robert Hutchins said:

> The great bulk of the students in American universities are there in order to meet these requirements. The public acquiesces in them, first, because it is accustomed to acquiesce in the demands of pressure groups, and second because it has a vague feeling that the members of certain occupations at least should be certified, or sanctified, in some way before they are let loose upon the public. The public is unwilling, often for good reasons, to trust these occupations to certify their own members. The universities acquiesce in these arrangements because

they wish to increase their enrollments; students bring in income, and anyway there is a general feeling that excellence in educational institutions, as in most other things, increases in proportion to size. The trades, occupations, businesses, and professions promote these arrangements in order to restrict competition and enhance their prestige. [Hutchins, 1953, p. 31]

Before we return to a consideration of integrative development, it is important to understand first the consequences of this specialized emphasis of higher education on student learning and development. In considering the student careers that are spawned and shaped in the university community and the university's responsibility for the intellectual, moral, and personal development of its members, we have often emphasized the unitary linear trend of human growth and development at the expense of acknowledging and managing the diverse developmental pathways that exist within different disciplines and professions. These paths foster some developmental achievements and, as we shall see, inhibit others. The channels of academic specialization are swift and deep., the way between them tortuous and winding. For example, these days, the major career transitions in college occur from science to the humanities (Davis, 1965). Several years ago, I served as a freshman advisor to undergraduates in a technological university. Two or three of my students in each group faced the awkward realization near the end of their freshman year that a career in engineering was not quite what they had imagined it to be. What to do? Transfer to a liberal arts school and possibly lose the prestige of a technological education? Endure the institute's technological requirements and "bootleg" a humanities major? Switch to management? Most decided to wait and see, but with a distinct loss of energy and increase in confusion. I felt powerless about what to advise or even how to advise.

It was only later that I was to discover that these shifts represented something more fundamental than changing interests—that they stemmed in many cases from fundamental mismatches between personal learning styles and the learning demands of different disciplines. That disciplines incline to different styles of learning is evident from the variations among their primary tasks, technologies, and products, criteria for academic excellence and productivity, teaching methods, research methods, and methods for recording and portraying knowledge. Disciplines, as we have seen, show sociocultural variation—differences in faculty and student demographics, personality, and aptitudes, as well as differences in values and group norms. For students, education in an academic field is a continuing process of selection and socialization to the pivotal norms of the field governing criteria for truth and how it is to be achieved, communicated, and used, and secondarily, to peripheral norms governing personal styles, attitudes, and social relationships. Over time, these selection and socialization pressures combine to produce an increasingly impermeable and homogeneous disciplinary culture and correspondingly specialized student orientations to learning. This chapter will explore the dynamics of this specialized developmental process in undergraduate and professional education.

SPECIALIZED DEVELOPMENT AND THE PROCESS
OF ACCENTUATION

The major developmental dynamic in specialized education is the selection and socialization of students into specialized areas of social knowledge commensurate with their interests and talents. This development takes place through a process of *accentuation*. In their comprehensive review of the effect of college on students, Feldman and Newcomb describe the accentuation process as it affects the college experience:

> *Whatever the characteristics of an individual that selectively propel him toward particular educational settings—going to college, selecting a particular one, choosing a certain academic major, acquiring membership in a particular group of peers—these same characteristics are apt to be reinforced and extended by the experiences incurred in those settings. [Feldman and Newcomb, 1969, p. 333]*

Thus, if students with a particular learning style choose a field whose knowledge structure is one that prizes and nurtures their style of learning, then accentuation of that approach to learning is likely to occur. The result is an educational system that emphasizes specialized learning and development through the accentuation of the students' skills and interests. Students' developmental pathways are a product of the interaction between their choices and socialization experiences in academic fields such that choice dispositions lead them to choose educational experiences that match these dispositions, and the resulting experiences further reinforce the same choice disposition for later experiences.

Some examples will serve to illustrate this process of specialization in learning style as a result of accentuation. In a first attempt to examine the details of this process, Plovnick (1971) studied a major university department using the concept of convergence and divergence defined by Hudson (1966). He concluded that the major emphasis in physics education was on convergent learning. He predicted that physics students who had convergent learning styles would be content with their majors, whereas physics majors who were divergent in their learning styles would be more uncertain of physics as a career and would take more courses outside the physics department than would their convergent colleagues. His predictions were confirmed. Those students who were not fitted for the convergent learning style required in physics tended to turn away from physics as a profession, while those physics students having a convergent style tended to continue to specialize in physics, both in their course choices and their career choices.

In another unpublished study, we examined the accentuation process as it operated at the molecular level of course choice. This research examined the choice of sensitivity training by graduate students in management. When we gathered the Learning Style Inventory (LSI) scores of students who chose a voluntary sensitivity-training laboratory, we found that they tended to be more concrete and reflective than those who chose not to attend the lab. When those with divergent learning styles completed the training sessions, their LSI scores became even more concrete and reflective on a post-test, accentuating their disposition toward divergent learning experiences.[1]

Witkin and his associates (Witkin, 1976) have shown that global (field-dependent) students choose specializations that favor involvement with people—such as teaching, sales, management, and the humanities—whereas analytical (field-independent) students choose areas that favor analysis, such as the physical sciences, engineering, and technical and mechanical activities. Clinical-psychology graduate students tend to be global, and experimental-psychology graduate students are analytical. In addition, Witkin found that when cognitive style matches the demands of a given career specialization, higher performance results.

It is important to note not only that the content of choices is associated with cognitive style, but also that there is an association between the choice *process* and cognitive style. Thus, global students make choices preferred by their peer group, whereas analytical students are more likely to use systematic planning and goal setting. Plovnick (1974) found a similar pattern when he used the LSI to study medical students' choice of medical specialty. There were significant relationships between the LSI scores and specific choices made: Accommodators chose medicine and family care; assimilators chose academic medicine; divergers chose psychiatry; and convergers chose medical specialties. In addition, LSI scores were related to the process of choosing: Concrete students tended to base their choices on role models and acquaintances, abstract students relied on theoretical material and interest in subject matter.

Robert Altmeyer (1966) has dramatically illustrated the result of the accentuation process on cognitive abilities in his comparative study of

---

[1]Another set of questions is raised by the choice/experience cycle in development. Although the results of these studies show that the majority of students seem to be involved in a series of choices and experiences that accentuate their learning-style tendencies, many students deviate from this dominant trend. If we are to understand the role of learning styles in the development process, we need to understand not only dominant trends but also the causes for deviation from these trends. More specifically, we may gain from this kind of analysis more insight into the relative importance of choices and experiences in human change and development. Until now, much emphasis has been placed on the primary importance of experience as the cause of change. This orientation has given rise to countless research studies seeking to measure with before-after change measurements the effects of various educational experiences. But suppose that a person was changed as much by his choices of experiences as by the experiences themselves. Take, for example, a person interested in mathematics. His interests and aptitudes in mathematics may lead him to seek educational experiences that will enhance these dispositions. In addition, he may be screened formally and informally for admission to this educational program, gaining entry only if he has mathematical aptitude. Thus, by the time his choice has been realized, he will already (1) have gone through a process of consciously recognizing an aspect of himself that he wanted to develop (i.e., his mathematical ability); (2) have done some planning about how to develop this aspect; and (3) perhaps have begun learning mathematics in order to pass selection tests. All these processes will have occurred before the "before" measurement in the typical study designed to assess the effects of an educational experience. Yet they may be as important in determining the directions of development.

engineering/science and fine-arts students at Carnegie Tech. In a cross-sectional study, he administered two batteries of tests to students at all levels in the two schools; one battery measured analytical reasoning, the other creative thinking. As predicted, engineering/science students scored highest on analytic reasoning and fine-arts students highest on creative thinking; and over the college years, these gaps widened: Engineering/science students became more analytical and arts students more creative. The surprising finding was that engineering/science students decreased in creative thinking and fine-arts students decreased in analytic reasoning over the college years. Thus, educational processes that accentuated one set of cognitive skills also appeared to produce loss of ability in the contrasting set of skills.

The corollary to the accentuation process of development in which skills and environmental demands are increasingly matched is the alienation cycle that results when personal characteristics find no supportive environment to nurture them. In this emerging information society, severe alienation can result when there is an incongruity between personal knowledge and social knowledge. This is illustrated most dramatically by the alienation of the poor, whose streetwise way of learning doesn't fit with the symbolic/technological knowledge of the university; or more subtly, it is illustrated by the creative writer who is "turned off" by the pedantic critical climate of her English literature department, or the adult who returns to college and finds little recognition for a lifetime of learning by experience.

UNDERGRADUATE STUDENT DEVELOPMENT IN A TECHNOLOGICAL UNIVERSITY

Thus far we have seen that experiential learning theory characterizes differences in the learning/inquiry norms of different academic fields and that student development and learning are shaped by these fields through a process of accentuation. To examine in greater detail the role of student learning styles in the educational process and to explore the consequences of matches and mismatches between learning styles and the knowledge structure of academic disciplines, let us now examine a case study of undergraduate students in a well-known technological university (TECH).[2]

Data for the study (except for cumulative grade averages, which were obtained from the registrar's office) were collected by means of a questionnaire that was sent to the 720 TECH seniors two months before graduation. Four hundred and seven students (57 percent) responded to the questionnaire. Of these responses, 342 (43 percent) were complete enough to test the hypotheses in this study. The questionnaire included the Learning Style Inventory, two scales measuring political alienation and anomie, questions about plans for next year, career choice, degree of commitment to that career,

[2]For a detailed report, see Kolb and Goldman, 1973.

undergraduate major, perception of academic workload, and involvement with peers. These variables will be described in detail as the results are presented. Figure 7.1 shows the LSI scores of students with different departmental majors in those departments with ten or more students. Analysis of variance for the six learning-style dimensions by departmental major shows that reflective observation, active experimentation, and the combination score active-reflective all vary significantly by departmental major. Differences on the abstract-concrete dimensions show no significance. This lack of significant differentiation may well be because of more uniform selective and normative pressures toward abstraction that operate across all the university departments. TECH's reputation as a scientific institution is strongly based on scholarship and the advancement of scientific knowledge. Humanities, architecture, and management are the most concrete departments in the university, and our observations would indicate that these are all quite scholarly in comparison with more concrete programs in other, less "academic" schools such as fine arts, drafting, or business administration. Selective and normative forces on the active-reflective dimension are more diverse, representing the tension in the university between basic science and practical application. With the exception of electrical engineering, the engineering departments are the most active in the university. With the exception of chemistry, the basic sciences and mathematics are more reflective.

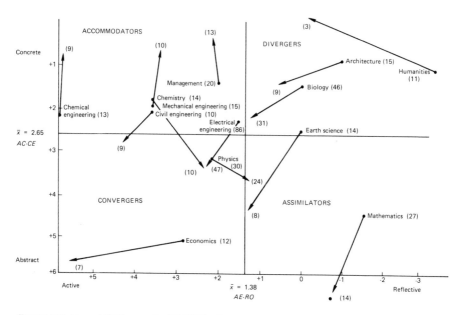

Figure 7.1 Mean LSI Scores for TECH Seniors on Abstract/Concrete and Active/Reflective by Departmental Major.

When the pattern of relationships among departments at TECH is compared with the Carnegie Commission data representing colleges and universities of all types (Figure 5.4), one is immediately struck by the fact that with the exception of architecture and humanities, the concrete disciplines in Figure 5.4 are not represented at this university (there are philosophy, political science, and psychology departments, but they had only two or three students each in our sample). Otherwise, there is a general correspondence with previous studies. Humanities falls in the diverger quadrant, mathematics is assimilative, management is clearly accommodative. Although the engineering departments all fall on the lower edge of the accommodator quadrant rather than the converger quadrant as predicted, this is most likely a function of the general abstract bias of the university as a whole. Physics and chemistry are not as abstract and reflective as predicted, although if the LSI scores of only those students planning to attend graduate school are used (as indicated by the arrowheads in Figure 7.1), the pattern is more consistent with prediction. Economics is somewhat more abstract and active than the Carnegie data, although, as we will describe later, this is probably a function of the unique nature of the TECH department. The architecture department's position in the divergent quadrant is also to some extent a function of the unique nature of the department, with its emphasis on creative design and photography as well as the more convergent technical skills of architecture.

Learning Styles and Career Choice

Figure 7.1 gives an indication about career paths of the students in each of the departments. The arrowheads indicate for each department the average LSI scores for those students who are planning to attend graduate school. We would predict that those who choose to pursue a given discipline further through graduate training should show an accentuation of the learning style characteristic of that discipline. That is, the arrows for those departments falling in the accommodative quadrant should point toward the concrete and active extremes of the LSI grid, the arrows for divergent departments toward the concrete and reflective, the arrows for the assimilative departments toward the abstract and reflective, and the arrows for the convergent departments toward abstract and active extremes of the LSI grid. The actual results are not so clearcut. Chemical engineering, mechanical engineering, management, humanities, mathematics, and economics all show in varying degrees the predicted accentuation pattern. Potential graduate students in chemistry, civil engineering, and electrical engineerig score in the convergent quadrant rather than becoming more accommodative. Architecture, biology, and earth science potential graduate students move toward the convergent rather than becoming more divergent. Physics moves into the assimilative quadrant.

The results above should be viewed as only suggestive, since several measurement problems prevented a more accurate test of the accentuation hypothesis. The first problem was that it was difficult to determine whether or not a mathematics student planning graduate work in artificial intelligence would continue studying mathematics. Even though most students clearly planned graduate training in the field of their major, the few borderline cases do contaminate the results. A second measurement problem lies in the fact that graduate study in general for TECH students is associated with an abstract and active orientation. Since all six of the departments that did not follow the accentuation prediction showed a tendency toward abstractness, and four of the six showed a tendency toward the active orientation, this general tendency for graduate study may well have overshadowed the accentuation process in those departments. The final measurement problem has to do with the prediction of learning demands for those departments like electrical engineering whose students score close to the middle of the LSI grid.

To deal with these problems in the measurement of the accentuation process, four departments were selected for more intensive case study. Several criteria were used to choose departments whose learning-style demands matched the four dominant learning styles. The first criterion used the average learning-style scores of the students in a given department as an indicator of the learning-style requirements of that department. This criterion assumes that *on the average,* students will over their college careers select themselves and be selected into fields that match their learning styles. The criterion clearly identified three TECH departments that matched three of the learning types— humanities was divergent in its learning demands, mathematics was assimilative, and economics was convergent (see Figure 7.1).

The fourth department that was ultimately chosen, mechanical engineering, was accommodative but was not clearly different from other departments in the accommodative quadrant. To pick the most representative accommodative department, three other criteria were applied. The first was to pick a department whose students going to graduate school showed an accentuation of the departmental learning style. Three departments in the accommodative quadrant showed this accentuation process—chemical engineering, mechanical engineering, and management—as did the three departments already chosen to represent the other styles. Of these three accommodative departments, chemical engineering seemed most representative, but we had to eliminate it because all but two of the students in the department had accommodative learning styles. This made impossible comparisons between students who matched the departmental norms and those who did not. The other candidate, management, was eliminated because a closer examination of students in that department showed that it comprised two separate and distinct groups: behavioral-science and management/computer-science majors. Thus, students would not be reacting to a single set of departmental learning-style demands.

As a final check, the educational objectives and curricula of the four departments selected by the criteria above were examined for indications of their learning-style demands. Humanities and mathematics showed strong indications of divergent and assimilative orientations, respectively, as our previous data and theory would predict. For example, course descriptions in humanities often emphasize "different perspectives" of a literary work. In mathematics, the emphasis is on basic theory and research, as this quote from the *TECH Bulletin*'s description of the undergraduate mathematics program indicates:

> *The immediate educational aims are to provide an understanding of a substantial part of the existing body of mathematical knowlede and an ability to impart this knowledge to others. But most important, the department hopes to inspire a deep interest in the discovery or invention of new mathematics or interpretation of mathematics to a new field.*

By indication of the learning styles of its students, the economics department at TECH is considerably more convergent—abstract and active— than economics majors in our previous research (Kolb, 1973). This convergent emphasis is borne out, however, by the objectives and curricula of the department. The department places a very strong emphasis on the quantitative/ theoretical and policy-formation aspects of economics and considerably less on the more liberal-arts approach (for example, economic history).

Although our previous work showed that engineers on the average fall in the convergent quadrant of the LSI, we were able to obtain no differentiation among the various forms of engineering. One advantage of studying a technical institute like TECH is that we can begin to differentiate among these types. One would expect, for example, that mechanical engineering, with its relatively small theory base, would be more concrete than electrical engineering, where theory plays a larger role. The concrete orientation of mechanical engineering can be illustrated by the following quote, excerpted from the *TECH Bulletin* description of undergraduate study in mechanical engineering:

> *. . . the student must experience the ways in which scientific knowledge can be put to use in the development and design of useful devices and processes. To teach this art, largely by project-oriented work of creative nature, is the primary object of subjects in laboratory and design.*

To study the career choices of the students in the four departments, we used each student's LSI scores to position him/her on the LSI grid with a notation of the career field he/she had chosen to pursue after graduation. If the student was planning to attend graduate school, the career field was circled (the results of this analysis are shown in Figures 7.2 through 7.5). If the accentuation process were operating in the career choices of the students, we should find that those students who fall in the same quadrant as the norms of their academic major should be more likely to pursue careers and graduate training directly related to that major, while students with learning styles that differ from their discipline norms should be more inclined to pursue other careers and not

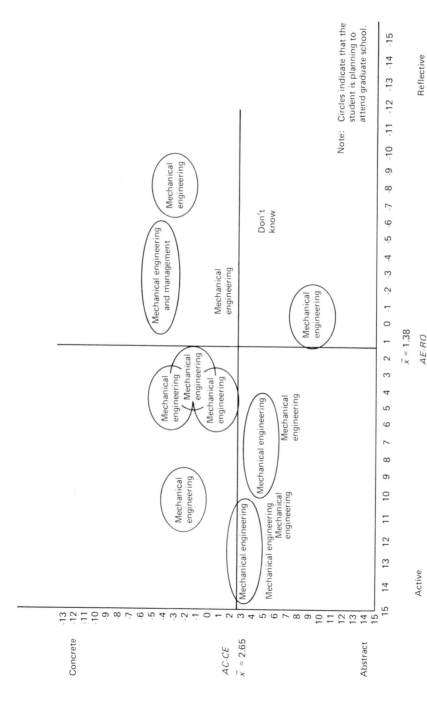

Figure 7.2 Career-Field and Graduate-School Plans for Mechanical-Engineering Majors as a Function of Their Learning Style

171

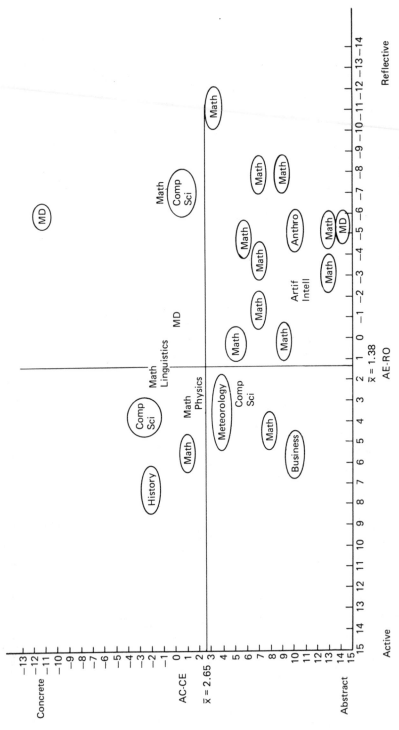

Figure 7.3 Career-Field and Graduate-School Plans for Mathematics Majors as a Function of Their Learning Style

172

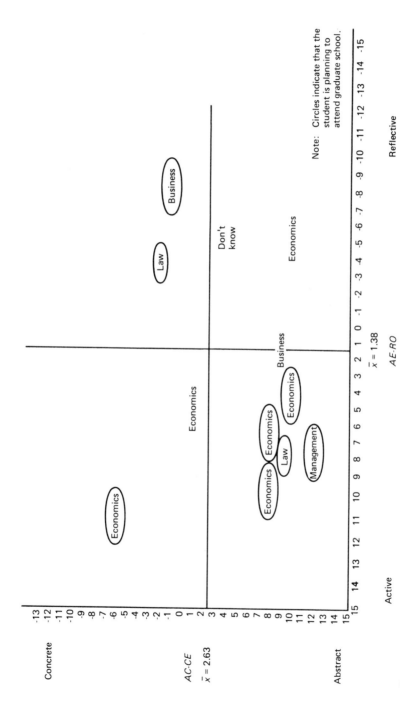

Figure 7.4 Career-Field and Graduate-School Plans for Economics Majors as a Function of Their Learning Style

173

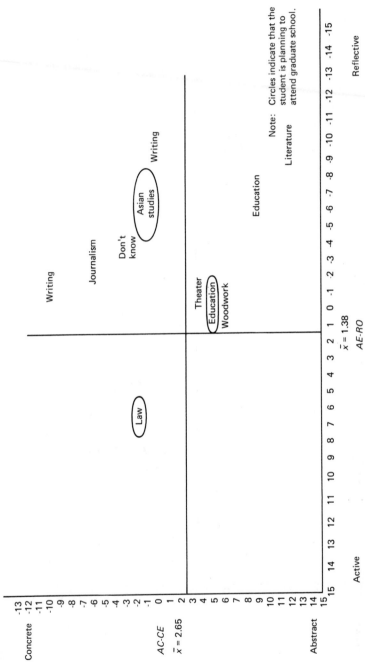

Figure 7.5 Career-Field and Graduate-School Plans for Humanities Majors as a Function of Their Learning Style

Concrete
-13
-12
-11
-10
-9
-8
-7
-6
-5
-4
-3
-2
-1
AC-CE
x̄ = 2.65
0
1
2
3
4
5
6
7
8
9
10
11
12
13
Abstract
14
15

Active
15 14 13 12 11 10 9 8 7 6 5 4 3 2 1 0 -1 -2 -3 -4 -5 -6 -7 -8 -9 -10 -11 -12 -13 -14 -15
Reflective

x̄ = 1.38
AE-RO

Writing

Journalism

Don't
know

Asian
studies

Writing

Theater
Education
Woodwork

Education

Literature

Law

Note: Circles indicate that the
student is planning to
attend graduate school.

174

attend graduate school in their discipline. Although the sample size is small and most students plan some form of mechanical-engineering career, this career-choice pattern can be seen in the mechanical-engineering department (Figure 7.2). All four of the students in the accommodator quadrant (100 percent) plan careers in mechanical engineering and graduate training as well. Only four of the ten students (40 percent) whose learning styles do not fit mechanical engineering are committed both to straight engineering careers and graduate training. The pattern is more clear in the mathematics department, where we have somewhat larger sample (Figure 7.3). Ten of the 13 mathematics students (80 percent) whose learning styles are congruent with departmental norms choose careers and graduate training in mathematics. Only two of the 13 students (15 percent) whose learning styles are not congruent plan both careers and graduate training in math (these differences are significant using the Fisher Exact Test, $p < .01$). Figure 7.4 shows the same trend in the economics department, although to a lesser degree. Three of the six economics students (50 percent) with congruent learning styles plan graduate training and careers in economics, but only one of the six (17 percent) with different learning styles has such plans.

The pattern in the humanities department (Figure 7.5) is somewhat more difficult to interpret. One is immediately struck by the fact that only three of the eleven students (27 percent) in the humanities department plan to attend graduate school. This is in contrast to the fact that 63 percent of all TECH seniors plan graduate training. In addition, all of the humanities students' career choices are somewhat related to the humanities but are definitely unrelated to the core curricula of TECH. In this sense, the humanities department as a whole seems not to fit with the learning demands of the rest of the institution. The concrete/reflective orientation of humanities seems in conflict with the abstract and active orientation of a technical school. We will explore this hypothesis further in the next section of results on performance and adjustment at TECH.

To further test the accentuation process in the four departments, we examined whether the student's choice-experience career-development cycle, indeed, operated as an accentuating positive feedback loop. If this were so, then those students whose learning-style dispositions matched and were reinforced by their discipline demands should show a greater commitment to their choice of future career field than those whose learning styles were not reinforced by their experiences in their discipline. As part of the questionnaire, students were asked to rate how important it was for them to pursue their chosen career field. They expressed their answers on a 1-5 scale, where 5 equaled "great importance." The average ratings for students whose learning styles matched discipline demands and those whose styles did not match the norms of their discipline are shown for the four departments in Figure 7.6. In all four departments, the average importance rating was higher for the students with a match between learning style and discipline norms (the differences being statistically significant in the mechanical-engineering and economics departments). Thus, it seems that learning experiences that reinforce learning-style

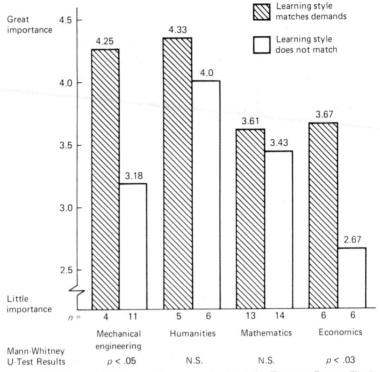

Figure 7.6 Students' Rating of How Important It Is for Them to Pursue Their Career Choice as a Function of Match Between Discipline Demands and Learning Style in Four Undergraduate Departments

dispositions tend to produce greater commitment in career choices than those learning experiences that do not reinforce learning-style dispositions.

Taken as a whole, these data present enticing, if not definitive, evidence that career choices tend to follow a path toward accentuation of one's specialized approach to learning. Learning experiences congruent with learning styles tend to positively influence the choice of future learning and work experiences that reinforce that particular learning style. On the other hand, those students who find a learning environment incongruent with their learning styles tend to move away from that kind of environment in future learning and work choices.

Learning Styles, Academic Performance, and Adaptation to the University

The final question to be explored in this research study was whether a student's learning style was an important determinant of social adaptation and performance in the university. To answer this, we compared, on a number of variables, the students whose learning styles fit their discipline demands with the students whose learning styles did not fit in the four departments mentioned above. To begin with, student cumulative grade averages were examined (see Figure 7.7). The mechanical-engineering and economics departments both showed results consistent with prediction; accommodative students in mechanical engineering had higher grades ($p < .10$) than mechanical-engineering students with other learning styles, and convergent students in economics had much higher grades ($p < .001$) than economics students with other learning styles. In the mathematics department, however, there was no difference between the two groups of students, and in humanities, the six students whose learning style was not divergent had somewhat higher grades. Although the humanities department results represent a reversal of our original prediction, they offer further evidence for the hypothesis that humanities and the divergent learning style associated with it are incongruent with the abstract and active norms of TECH as a whole. This latter hypothesis would suggest that humanities students who are not divergers should perform better academically.

The same pattern of results is found when another aspect of academic performance, student perceptions of how heavy the academic workload is, is examined (see Figure 7.8). Students rated their perception of academic workload on a 1-5 scale, where 1 equaled "very great" and 5 equaled "light." In

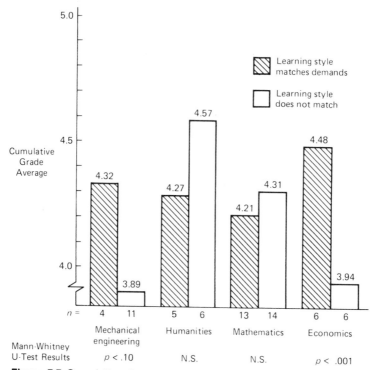

Figure 7.7 Cumulative Grade Average as a Function of Match between Discipline Demands and Learning Style in Four Undergraduate Departments

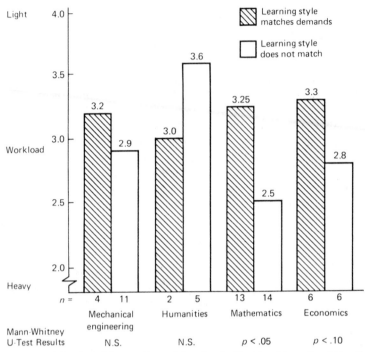

Figure 7.8 Students' Perception of Academic Workload as a Function of Match Between Discipline Demands and Learning Style in Four Undergraduate Departments

mechanical engineering, mathematics, and economics, those students whose learning styles were congruent with their discipline norms felt the workload to be lighter than did those students whose learning styles did not "fit." (Statistical significance levels in mathematics and economics are $p < .05$ and $p < .10$ respectively.) Again, the humanities department showed a trend in the opposite direction.

Mismatches between learning styles and discipline demands are apt to affect a student's social adaptation to the university. An incongruence between a student's learning style and the norms of his or her major might well undermine feelings of belonging to the university community and alienate him or her from the power structure (faculty and administration). To test these hypotheses, we used a version of Olsen et al.'s political alienation scale (1969) and McCloskey and Schaar's anomie scale (1963) that were adapted to apply specifically to the TECH environment (see Kolb, Rubin and Schein, 1972, for complete details of these scales). These scales measure two uncorrelated aspects of alienation that influence student adaptation. Political alienation results from the failure of authorities, teachers, administrative officials, and the system as a whole to meet the student's needs. The politically alienated student feels that the authority structure of the university is not legitimate because it is unconcerned about students, because it does not involve them in its decision procedures, because it allows its priorities to be set by vested interests, and because it is incapable of solving the problems it faces. Anomie stems not from dissatisfaction with the formal authority system but from a lack of contact with the norms and values that determine and direct behavior of individuals in the university. These norms and values are communicated most directly through contact with one's peers. We have found, for example, that feelings of anomie among TECH students are strongly associated with lack of involvement in a personally important group of peers (Kolb et al., 1972). Anomic students feel lonely, isolated, and out of place at TECH. They have difficulty determining what is expected of them and what they believe.

Figures 7.9 and 7.10 show the anomie scores and political alienation scores respectively in the four departments for students whose learning styles are congruent and incongruent with their discipline demands. The results are generally consistent with the prediction that there would be higher anomie and political alienation among those students whose learning style is incongruent with their discipline norms. (None of the political-alienation differences are significant statistically, however. Anomie significance levels for humanities and economics were $p < .10$ and $p < .01$ respectively.) One interesting fact in Figure 7.10 is the very high political alienation scores of all students in the humanities department. Humanities, in fact, scored highest on this variable of all the departments in the institute. This further develops the pattern of humanities as a deviant learning environment at TECH.

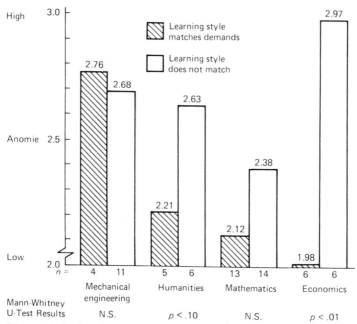

Figure 7.9 Students' Feelings of Anomie as a Function of Match Between Discipline Demands and Learning Style in Four Undergraduate Departments

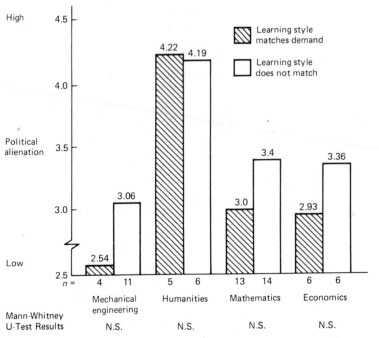

Figure 7.10 Students' Feelings of Political Alienation as a Function of Match Between Discipline Demands and Learning Style in Four Undergraduate Departments

Further insight into the effect of learning styles on social adaptation can be gained by examining student involvement with an important peer group (Figure 7.11). Students were asked to rate on a 1-to-5 scale (5 = very involved) how involved they were with their most important peer group. As has already been noted, previous research showed high involvement with peers to be associated with low anomie. As Figure 7.11 shows, in all four departments, students with learning styles matching departmental norms tended to be highly involved with their peers. This pattern was most pronounced in the humanities ($p < .05$) and economics ($p < .01$) departments. These results suggest that student peer groups may be an important vehicle for the communication of the learning-style requirements of a department, although, as we already know from many studies of formal and informal organizations, peer-group norms may sometimes run counter to the formal organizational requirements. Some evidence for this special role of the peer group can be seen in a comparison of the economics and humanities departments. In both these departments, students whose learning style fits with the discipline demands are very involved with their peers; and both groups of students score very low in anomie, as we would predict. Yet the convergent economics students score very low in political alienation, whereas the divergent humanities students feel extremely politically alienated from the university. Thus, in humanities, student peer-group solidarity among divergers

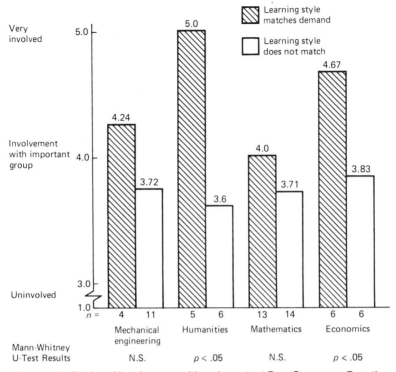

Figure 7.11 Students' Involvement with an Important Peer Group as a Function of Match Between Discipline Demands and Learning Style in Four Undergraduate Departments

is based on norms of alienation and rebellion from the university, and in economics, the convergent peer-group norms support the goals and procedures of the formal authorities. This may in part account for the fact that the grades of the divergent humanities students are poor relative to those of other humanities students, while the grades of the convergent economics students are far better than those of other students in economics.

The research above illustrates the usefulness of experiential learning theory for describing specialized developmental processes in undergraduate education by describing variations in the ways people learn, and corresponding variations in the learning demands of different academic disciplines. This study of TECH undergraduates shows that, at least in this one institution, the experiential learning theory typology is useful for describing the learning-demand characteristics of different academic departments and for predicting the direction of student career choices; and through examination of the matches and mismatches between student learning styles and departmental learning demands, the typology helps to explain variations in academic performance and adaptation to the university. These results suggest that the experiential learning model may well provide a useful framework for the design and management of learning experiences. As was already noted, the dominant trend in research on the "climate" of learning environments has been to focus on the effect on performance and adaptation of social-emotional variables such as motivation, attitudes, participation, liking for the teacher, and social isolation. Many of these variables have been shown to be important. However, the results of this study suggest that the climate of learning environments might as productively be examined in terms of its effect on the learning process itself, and, in particular, on the learning styles of students. Rather than being a cause of successful academic performance, motivation to learn may well be a result of learning climates that match learning styles and thereby produce successful learning experiences. Similarly, the sources of student alienation may lie as much in failures to achieve the university's central mission—learning—as they do in its social milieu.

PROFESSIONAL EDUCATION AND CAREER ADAPTATION

Specialization through the process of accentuation is a major force in undergraduate university education in general, but there is reason to suspect that this process is even more central to professional education. From a social control point of view, professions seem to have originally emerged in the areas of human activity—medicine, religion, law—where it is not feasible to judge performance on the basis of outcomes. Since one cannot judge a doctor on whether or not a specific patient dies or a lawyer on whether a specific case is won or lost, the emphasis in professions is on controlling the means of performance rather than the outcomes. One is therefore professionally competent if he or she performs the accepted professional activities or methods adequately, regardless of their results. As professions have expanded into other areas of human activity, this emphasis on means and methods has been retained. One result of this emphasis on means of performance is that schools of professional education have the primary responsibility for the development and certification of professional competence. Although programs of peer review, periodic licensing, and continuing education are now appearing in some professions, for the most part the professional student on graduation is presumed competent for life. This responsibility causes professional schools to make every possible effort to incorporate the appropriate knowledge, skills, and attitudes deemed necessary for professional competence.

As a result, the process of socialization into a profession becomes an intense experience that instills not only knowledge and skills but also a fundamental reorientation of one's identity. We refer to this orientation as a professional mentality. This mentality is pervasive throughout all areas of the professional's life; it includes standards and ethics, the appropriate ways to think and behave, the criteria by which one judges value, what is good or bad. Learning style is an important part of professional mentality. It represents the generic learning competencies that facilitate the acquisition of the specific performance skills required for effectiveness in the core professional role.

Through processes of selection and socialization, professional schools make every effort to ensure the proper professional mentality in their graduates. This education is a major social control on the quality of the professional service.

A problem arises, however, when we consider the nature of professional careers in a rapidly changing society. As Whitehead observed, "The fixed person for the fixed duties, who in older societies was such a godsend, in the future will be a public danger" (1926, p. 282). Few professionals remain for a lifetime in the core professional role for which they were trained. In engineering, for example, the typical career path requires a transition to management, a job role requiring a different portfolio of competencies and a different learning style from the convergent professional mentality so suited to engineering work. This lifelong career perspective poses a serious dilemma for professional education. Should it continue to emphasize intensive socialization in the specialized role requirements of the profession, or should some of this rigorous specialized training give way to the broader development of learning competencies required for lifelong learning? The choice for broader development may mean less specialized education at a time when the knowledge required for professional competence is increasing. The specialized choice may result in professional deformation—in the intensive overlearning of a specialized professional mentality that actively hinders adaptation to the changing requirements of one's career.

The dilemma has been central to much of the self-examination, social criticism, and student/alumni evaluation of professional education. Schein, for example, has outlined eight problems of professional education, all of which are related to the dilemma of specialized vs. integrative education:

1 The professions are so specialized that they have become unresponsive to certain classes of social problems that require an interdisciplinary or interprofessional point of view—e.g., the urban problem.

2 Educational programs in professional schools, early career paths, and formal or informal licensing procedures have become so rigid and standardized that many young professionals cannot do the kind of work they wish to do.

3 The norms for entry into the professions have become so rigid that certain classes of applicants, such as older people, women, and career switchers, are in effect discriminated against.

4 The norms of the professions and the growing base of basic and applied knowledge have become so convergent in most professions that it is difficult for innovations to occur in any but the highly specialized content areas at the frontiers of the profession.

5 Professionals have become unresponsive to the needs of many classes of ultimate clients or users of the services, working instead for the organization that employs them.

6 Professional education is almost totally geared to producing autonomous specialists and provides neither training nor experience in how to work as a member of a team, how to collaborate with clients in identifying needs and

possible solutions, and how to collaborate with other professionals on complex projects.

7 Professional education provides no training for those graduates who wish to work as members of and become managers of intra- or interprofessional project teams working on complex social problems.

8 Professional education generally underutilizes the applied behavioral sciences, especially in helping professionals to increase their self-insight, their ability to diagnose and manage client relationships and complex social problems, their ability to sort out the ethical and value issues inherent in their professional role, and their ability to continue to learn throughout their careers. [Schein, 1972, p. 59]

A COMPARATIVE STUDY OF PROFESSIONAL EDUCATION IN SOCIAL WORK AND ENGINEERING

To explore this dilemma and its attendant problems, we examined the effect of professional education on career adaptation by surveying the alumni of two professional education programs from a single university.[3] The alumni from the university's social-work and engineering schools in the graduating classes of 1975, 1970, 1965, 1960, and 1955 were studied by means of questionnaires, tests, and interviews (see Kolb, Wolfe, et al., 1981, for detailed methodologies). The professions of social work and engineering were chosen for study because they typify the social and science-based professions respectively. Thus, we could examine specialized education in two different professions with different knowledge structures and learning styles—the contextualist/accommodative orientation in social work and the formist/convergent orientation in engineering—and examine the consequences of this education on later career development.

The science-based professions, and especially engineering, require a highly developed capacity for working with abstract conceptualizations in the utilization of advanced technology for solving real-world problems. The work itself results not so much in further conceptualization (the province of the basic sciences) but rather in action taken to solve practical problems and to develop and construct physical structures, products, and technical processes. Thus, a well-developed competence in active experimentation is equally essential for effective work in the science-based professions. The adaptive competencies—symbolic complexity and behavioral complexity—combine to make up the convergent style that is the forte of the professional engineer.

Career advancement for engineers often involves a promotion to managerial positions that generally require a substantially different mix of

---

[3]The research reported in this section is part of a larger research program on professional education and career development (see Kolb and Wolfe et al., 1981). The data reported here were analyzed in collaboration with Ronald Sims.

competencies. Much less of these managers' time is devoted to the direct application of scientific knowledge. Although there is a continuing concern for action, the focus is much more on the concrete realities of managing people, planning for various contingencies, setting priorities, and handling administrative tasks. The emergent need, in this transition to management, is for increased competence in handling the complexities and vagaries of concrete experience. The convergent modality must give way to an accommodative style of adaptation, based on competencies in affective complexity (concrete experience) coupled with behavioral complexity (active experimentation). Evidence for this transition in engineering careers is seen in the current job roles of engineering alumni in our study. Of new engineers three years on the job (the 1975 alumni), only 31 percent are managers. This percentage rises steadily over time to the 1955 alumni group, where 76 percent are managers.

Professional work in human-services fields (such as social work) is predicated on highly developed accommodation skills. The emphasis is on dealing with the social and emotional complexities of people in need. The helping process calls for heightened sensitivity to the concrete realities of the human condition, matched with active problem solving. These generic competencies are required for the effective delivery of services to the disadvantaged, the troubled, and the needy.

Career advancement for human-service professionals may also involve taking on managerial responsibilities, but in this case, a change in basic adaptive style may or may not be required. Although a newly appointed director of a social agency generally has many new things to learn, his or her accommodative style is generally appropriate for most of the developmental agenda in this transition. Nonetheless, for many who are promoted from direct-service delivery to administrative or policy-formation assignments, some increase in abstract analytic competencies is called for. One must back away from some of the concrete details of casework with individuals in order to gain a larger perspective. The basic accommodator style begins to require a backup of converger skills or perhaps even assimilator (social-planning) skills. The study of social-work alumni shows a less clear picture of career transition in that field. The percentage of managers in all five alumni groups ranges from 43 to 63 percent, with no clear transitional pattern. These data, along with observations of individual career histories, suggest that careers in social work are primarily of a dual-track nature. People enter the profession with an orientation to management or direct service and tend to stay in that job role more than is the case in engineering.

Thus, engineering and social work seem to have very different career paths. In engineering, there is a definite general progression from direct engineering work to managerial positions over the cohort years, whereas social work appears to have two tracks, administrative and direct service, that begin in graduate school and continue equally in early and late career with less distinct progression from one role to the next. Since professional education must prepare people not only for early career demands but also for the often quite different demands of later career responsibilities, the different structure of career paths in these two fields offers contrasts of great interest for the study of career adaptation.

Professional Mentality and Professional Deformation

When we examine the Learning Style Inventory scores of social-work and engineering alumni (Figure 7.12), we see that the difference between the two professions in adaptive orientation is dramatically illustrated, particularly in their emphasis on abstractedness (knowing via comprehension) versus concreteness (knowing via apprehension). Engineering alumni fall mostly in the convergent learning style (41 percent); social-work alumni fall in the divergent

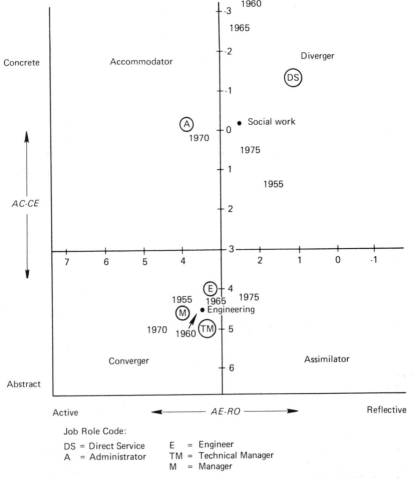

Figure 7.12 Learning Style Inventory Scores for Engineers and Social Workers by Alumni Year and Job Role

(34 percent) and accommodative (29 percent) quadrants. The science-based profession of engineering and the social profession of social work are thus markedly different in the way they acquire and use knowledge, at least as measured by the learning styles of alumni educated in these two professions.

Equally relevant to our consideration of specialized professional education and its effect on career adaptation is the degree of variation in learning style among social workers and engineers within their professional specialties. In engineering, we were surprised to find a great deal of homogeneity in learning style. There was significantly less variance in LSI scores than in social work. More important, there were no significant differences among alumni cohort years (note that the averages for the five cohort years are all tightly grouped about the engineering mean in Figure 7.12) or among the three major job roles currently held by engineering alumni—manager, technical manager, and "bench" engineer. Insofar as learning style is a part of the professional mentality of engineering, we see here a very consistent professional mentality that varies little even in the face of age, years of work experience, and different job demands. The social-work professionals show much greater variation in learning style. There is wide (although not statistically significant) variation among cohort-year averages, and the two major job roles in social work, administration and direct client service, are significantly differentiated on the active-reflective dimension of the LSI ($p < .02$), as one might predict from an analysis of demands of these jobs. Administrative job holders are primarily accommodative in their approach to learning, whereas direct-service personnel emphasize the divergent learning style.

Taken together, the results above portray engineering as a field with a highly paradigmatic, coherent professional mentality shaped by the selection and socialization forces of accentuation. A paradigm refers to the body of theory about cause and effect that is subscribed to by all members of the field (Kuhn, 1962). This paradigm serves two important organizing functions: It provides a consistent account of most of the phenomena of interest in a particular area, and it defines those problems that require further research. From these data we would also infer that the social-work profession is a less established and paradigmatic profession than engineering. Schein (1972) identified three trends of maturing professions: (1) They become more convergent in their knowledge base and standards of practice; (2) they become more highly differentiated and specialized; and (3) they become more bureaucratized and rigid with respect to the career alternatives they allow. On all three criteria, the social professions, including social work, are less mature and paradigmatic than are the science-based professions.

Adaptive Competence and Career Adaptation

Given these differences in the maturity and paradigmatic nature of social work and engineering, we would expect different problems of career adaptation in the two fields. To the extent that the specialized professional mentality inculcated in the student becomes a central part of his or her identity, that student may become inflexible and intolerant toward styles that conflict with that mentality. This rigidity may actively inhibit one's ability to adapt to changing career demands. This problem would seem to be most serious for the established paradigmatic professions that have clearly identified "ways of doing things" and the most intensive selection/socialization processes. Less paradigmatic professions would appear to allow for greater flexibility and variability in their graduates, but in many cases this advantage may be offset by the lack of powerful models, tools, and technologies for achieving the core mission of the professions.

One way to assess career adaptation is to measure how well the competencies of the individual professional meet the demands of his or her current job. On the alumni questionnaire, respondents were asked to describe the demands of their current job and their corresponding level of ability to meet these job demands. The technique used was an earlier version of the competency circle described in Chapter 4 (p. 93 and Figure 4.10). Although, as was indicated earlier, these self-ratings of job demand and personal competence would obviously be enhanced by objective independent assessments, the responses of social work and engineering professionals nonetheless reveal interesting patterns of career adaptation. To begin with, differences in job demands were analyzed. The different job roles making up careers in engineering and social work require different portfolios of performance competencies. Engineering jobs require predominately convergent competencies associated with the symbolic and behavioral learning competencies. Managerial jobs in engineering require more affective and behavioral competencies. Direct-service social work requires highly developed affective competencies, and administrative jobs emphasize behavioral competencies more strongly.

To test this hypothesis, one-way analyses of variances were done between the job demands of the different job roles in social work and engineering, and the mean scores were plotted on the competency-circle graphs (Figures 7.13 and 7.14). Figure 7.13 shows great differences in the different job roles comprising engineering careers. Using a Scheffe procedure at .05 level, the significant subsets between job roles are circled. As can be seen in Figure 7.13, professional engineers in the job roles of engineer, technical manager, and manager do perceive their jobs as having different demands in the competencies of dealing with people, being personally involved, and being sensitive to people's feelings, seeking and exploiting opportunities, making decisions, and setting goals, designing experiments, testing theories, and gathering information. Generally, managerial jobs require greater affective and behavioral competencies, and direct engineering work requires greater symbolic and perceptual competencies.

For social workers, the analysis of variance procedures showed significant differences between job roles on making decisions, seeking and exploiting opportunities, analyzing quantitative data, sensitivity to people's feelings, and testing theories and ideas (Figure 7.14). Direct-service social workers and

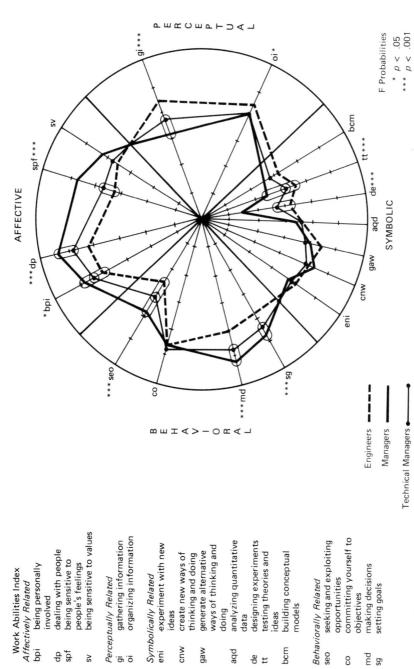

Work Abilities Index

Affectively Related
bpi   being personally
      involved
dp   dealing with people
spf   being sensitive to
      people's feelings
sv   being sensitive to values

Perceptually Related
gi   gathering information
oi   organizing information

Symbolically Related
eni   experiment with new
      ideas
cnw   create new ways of
      thinking and doing
gaw   generate alternative
      ways of thinking and
      doing
aqd   analyzing quantitative
      data
de   designing experiments
tt   testing theories and
      ideas
bcm   building conceptual
      models

Behaviorally Related
seo   seeking and exploiting
      opportunities
co   committing yourself to
      objectives
md   making decisions
sg   setting goals

Figure 7.13 Comparison of Job Demands for Engineers, Technical Managers, and Managers

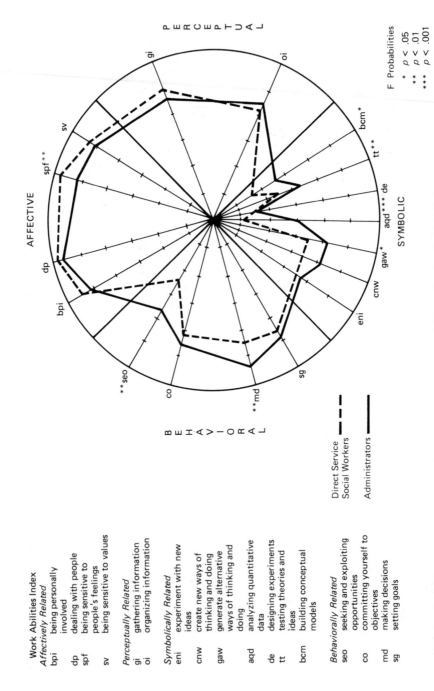

Work Abilities Index

Affectively Related
bpi   being personally involved
dp   dealing with people
spf   being sensitive to people's feelings
sv   being sensitive to values

Perceptually Related
gi   gathering information
oi   organizing information

Symbolically Related
eni   experiment with new ideas
cnw   create new ways of thinking and doing
gaw   generate alternative ways of thinking and doing
aqd   analyzing quantitative data
de   designing experiments
tt   testing theories and ideas
bcm   building conceptual models

Behaviorally Related
seo   seeking and exploiting opportunities
co   committing yourself to objectives
md   making decisions
sg   setting goals

Direct Service Social Workers ------

Administrators ——

Figure 7.14 Comparison of Job Demands for Administrators and Direct-Service Social Workers

F Probabilities
* $p < .05$
** $p < .01$
*** $p < .001$

administrators perceive their jobs as having different job demands. Direct-service professionals see their jobs as more demanding affectively than do administrators. Administrators perceive their jobs as more demanding behaviorally—for instance, seeking and exploiting opportunities, committing themselves to objectives, and making decisions.

By comparing alumni's self-ratings of their work abilities with their descriptions of the demands of their current jobs, it is possible to determine the percentage of alumni in different job roles who see themselves as being underqualified in each of the four clusters of performance competencies. These data are shown in Table 7.1.

Table 7.1 Percentage of Those in Different Job Roles Whose Work Abilities Do Not Meet Job Demands

| | Job Demands | | | |
Job Roles	Affective	Behavioral	Symbolic	Perceptual
Engineering:				
Engineer	24%	20%	18%	43%
Technical manager	33%	35%	6%	34%
Manager	42%	31%	22%	15%
Social work:				
Direct service	45%	29%	15%	27%
Administrator	33%	44%	30%	40%

The data for engineers suggest problems in career adaptation. One-third or more of the technical managers and managers in the engineering alumni sample report that they are underqualified in affective and behavioral competencies. These percentages are greater than the corresponding percentages of bench engineers who are underqualified in affective and behavioral competencies, suggesting that the larger number of underqualified managers in these areas results from a failure to learn how to respond to the increased affective and behavioral demands characteristic of managerial jobs (Figure 7.13). The fact that the number of affectively and behaviorally underqualified managers is greater than symbolically and perceptually underqualified managers suggests that professional education more adequately prepares professionals in symbolic and perceptual competencies than in affective and behavioral competencies (see the following section on learning at school and at work).

In social work, 44 percent of the administrators report that they are underqualified in the behavioral competencies. The increase in the number of behaviorally underqualified administrators over behaviorally underqualified direct-service workers would seem to result from a failure to learn how to respond to the increased behavioral demands of administrative jobs (see Table 7.1). However, a large percentage of administrators see themselves as underqualified in the other three areas of competence, as well as in the behavioral area that appears to be neglected in professional social-work education (Figure 7.16). This suggests that failures of career adaptation in social work are as much a result of a generalized lack of competencies to deal with the professional tasks in the administrative role that are often nearly impossible, as they are a result of professional deformation.

Thus we see differences in how professionals in social work and engineering adapt to the changing demands of their careers. The job roles in engineering and social work require quite different portfolios of performance competencies. Engineering jobs require strong capabilities in symbolic and perceptual areas; direct-service social work emphasizes affective and perceptual competencies. Administrative and managerial jobs across the two professions are very similar, requiring highly developed affective and behavioral competencies.

Both professions seem to have problems of career adaptation, although for different reasons. In social work, it appears that many incumbents of jobs at all levels feel somewhat overwhelmed by the requirements of their jobs. The challenge for professional education would seem to lie in the development of more powerful "social technologies" and educational methods for responding to our country's increasing social problems in a time of scarce resources.

The problem in engineering may more properly be considered one of professional deformation. The scientific technologies of the various engineering fields with their attendant scientific problem-solving mentality have proven their potency repeatedly. Career adaptation problems in engineering stem more from overspecialization in these learning competencies, often to the point where professionals in the field have difficulty performing in managerial job roles that require greater affective and behavioral competence.

Learning in School and at Work

The specialized development that characterizes most higher educational experiences usually carries forward into one's early career. First jobs often are continuing apprenticeships for the refinement of the specialized skills and knowledge acquired in preparatory education. The acquisition of the knowledge, skills, and values that began in school is carried forward in the workplace, as successful performance in a specialized area of expertise is rewarded by the assignment of increasingly complex challenges in that area. Yet, as has been noted, there is a transition point in most career paths where the demands of job roles change, requiring an increasingly integrative perspective on learning. A study of the accounting and marketing professions conducted by Clarke et al. (1977) illustrated this change in learning style in the later stages of one's career. Their study compared cross-sectional samples of accounting and marketing students and professionals in school and at lower-, middle-, and senior-level career stages. The learning styles of marketing and accounting M.B.A. students were similar, being fairly balanced on the four learning modes.

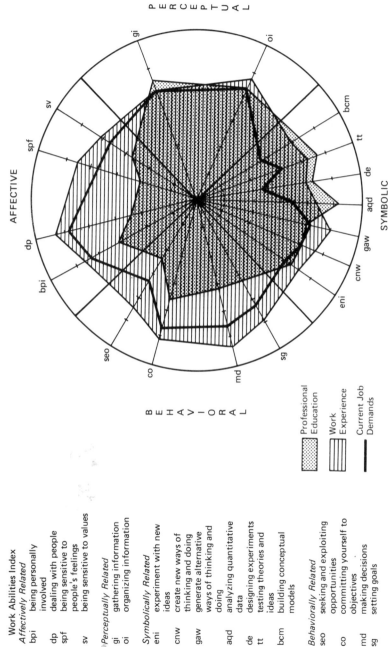

Work Abilities Index

Affectively Related
bpi   being personally involved
dp   dealing with people
spf   being sensitive to people's feelings
sv   being sensitive to values

Perceptually Related
gi   gathering information
oi   organizing information

Symbolically Related
eni   experiment with new ideas
cnw   create new ways of thinking and doing
gaw   generate alternative ways of thinking and doing
aqd   analyzing quantitative data
de   designing experiments
tt   testing theories and ideas
bcm   building conceptual models

Behaviorally Related
seo   seeking and exploiting opportunities
co   committing yourself to objectives
md   making decisions
sg   setting goals

Figure 7.15 Contributions of Work Experience and Professional Education to the Development of the Performance Competencies of Engineering Alumni

193

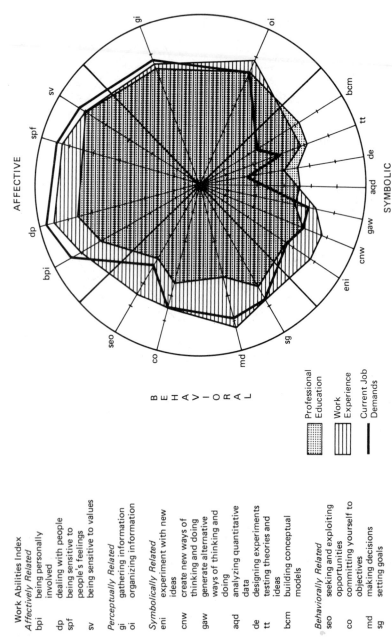

Work Abilities Index

Affectively Related
- bpi being personally involved
- dp dealing with people
- spf being sensitive to people's feelings
- sv being sensitive to values

Perceptually Related
- gi gathering information
- oi organizing information

Symbolically Related
- eni experiment with new ideas
- cnw create new ways of thinking and doing
- gaw generate alternative ways of thinking and doing
- aqd analyzing quantitative data
- de designing experiments
- tt testing theories and ideas
- bcm building conceptual models

Behaviorally Related
- seo seeking and exploiting opportunities
- co committing yourself to objectives
- md making decisions
- sg setting goals

Figure 7.16 Contributions of Work Experience and Professional Education to the Development of the Performance Competencies of Social-Work Alumni

Lower-level accountants had convergent learning styles, and this convergent emphasis was even more pronounced in middle-level accountants, reflecting a highly technical emphasis in the early and middle stages of accounting careers. The senior-level accountants, however, were accommodative in their learning style, reflecting a greater concern with client relations and administration than with technical functions. Marketing professionals at the lower level also were convergent in learning style but became highly concrete at middle-level responsibilities, reflecting a shift from technical to creative concerns. The senior marketing personnel had accommodative learning styles similar to those of senior accountants, probably reflecting the same client and management concerns.

There is a similar transition in the learning orientations of engineers and social workers over the course of their careers. In a selected interview study of the engineering and social-work alumni, Gypen found that:

> As engineers move up from the bench to the management positions, they complement their initial strengths in abstract conceptualization and active experimentation with the previously non-dominant orientations of concrete experience and reflective observation. As social workers move from direct service into administrative positions, they move in the opposite direction of the engineers. [Gypen, 1980, p. ii]

Furthermore, Gypen found that these changes in learning style were directly related to the changing demands of one's current job.

These results give a somewhat more optimistic picture of professional career adaptation than the just-reported data showing that large numbers of professionals describe themselves as underqualified for their current job demands (see Table 7.1). From this perspective, the developmental "glass" appears half full rather than half empty. Some change in the direction of career adaptation does occur after professional education, most likely through *learning on the job.*

To explore how the social-work and engineering alumni developed their current portfolios of competencies, the alumni questionnaires asked respondents to rate how much their professional education had contributed to the development of each of the performance competencies described in the last section and how much their work experience had contributed to the development of these competencies. Their responses are plotted on the competency circle for engineering alumni in Figure 7.15. The dark shaded area represents contributions of professional education to competencies, and the lined area shows contributions of work experience to the development of competence. The dark line shows the average current job demand for each competence. The figure shows dramatic differences in the competencies acquired in education and work. Engineering education seems to prepare or, in several cases, overprepare people for the demands of their jobs in symbolic and perceptual competencies but makes little contribution to the development of affective and behavioral competencies. These seem to be acquired primarily in the work setting.

Figure 7.16 shows the same analysis for social-work alumni. Here, the shaded area representing the contribution of social-work professional education is larger than in engineering, but it is still biased toward the development of perceptual and symbolic skills. Work experience contributes more to the development of affective and particularly behavioral skills, as in the engineering figure.

Surprisingly, these patterns were not significantly different for different alumni years; alumni only three years out of school (the class of 1975) showed the same pattern as alumni 23 years out (the class of 1955). Engineering alumni in all cohort groups reported that their professional education emphasized the development of symbolic and perceptual skills while neglecting affective and behavioral skills. Social-work alumni in all cohort groups felt that their professional education had developed required competencies in the affective, perceptual, and symbolic areas but had neglected the development of behavioral competencies. Both social-work and engineering alumni consistently felt that they had made up for these deficits as well as supplemented their strengths through experiential learning on the job. In another study, Sims (1981) found that this on-the-job learning is facilitated in those organizations with a strong growth climate characterized by good supervision, advancement potential and autonomy, and a chance to grow and develop, and is inhibited in organizations whose climate is not supportive of learning and development. These results showing the critical role of organization climate have been independently replicated by Margulies and Raia (1967). Lifelong learning is not automatic but must be nurtured in a supportive learning environment, both in school and at work.

MANAGING THE LEARNING PROCESS

To conduct the educational process in universities in a manner that attends to the individual learning styles of students and fosters student development requires identification and management of those aspects of the educational system that influence the learning process. Such a management system must be soundly built on a valid model of the learning process. There has been a great burgeoning of educational techniques designed to assist the learning process in recent years: computer-aided instruction, experienced-based learning materials in math, science, and psychology, programmed instruction, games, multimedia curricula, open classrooms, and so on. Although these techniques tend to be highly sophisticated and creative applications of their own particular fields of expertise, be it computer science, psychology, or architecture, they are much less sophisticated about how they enhance human learning. The weakness of nearly all these techniques is the failure to recognize and explicitly provide for the differences in learning styles that are characteristic of both individuals and subject matters. Even though many of these educational innovations have been developed in the name of individualized education and self-directed learning, there has been little attempt to specify along which dimensions individualization is to take place. For example, although computer-aided instruction and programmed learning provide alternative learning routes or branches for the individual learner, these branches tend to be based primarily on various elaborations of the subject matter being taught (for example; a wrong answer puts the learner on a branch giving him more information about the question). Little has been done to provide the individual learner with branches that provide alternative learning methods (such as pictoral versus symbolic presentation) based on the person's learning style. In addition, there has been little research to assess how the effectiveness of various teaching methods is contingent on either individual learning styles or the type of subject matter being taught. (Two significant exceptions in the case of learning styles are the works of David Hunt, 1974; and Liam Hudson, 1966.)

Learning Environments

Experiential learning theory provides one such system for managing the learning process in Fry's concept of the learning environment (Fry, 1978). Any educational program, course design, or classroom session can be viewed as having degrees of orientation toward each of the four learning modes in the experiential learning model, labeled as affective, perceptual, symbolic, and behavioral, to connote the overall climate they create and the particular learning skill or mode they require (Kolb and Fry, 1975). Thus an affective environment emphasizes the experiencing of concrete events; a symbolic environment emphasizes abstract conceptualization; a perceptual environment stresses observation and appreciation; a behavioral environment stresses action taking in situations with real consequences. Any particular learning experience can have some or all of these orientations, to differing degrees, at the same time. A typical lecture obviously has perceptual and symbolic orientations, because it requires students to listen to and interpret the presentation (reflective observation skills) and to reason and induce conceptual relationships from what they hear (abstract conceptualization skills). But there may be an affective orientation as well. Some students may be experiencing the teacher doing the lecturing as a role model. Or if we direct questions or pose dilemmas to the class, we increase the behavioral orientation by urging students to take action by speaking up and testing their ideas out in public.

Fry has found that each type of environmental orientation can be measured by observing the following variables in the context of a course: the purpose of the major activities, the primary source or use of information, the rules guiding learner behavior, the teacher's role, and the provision for feedback. These are useful cues, because to a great extent they are controlled by the instructor, faculty, or administration, independently of the learner. Most decisions affecting these aspects of learning environments are made before learner-classroom interactions take place. Using these variables, the following pictures of different types of environments result.

Affectively complex learning environments are ones in which the emphasis is on experiencing what it is actually like to be a professional in the field under study. Learners are engaged in activities that simulate or mirror what they would do as graduates, or they are encouraged to reflect upon an experience to generate these insights and feelings about themselves. The information discussed and generated is more often current/immediate. It often comes from expressions of feelings, values, opinions by the learner in discussions with peers or the teacher. Such expressions of feelings are encouraged and seen as productive inputs to the learning process. The learner's activities often vary from any prior schedule as a result of the learner's needs. The teacher serves as a role model for the field or profession, relating to learners on a personal basis and more often as a colleague than an authority. Feedback is personalized with regard to each individual's needs and goals, as opposed to comparative. It can come from both peers and the teacher. There is accepted discussion and critique of how the course is proceeding, and thus, specific events within a single class session are often more emergent than prescribed.

Perceptually complex learning environments are ones in which the primary goal is to understand something: to be able to identify relationships between concepts, to be able to define problems for investigation, to be able to collect relevant information, to be able to research a question, and the like. To do this, learners are encouraged to view the topic or subject matter from different perspectives (their own experience, expert opinion, literature) and in different ways (listen, observe, write, discuss, act out, think, smell). If a task is being done or a problem is being solved, the emphasis is more on how it gets done, the process, than on the solution. Success or performance is not measured against rigid criteria. Learners are instead left to conclude, answer, define criteria of success for themselves. Individual differences in this process are allowed and used as a basis for further understanding. Learners are thus free to explore others' ideas, opinions, and reactions in order to determine their own perspective. In this process, the teacher serves as a "mirror" or "process facilitator." He or she is nonevaluative, answers questions with questions, suggests instead of critiquing, and relates current issues to larger ones. The teacher creates a reward system that emphasizes methodology of inquiry versus getting a particular answer. In class sessions, there is planned time spent on looking back at previous steps, events, or decisions in order to guide the learner in future activities.

Symbolically complex learning environments are ones in which the learner is involved in trying to solve a problem for which there is usually a right answer or a best solution. The source of information, topic, or problem being dealt with is abstract, in that it is removed from the present and presented via reading, data, pictures, lecture inputs, and so on. In handling such information, the learner is both guided and constrained by externally imposed rules of inference, such as symbols, computer technology, jargon, theorems, graphical keys, or protocols. There is often a demand on the learner to recall these rules, concepts, or relationships via memory. The teacher is the accepted representative of the body of knowledge—judging and evaluating learner output, interpreting information that cannot be dealt with by the rules of inference, and enforcing methodology and the scientific rigor of the field of study. The teacher is also a timekeeper, taskmaster, and enforcer of schedules of events in order that the learner can become immersed in the analytical exercise necessary to reach a solution and not worry about having to set goals and manage his or her own time. Success is measured against the right or best solution, expert opinion, or otherwise rigid criteria imposed by the teacher or accepted in the field of study. Decisions concerning flow and nature of activities in the class session are essentially made by the teacher and mostly prior to the course.

Behaviorally complex learning environments are those in which the emphasis is upon actively applying knowledge or skills to a practical problem. The problem need not have a right or best answer, but it does have to be something the learner can relate to, value, and feel some intrinsic satisfaction from having solved. This would normally be a "real-life" problem, case, or simulation that the learner could expect to face as a professional. In the attack on the problem, the focus is on doing. Completing the task is essential. Although there may be an externally imposed deadline or periodic checkpoints for which reports or other information are required, most of the learner's time is his to manage. He is thus concerned with what effect his present behavior will have vis-à-vis the overall task to be done. The next activity he engages in will not occur independent of the one he is presently in. In this way, the learner is always left to make decisions/choices about what to do next or how to proceed. The teacher can be available as a coach or advisor, but primarily in the learner's request or initiative. Success is measured against criteria associated with the task: how well something worked, feasibility, sellability, client acceptance, cost, testing results, aesthetic quality, and so on.

Learning environments vary in the degrees to which they are oriented to any of the four pure types described above. In a study of a landscape-architecture department (Fry, 1978), ten courses were measured to determine the degree of environmental complexity or the tendency of a course to be oriented in one or more ways. The results indicated that all the courses had degrees of orientation in each area and that it was even possible for a given course to be very affectively and symbolically oriented at the same time. Consistent patterns of environmental orientation showed up in the following combinations: perceptual and symbolic—an "investigative" or "inquiry" climate with the emphasis on inductive theory building and on understanding why things happen (this was most characteristic of lecture and seminar course sessions in this setting); symbolic and behavioral—a "mastery" climate where emphasis was on mastering techniques by practice in problem solving (this was most characteristic of laboratory and recitation sections of courses in this study); behavioral and affective—a "simulative" climate where situations were created to put the learner in the role expected of a graduate in a work setting (this was most characteristic of courses requiring field experience, site visits, and interaction with others outside the classroom in this setting).

Learner-Environment Interactions

When experiential learning theory is used to view the learner and instructional environment in the terms discussed above, useful relationships begin to emerge concerning the design of learning situations. Studies of the preferences of M.B.A. students and graduate students in architecture (Fry, 1978; Kolb, 1976) suggest that what we considered to be characteristics of affective, perceptual, symbolic, and behavioral orientations in the environment do relate to and require learner skills in concrete experience, reflective observation, abstract conceptualization, and active experimentation, respectively (see Table 7.2).

The students who scored high in concrete experience as a preferred learning mode indicated that their ability to learn was enhanced by affectively related factors such as personalized feedback, sharing feelings, teachers behaving as friendly helpers, activities oriented toward applying skills to real-life problems, peer feedback, and the need to be self-directed and autonomous. An environmental factor that hindered their learning ability was theoretical reading assignments.

The learners scoring highest in reflective observation reported perceptually related environmental factors as being helpful. These included teachers providing expert interpretations and guiding or limiting discussions, output being judged by external criteria of field or discipline, and lecturing. Reflective learners are not helped by task-oriented situations where information generation was focused on getting some job done.

The learners scoring highest in abstract conceptualization cited symbolically related factors such as case studies, thinking alone, and theory readings as contributing to their ability to learn. They also felt that several elements of affectively and behaviorally oriented environments hindered their ability to learn. These included group exercises and simulations, the need to be self-directed or autonomous, personalized feedback, teachers being models of the profession, sharing personal feelings about subject matter, dealing with "here-and-now" information, and activities oriented toward experiencing being a professional in the field.

Finally, the learners with the strongest active-experimentation tendencies identified several factors as helpful that one would associate with a behaviorally oriented learning environment. These included small-group discussions, projects, peer feedback, homework problems, the teacher behaving as a model of the profession, being left to judge one's work by oneself, and activities designed to apply skills to practical problems. Things these students reported as hindrances to their ability to learn included lectures, teachers serving as taskmasters, and having their work evaluated as simply right or wrong.

Table 7.2 Learning Environment Characteristics that Help or Hinder Learners with Different Learning Styles

Learning Environment Characteristics	Concrete Experience	Reflective Observation	Abstract Conceptualization	Active Experimentation
			Learning Styles	
"Typical" educational events: (Harvard M.B.A.s)	Theory readings—*not helpful* (−.21[b]) Peer feedback helps (.15a)	Lectures help (.18[a])	Case studies help (.22[b]) Theory readings help (.34[c]) Exercises & simulations—*not helpful* (−.15) Thinking alone helps (.17[a]) Expert talks—*not helpful* (−.15)	Lectures—*not helpful* (−.25[c]) Small-group discussions help (.16[a]) Projects help (.18[a]) Peer feedback helps (.20[b]) Homework helps (.19[a])
Situational factors: (Architecture grad. students)	When: Feedback is personalized (.45[c]) Feelings are shared (.20) Purpose of activities is to apply skills (.24[a]) Teacher is coach/helper (.36[b]) Learner expected to be self-directed, autonomous (.37[b])	When: Teacher provides expert interpretation (.23[a]) Info. focused on task—*not helpful* −.33[b] Performance judged by external criteria of field (.23[a]) Teacher serves as taskmaster/guide (.20)	When: Learner is expected to be self-directed/autonomous—*not helpful* (−.39[b]) Teacher is coach/helper—*not helpful* (−.22[a]) Purpose of activity to apply skill to solve problem—*not helpful* (−.23[a]) Personalized feedback—*not helpful* (−.47[c]) Teacher is model of profession—*not helpful* (−.21[a]) Sharing feelings—*not helpful* (−.43[b]) Info. source is "here and now"—*not helpful* (−.29[a]) Purpose of activity is to experience being a professional—*not helpful* (−.26[a])	When: Teacher is a model of profession (.22[a]) Learner left to determine own criteria of relevance (.21[a]) Purpose of activity to apply skills to solve problem (.37[b]) Info. focused on task completion (.37[b]) Performance judged right or wrong—*not helpful* (−.25[a]) Teacher serves as taskmaster/guide—*not helpful* (−.37[b])

[a] $p < .05$ Pearson Correlation
[b] $p < .01$ Pearson Correlation
[c] $p < .001$ Pearson Correlation

People enter learning situations with an already-developed learning style. Associated with this learning style will be some more or less explicit theory about how people learn, or more specifically, about how they themselves learn best. Learning environments that operate according to a learning theory that is dissimilar to a person's preferred style of learning are likely to be rejected or resisted by that person. Many students, for example, resist required courses designed to broaden their interests. One way to deal with this problem is for teacher and student to share explicitly their respective theories of learning. From this discussion, the student can gain an insight into why the subject matter is taught as it is and what adjustments he need make in his approach to learning this subject. The discussion can help the teacher to identify the variety of learning styles presented in the class and to modify his/her approach to accommodate these differences. A third benefit from explicit discussion of the learning process as it applies to the specific subject matter at hand is that both teacher and students are stimulated to examine and refine their learning theories. Learning becomes a skill that can be improved and coached. Perhaps the most important implication of the interaction between learning styles and learning environments is that empathy and communication are central to the teaching process. To educate means literally "to draw out." This requires an ability on the part of the teacher to make contact with the students' inner resources, attitudes, and ideas and through dialogue to develop and refine their knowledge and skills.

A second practical concern that emerges from our research on learner-environment transactions is the need to individualize instruction. Most traditional classroom teaching methods are too homogeneous as learning environments, appealing to only a single learning style while handicapping those who would prefer to learn another way. Approaches that individualize the learning process to meet the student's goals, learning style, pace, and life situation will pay off handsomely in increased learning. One key to this individualization is a shift in the teacher role from dispenser of information to coach or manager of the learning process. Modern technology, particularly the microcomputer revolution, is facilitating this role transition by providing alternative modes for delivery of content.

Specialized vs. Integrative Developmental Goals

Matching student learning styles with corresponding learning environments seems an easy and practical way to improve the learning process. But does this mean we should alter our course designs to accommodate the type of learner that comes into them, and/or require specialized learning skills that typify the inquiry norms of a given profession or field of study?

To answer this question, it is necessary to consider the goals of the educational program. In curriculum design, three classes of learning objectives must be considered: content objectives, learning-style objectives, and growth and creativity objectives. Very often in the design of curricula, it is only the content objectives that are explicitly considered: What material should be covered? What concepts should be introduced? What facts does the student need to know? Yet in most academic disciplines, there are also important norms about learning style. Students are expected to adopt certain perspectives on their work. They must learn to think like a mathematician or feel like a poet or make decisions like an executive. Thus, the learning style that is felt to be appropriate for a given area of study must also be considered when educational objectives are set.

To complicate matters further, the third class of objectives must be considered, objectives for growth and creativity. In addition to specialized developmental training, teachers often have objectives concerning the growth and creativity of their students. In making students more "well-rounded," the aim is to develop the weaknesses in the students' learning style to stimulate growth in their ability to learn from a variety of learning perspectives. Here, the goal is something more than making students' learning styles adaptive for their particular career entry job. The aim is to make the student self-renewing and self-directed; to focus on integrative development where the person is highly developed in each of the four learning modes: active, reflective, abstract, and concrete. Here, the student is taught to experience the tension and conflict among these orientations, for it is from the resolution of these tensions that creativity springs.

The dilemma in making choices among these three levels of objectives is illustrated by Plovnick's study, cited earlier, which concluded that the major emphasis in physics education was on convergent learning, and that physics students who had convergent learning styles were more content with their majors than students whose learning styles did not match the inquiry norms of physics. The dilemma for the physics department is this. To contribute in physics today, one must know many facts, so content learning is important and takes time, time that might be spent developing the convergent skills of divergers. So isn't it simpler to select (implicitly or explicitly) people who already possess these convergent experimental and theoretical skills? Perhaps, but in the process, what is lost is the creative tension between convergence and divergence. The result of this process may be a program that produces fine technicians but few innovators. Kuhn (1962) put the issue this way: "Because the old must be revalued and reordered when assimilating the new, discovery and invention in the sciences are usually intrinsically revolutionary. Therefore they do demand just that flexibility and open-mindedness that characterize and indeed define the divergent." It just may be that one of the reasons that creative contributions in the sciences are made primarily by younger persons (Lehman, 1953) is that the learning styles of older adults have been shaped by their professional training and experience, so that they adapt well to the inquiry norms of their profession but the creative tension is lost.

IMPLICATIONS FOR HIGHER EDUCATION

As we have seen, higher education today encourages early specialization, which necessarily accentuates particular interests and skills. Should we continue to follow the trend toward increasingly specialized education, or should we be creating new educational programs that reassert the integrative emphasis lost in the demise of classical education? Recently, Derek Bok's *President's Report* for Harvard University (Bok, 1978) outlined a revised undergraduate curriculum plan—a plan that some have characterized as a return to classical education, with its compulsory core courses in science and mathematics, literature and the arts, history, philosophy and social analysis, and foreign cultures. The pendulum swing toward specialization that Charles Eliot began in 1869 with the modest introduction of electives and the concept of a major may have reached its peak in the late 1960s in the course proliferation that came with students' demands for relevance and participation in the educational decisions that affected their lives. The "back-to-basic-skills" climate that seemed to permeate American education at all levels in the 1970s may signal, among other things, the reassertion of an integrative emphasis in the educational process.

There is little question that integrative development is important for both personal fulfillment and cultural development. It appears essential for growth and mastery of the period of adult development that Erikson has called the crisis of generativity versus stagnation. The educational issue is how and when to intervene in a way that facilitates this development. The "hows" are not easy. Bok compared the introduction of the new core curriculum to "reorganizing a graveyard." Specialization in the university is greatly reinforced by faculty reward systems, selection and evaluation criteria, and disciplinary values. The result of these organizational processes is brought into sharp focus when we examine the difficulties and obstacles that attend the establishment of truly interdisciplinary programs of research or teaching, or the struggles for survival and viability that face "deviant" disciplines in an institution where attention, resources, and prestige are focused on the dominant academic culture. Even at a scientific institute like TECH, where the humanities are firmly established with a distinguished faculty, we see intense student alienation, departmental evaluation standards that appear more attuned to the inquiry norms of engineering than to the humanities, and a subtle but powerful imperialism of the dominant scientific culture on research and teaching activities. However useful scientific analyses of the humanities (for example, computer models of Greek myths) may be in their own right, one must ask how well such activities serve to broaden the world view of the science or engineering specialist.

In the words of Robert Hutchins:

> The reverence that natural science has inspired is in large part responsible for the steady narrowing of education that the progress of specialization has caused during the last thirty years. The progress of specialization has meant that the world and ourselves have been progressively taken apart, and at no point

have they been put together again. As the progress of the scientific method has discredited the methods of history, philosophy, and art, so the specialism essential to science has discredited a generalized approach to history, philosophy, art and all other subjects, including science itself. This means that comprehension has been discredited, for it cannot be attained by splitting the world into smaller and smaller bits. [Hutchins, 1953, p. 25]

The Institutional Context and Integrative Development

So far, this discussion has focused primarily on the course-level units of learning environments. It is more difficult to conceptualize the effect of the larger institutional context on student learning, although the effect is considerable. Included here is the organization and management of departments, including such things as student and faculty interaction patterns, emphasis on research, teaching or practical application, the structure and number of required courses, emphasis on grades, and so on. Beyond departments, one must consider the university structure, its mission and philosophy of education, the alternative learning environments available, the selection/evaluation criteria for faculty and students, social networks outside of classes, campus atmosphere, and the like. Some evidence suggests that these large-system phenomena may be particularly connected with the affective and behavioral orientations. For example, faculty members in engineering have suggested to us that concrete experience and active experimentation skills in their students may be developed not as part of their formal curriculum of courses but rather in social groupings in fraternities, one-on-one relationships with faculty mentors, summer work experiences, and other extracurricular campus activities.

Liam Hudson has examined the effect of relationship between departments and larger organizational processes on the educational process:

> At the pragmatic level, for instance, one makes no sense of a certain course in the behavioral sciences, until one sees it as a compromise reached between a number of university departments, each of which has a legitimate interest in its content. The curriculum, simply, is a by-product of a process that is starkly political. And at the conceptual level we find ourselves continually confronting mysterious notions, like that of a "discipline." To begin to grasp what happens inside universities, we find ourselves compelled to grapple with the boundary rules which surround bodies of knowledge like history, medicine, chemistry or psychology, and to make interpretative sense of their function. We need, too, to come to terms with what one might describe as the politics of knowledge—that territory in which such disciplines take shape, in which schools of thought do battle with one another, and in which certain views of mankind are rendered legitimate, while others are cast beyond the pale. [Hudson, 1976, p. 219]

Thus, it would seem that a central function for the larger university organization is to provide the integrative structures and programs that counterbalance the tendencies toward specialization in student development and academic research. Continuous lifelong learning requires learning how to learn, and this involves appreciation of and competence in diverse approaches to creating, manipulating, and communicating knowledge.

To assume that this integrated appreciation and competence can be achieved solely by distribution requirements or other legislative approaches is highly questionable. As with racial integration, we must closely scrutinize any strategy that requires students to do what we ourselves cannot or will not do. To build integrative programs of teaching and research requires that reward systems, selection and evaluation criteria, and inquiry values be confronted and adjusted to sustain interdisciplinary activity. In addition, some kind of focal point may be required for successful integrative education. Successful interdisciplinary programs I have seen have had a common reference point for integrative activity. At Alverno College, a common reference point is the student's development as a self-directed learner. The faculty have reconceptualized their liberal arts curriculum to focus on developing abilities, and have created classroom and off-campus learning experiences with sharp attention to the principles of experiential learning theory and practice (Doherty, Mentkowski, and Conrad, 1978). Results from longitudinal studies (Mentkowski and Strait, 1983) confirm that while students as a group enter college with predominant preferences for some learning styles over others, they show equal preferences for the four styles two years later. They shift in their preferences from more concrete to more abstract and from more reflective to more active. These changes have been directly linked to student performance in the curriculum. This suggests that the environmental press of a college dedicated to experiential learning concepts can cause students to be more balanced in their learning style preferences, and when they are ready to enter their specialized professional programs, they have already experienced multiple learning modes. Further, students as a group maintain their more balanced preferences during the last two years of college, even though practically all of them enter a particular career track. Type of major does not contribute to change. Further, alumnae report having to learn in a variety of modes at work, and being able to adapt to continued and unguided learning situations in a variety of settings (Mentkowski and Much, 1982). In the professions, this reference point is often the professional role itself, in which critical functions and tasks emphasize the need for specialized knowledge from various disciplines. In the "pure" academic disciplines, this focus can come through the broad application of a methodology such as systems analysis or through a research problem that requires multiple perspectives. In the humanities, this reference point may be experiential learning, a focus on the "common experiences of life," reversing a trend toward theorizing and formal specialization that has, in the opinion of W. Jackson Bates, nearly destroyed the field. Bates calls this trend:

. . . the most serious liability that literary study has been gradually creating for itself: the autonomous nature of literature (and the arts) as a separate preserve apart from the common experiences of life. Hazlitt had a point when he said that the arts resembled Antaeus in the fable, who was invincible as long as his *feet touched his mother Earth, but who was easily strangled by Hercules once he was lifted from the strength-giving ground. [Bates, 1982, p. 52]*

The "when" question may suggest even more fundamental changes. The continuing knowledge explosion and the corresponding rapid rate of change raise serious questions about the current strategy of "front-loading" educational experience in the individual's life cycle. When, as current labor statistics indicate, the average person will change jobs seven times and careers three times during his or her working life, it makes more sense to distribute educational experiences throughout adult life in order to assist in the preparation for and mastery of these changes. Younger students will need to intersperse more life/work experience between their years of preparation in formal education. Existing programs of field-experience education (internships, work/study, and so on) give testimony to the learning/development payoff of such a mix of academic and practical training (Hursh and Borzak, 1979). The older generation will need the adult work/study version of what used to be called a "liberal arts education" with fresh opportunities to harvest the many fruits of knowledge left behind on their respective climbs to the top. In this model, the university becomes a center for lifelong learning. Integrative learning experiences take on new meaning and vitality when they are directly connected with the integrative challenges of adult life. Discussions of human values and the quality of life are very different with high school graduates than they are with managers of an oil refinery. Quality patient care has one connotation to the idealistic premed student and quite another to the harried medical specialist. Perhaps the richest resources for integrative development lie in the dialogue across age levels that the university for lifelong learning can provide.

eight

Lifelong Learning and Integrative Development

But yield who will to their separation,
My object in living is to unite
My avocation and my vocation
As my two eyes make one in sight.
Only where love and need are one,
And the work is play for mortal stakes,
Is the deed ever really done
For Heaven and the future's sakes.
Robert Frost*

There has been in recent years a dramatic preoccupation with adult development and midlife transition issues, sparked in part by the arrival at the midpoint of life of the postwar baby-boom generation. This emphasis on adult learning and development has been labeled by some a "revolution in human development" (Brim and Kagan, 1980), and indeed, one cannot fail to be impressed by the burgeoning of self-development techniques and activities—from bookstores' shelves crowded with self-help books to workshops ranging from AA to TA to TM to Zen. Although some see a dangerous current of narcissism and "me" orientation in these developments, I prefer a more positive interpretation—namely, that the dialectic between social specialization and individual integrative fulfillment is itself reaching toward a higher-level synthesis.

*From "Two Tramps in Mud Time" from THE POETRY OF ROBERT FROST edited by Edward Connery Lathem. Copyright 1936 by Robert Frost. Copyright © 1964 by Lesley Frost Ballantine. Copyright © 1969 by Holt, Rinehart and Winston. Reprinted by permission of Holt, Rinehart and Winston, Publishers and Jonathan Cape Ltd.

The very diversity and intense specialization that threaten to tear us apart are grist for the integrative mill. Modern communication, the mass media, and the other fruits of the information revolution provide an instantaneous cornucopia of fantasies, ideas, perspectives, value conflicts, and crises that challenge and fuel the integrative capacities of us all. We seek to grow and develop because we must do so to survive—as individuals and as a world community. If there is a touch of aggressive selfishness in our search for integrity, it can perhaps be understood as a response to the sometimes overwhelming pressures on us to conform, submit, and comply, to the object rather than the subject of our life history.

The challenge of lifelong learning is above all a challenge of integrative development. Consider the careers of two great atomic scientists, the American Edward Teller and the Russian Andrei Sakharov, both of whom early in their careers were central in the development of their countries' nuclear capabilities. Teller went on to become one of our country's foremost advocates of nuclear power and a strong defense, whereas Sakharov, who gave his country the hydrogen bomb in the 1950s, was stricken by conscience and became a political dissident and a vigorous defender of human rights. Recently he was banished from Moscow for his protest against the presence of Soviet troops in Afghanistan.

These moral and ethical decisions to promote or reject one's own inventions, to support or protest against one's own country, are qualitatively different from the specialized problem-solving activities of the working scientist. As Piaget (1970) and others (such as Kuhn, 1962) have documented, the historical development of scientific knowledge has been toward increasing specialization, moving from egocentrism to reflection and from phenomenalism to constructivism—in experiential learning terms, from active to reflective and concrete to abstract. Yet the careers of highly successful scientists follow a different path. These people make their specialized abstract-reflective contributions often quite early in their careers. With recognition of their achievements comes a new set of tasks and challenges with active and concrete demands. The Nobel prizewinner must help to shape social policy and to articulate the ethical and value implications of his or her discoveries. The researcher becomes department chairperson and must manage the nurturance of the younger generation. So in this career, and most others as well, the higher levels of responsibility require an integrative perspective that can help shape cultural responses to emergent issues.

The challenges of integrative development are great, and not everyone is successful in meeting them, no matter how intelligent the person or how highly skilled in the professional specialty. In fact, as we have seen in Chapter 7, one's professional specialization may inhibit development of an integrative perspective. Charles Darwin, in his autobiography, was puzzled about his lost taste for literature, music, and the fine arts, suspecting that this loss was somehow related to his specialization:

My mind seems to have become a kind of machine for grinding general laws out of large collections of facts, but why this should have caused the atrophy of that part of the brain alone, on which the highest tastes depend, I cannot conceive. [Darwin, 1958, pp. 138-39]

Several observers have attributed the problems that Jimmy Carter encountered in his presidency to his strong professional identity as a scientist and engineer (Fallows, 1979; Pfaff, 1979) and his difficulties in adapting to the concrete and reflective demands of the presidency (Gypen, 1980). Clark Clifford, who has been a personal consultant and friend to several presidents, said of Carter:

He prided himself on being an engineer and scientist. . . . And every now and then he would say, "Now, as a scientist I would do this." "As a scientist I would do that." And he had good scientific training. What scientists do is, they start at A. And they go from A to B and B to C and C to D and D is their goal. And they know that if they just stay on the line, unquestionably they will reach D. I saw that in the President from time to time—that he had sufficient knowledge and experience to know that if he proceeded along a certain line the result would be there. The trouble is, it doesn't work in the White House. Because it doesn't take into consideration the House of Representatives, or the Senate of the United States, or the media, or the American people. . . . All these other factors come in. The problems of the President of the United States are not susceptible to scientific treatment. There's a lot more that goes into it. The fact is you almost have to disregard it. . . . President Carter came into the White House and after a while he got settled and began to feel more comfortable and began to look around for problems to solve. Well, one of them was the Panama Canal. . . . And that is a perfect issue for a president to bring up in the third year of his second term when he can be a statesman. And he can say, "This is right." And then he doesn't have to worry about commitments that he has made. But he picked this one out. Now, interestingly enough, he was right. . . . And courageous. But absolutely wrong to bring up at this time. Because he froze a very substantial part of the populace into a position of eternal and permanent enmity, as far as he was concerned. . . . A broader concept on his part of the presidency would have greatly facilitated that decision-making process. Another twenty-two water projects out in the West. . . . He took a look at that and my recollection is he said about 14 of these have no merit and maybe seven or eight have. Well, right about that time out went California, Oregon, Washington, Idaho, Montana, Colorado. [Bill Moyers Journal, 1981, pp. 6-7]

President Carter's later successes suggest significant progress toward an integrative response to the demands of his office, particularly in achieving a Mideast agreement through personal diplomacy in the Camp David accords. The early years of his term, however, appear to have suffered because of his specialized scientific perspective.

But the challenges of integrative development are not limited to scientists and presidents. A recent *Wall Street Journal* survey of chief executives asked them to identify the main strengths that determine a manager's potential for advancement (Allen, 1980). At the head of the list (cited by 36 percent of chief executives from large firms) was integrity, followed by an ability to get along with others and industriousness. Specialized technical experience or education was mentioned by only a few as critical for success. The article states, "The strong consensus among chief executives of companies of all sizes is that 'inner' character strengths matter most for success and advancement in business." In fact, there are integrative developmental challenges in all occupations, at all occupational levels, and in our private lives as well. Many first-line supervisors, for example, have created personal job definitions that transcend the specialized boundaries of their trade to include the development of younger workers and the building of meaningful community and family relationships.

These challenges become particularly acute in midlife, when as adults we face what Erikson has termed the crisis of generativity or stagnation:

> . . . For we are a teaching species. . . . Only man can and must extend his solicitude over the long parallel and overlapping childhoods of numerous offspring united in households and communities. As he transmits the rudiments of hope, will, purpose and skill, he imparts meaning to the child's bodily experiences; he conveys a logic much beyond the literal meaning of the words he teaches; and he gradually outlines a particular world image and style of citizenship. . . . Once we have grasped this interlocking of the human life stages, we understand that adult man is so constituted as to need to be needed lest he suffer the mental deformation of self-absorption, in which he becomes his own infant and pet. I have, therefore, postulated an instinctual and psychosocial stage of generativity. Parenthood is, for most, the first, and for many, the prime generative encounter; yet the continuation of mankind challenges the generative ingenuity of workers and thinkers of many kinds. [Erikson, 1961, pp. 159-60]

In acceptance of the fact that we are a "teaching species" as well as a "learning species," a kind of figure/ground reversal takes place at midlife. Our progressive independence from the care of others, our self-oriented pursuit of individual goals, fades from the foreground of our experience to be replaced by a growing concern for the care of others. In the process, other reversals occur as well. In Jung's terms, the shadow side of personality emerges and claims dominion in consciousness along with the specialized conscious identity of youth. This is a social as well as personal transition, for many forces in the structure of career paths call for personal reassessment and integrative development. For example:

☐ The career *cul de sac*—careers that provide advancement and opportunity only to a certain point and then require major adaptation and change, e.g., housewife/mother or engineering.

☐ Withdrawal of reward; e.g., up or out tenure systems.

☐ Withdrawal of opportunity—organizational career paths that have few opportunities for advancement and responsibility at middle and upper levels.

☐ The "fur-lined trap" and achievement addiction—organizational and career reward systems that so effectively reward specialized role performance that individuals have little energy remaining for broader development, family, and private life.

☐ Career demands for integrative development—the extent to which a given career requires and/or allows development beyond specialization. For example, management at top levels requires an integrative perspective and organizations have policies such as job rotation to facilitate the development of this perspective.

☐ Opportunities for creativity/role innovation (Schein, 1972)—the extent to which a career offers continuing challenges and opportunities for changing roles and job functions.

The developmental model of experiential learning theory holds that specialization of learning style typifies early adulthood and that the role demands of career and family are likely to reinforce specialization. However, this pattern changes in midcareer. Specifically, as people mature, accentuation forces play a smaller role. To the contrary, the approach of the middle years brings with it a questioning of one's purposes and aspirations, a reassessment of life structure and direction. For many, choices made earlier have led down pathways no longer rewarding, and some kind of change is needed. At this point, many finally face up to the fact that they will never realize their youthful dreams and that new, more realistic goals must be found if life is to have purpose. Others, even if successful in their earlier pursuits, discover that they have purchased success in career at the expense of other responsibilities (such as to spouse and children) or other kinds of human fulfillment. Continued accentuation of an overspecialized version of oneself eventually becomes stultifying—one begins to feel stuck, static, in a rut. The vitality of earlier challenges is too easily replaced by routinized application of well-established solutions. In the absence of new and fresh challenges, creativity gives way to merely coping and going through the motions. Many careers plateau at this time, and one faces the prospect of drying up and stretching out the remaining years in tedium. Finding new directions for generativity is essential.

Perhaps it is inevitable that specialization precede integration in development, inevitable that youth be spent in a search for identity in the service of society, until in a last reach for wholeness we grasp that unified consciousness that has eluded us. As William Butler Yeats so eloquently put it, "Nothing can be sole and whole that has not been rent." For wholeness cannot be fully appreciated save in contrast to the experience of fragmentation, compartmentalization, and specialization. Kurt Lewin's observation that pulsation from differentiation to integration is the throb of the great engine of development is writ large as a universal social pattern of socialization.

ADAPTIVE FLEXIBILITY AND INTEGRATIVE DEVELOPMENT

There is considerable agreement among adult-development scholars that growth occurs through processes of differentiation and hierarchic integration and that the highest stages of development are characterized by personal integration and integrity. From the perspective of experiential learning theory, this goal is attained through a dialectic process of adaptation to the world. Fulfillment, or individuation, as Jung calls it, is accomplished by expression of nondominant modes of dealing with the world and their higher-level integration with specialized functions. With integrative development comes an increasing freedom from the dictates of immediate circumstance and the potential for creative response. This structural potential is expressed behaviorally by the individual's adaptive flexibility. As Werner put it:

> In general, the more differentiated and hierarchically organized the structure of an organism is, the more flexible its behavior. This means that if an activity is highly hierarchized, the organism, within a considerable range, can vary the activity to comply with the demands of the varying situation. [Werner, 1948, p. 55]

Adaptive flexibility and the mobility it provides are the primary vehicles of integrative development. They are the means by which people transcend the fixity of their specialized orientation. Fixity can be inferred from the intrinsic trend of any evolution toward an end stage of maximum stability. Such maximum stability, as the end stage of a developmental sequence, implies the closing of growth—the permanence, for instance, of specialized reaction patterns. But fixity would finally lead to rigidity of behavior if not counterbalanced by adaptive flexibility. As most generally conceived, adaptive flexibility implies "becoming" as opposed to "being."

Assessing Adaptive Flexibility: The Adaptive Style Inventory

One consequence of integrative development for those scientists who wish to predict and control human behavior is a certain amount of frustration, for with integrative development and its attendant adaptive flexibility comes increasing difficulty in the prediction of behavior. It is easy to predict behavior consequences in a low-level system (say, turning on a light switch) but far more difficult to predict behavior of higher-level systems capable of hierarchic integration (as with a computer). This problem is confounded when the attempt is made to characterize individuals as whole persons at a given stage of development. Developmental theorists have recognized this problem and attempted to deal with it in a number of ways—for example, by ad hoc concepts, as in Piaget's concept of horizontal *decalage* (variability in cognitive structure from task to task in a given time period; compare Flavell, 1963, p. 23) or by simply averaging this variability and thus ignoring it.[1]

Another approach to these measurement problems is to use the level of adaptive flexibility itself as an indicator of the level of integrative development. Thus, if people show systematic variability in their response to different environmental demands, we can infer a higher level of integrative development. To accomplish this assessment, however, requires that two conditions be met. First, a holistic system of environmental demands that samples the person's actual and potential life space is required. As Scott (1966) has pointed out, adaptive flexibility is meaningful only if there is some situation or circumstance being adapted to. Variability alone is not necessarily adaptive flexibility; it must be systemic variation in response to varying environmental demands. Second, the dimensions of personal-response flexibility and situation demand should be defined in commensurate terms. Flexibility of response should be measured along a dimension so that situation/person matches or mismatches can be identified that are related to the situation responded to. The theory of experiential learning provides a framework within which these conditions can be met. Toward this end, a modified version of the Learning Style Inventory called the Adaptive Style Inventory (ASI) was created. This instrument profiles the transactions between persons and their environment by providing them with a series of situations in the form of sentence stems (for example, "When I start to do something new"), which they complete by choosing between two responses, each response representing an adaptive mode (such as, "I rely on my feelings to guide me"—concrete experience; "I set priorities"—abstract conceptualization).

The ASI instrument is divided into four situations that the respondent must "adapt" to. These situations correspond to the four learning styles— divergent situations, assimilative situations, convergent situations, and accommodative situations. Each situation is characterized by two sentence stems, each with six pairs of response choices that present the four adaptive-mode responses in paired comparison fashion. The ASI thus yields an adaptive profile for the four different learning-style environments and an average adaptive profile across all four situations.

Responses to the ASI can be portrayed in a way that shows one's adaptive orientations as points on a two-dimensional learning space. One point represents average responses across all situations. It is achieved by noting scores on the abstract-concrete dimension (AC-CE) and scores on the active-reflective dimension (AE-RO) and plotting a point at the juncture of these two points on the learning grid (see Figure 8.1). The same procedure is followed to

---

[1] This averaging of stage variability is Loevinger's approach: "One must immediately admit that most samples of behavior, e.g., test protocols, contain evidence of functioning on diverse levels. . . . Nonetheless, the first step in bringing the concept within scientific compass is measurement. A probabilistic modification of the hierarchies model both accommodates the complexities and assimilates them to the requirements of measurement" (1966, p. 202).

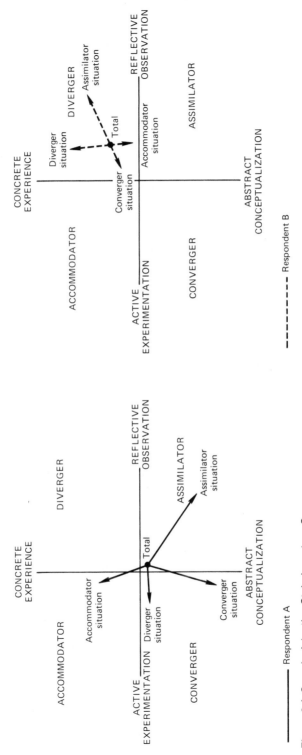

Figure 8.1 Sample Adaptive Style Inventory Scores

215

portray how the person responded in each of the four kinds of situations. Arrows are then drawn from the total score to each of the situational scores. These arrows indicate the direction of the person's response to each kind of situation. *The amount of adaptive flexibility from situation to situation is indicated by the length of the arrows.*

Figure 8.1 shows two sample responses to the ASI. Respondent A has a total score near the center of the grid, indicating a relative balance in the person's average adaptive style. The responses to each environmental press are consonant with the press in three of the four instances. The modal response to the diverger situations is heavily active and does not differ significantly from the total score on the abstract-concrete dimension. It could be said that this person responded to three situational presses—accommodator, converger, assimilator—in terms consonant with those presses; that is, she responded to the situations by increasing emphasis on the adaptive modes "pulled for." However, in diverger situations, the respondent responded primarily in an active mode, acting against the press of the situation.

Respondent B, on the other hand, has a total score well within the diverger quadrant, indicating a tendency to respond to all situations in a concrete and reflective mode. Each of the situational presses was responded to in terms other than conformity to the press of the environment (relative to the total score), except in converger situations. In diverger situations, this person responds to very concrete ways but also responds in slightly more active ways.

The response to diverger situations would be interpreted as more consonant with accommodator situations. (Admittedly, the response in terms of the total grid is still in the diverger quadrant, which makes the response still consonant with the situational press. However, the reference point for each person is not the theoretical center of the grid, but his or her own total score.) In accommodator situations, the person responds in a more abstract way and in a somewhat reflective way, contrary to the accommodator situational press, which demands a concrete and active response. In assimilator situations, respondent B responded in a reflective way, as would be demanded by the situation, but also responded in a concrete way, which is contrary to the assimilator situational press. Finally, this respondent responded to converger situations in ways appropriate to the converger situational press.

To assess the level of adaptive flexibility quantitatively, formulas were devised to determine how much the respondent varied his or her adaptive orientation from situation to situation. Five such variables were created, concrete experience adaptive flexibility (CEAF), reflective observation adaptive flexibility (ROAF), abstract conceptualization adaptive flexibility (ACAF), active experimentation adaptive flexibility (AEAF), and total adaptive flexibility (TAF).[2] CEAF, for example, is the extent to which people vary their concrete

---

[2] The specific formulas are reported in Kolb and Wolfe, 1981, pp. 117-18. Technical specifications for the ASI, including reliability and validity, are reported in the same publication, pp. 66-86. The study of adaptive flexibility and integrative development was done in collaboration with my friend and colleague, the late Glen Gish. In his life, he exemplified the ideals of integrative development of which we speak here.

experience orientation across the four situations. The total adaptive flexibility score (TAF) is the sum of CEAF, ROAF, ACAF, and AEAF. It should be noted that these scores do not take into account the direction of the person's adaptation to a given situational demand but simply the degree of variation in adaptive modes from situation to situation, since adaptive flexibility is composed of both movement toward the press of a situation and movement in other directions.

The Relation Between Adaptive Flexibility and Integrative Development

Armed with this ASI-based operational definition of adaptive flexibility, we can investigate the relation between adaptive flexibility and integrative development empirically. To do so, we studied three samples of midlife adults: a selected sample of 47 professional engineers and 23 professional social workers from the alumni study described in the last chapter, and a group of 39 midlife men and women of varying occupations who were participants in an intensive study of midlife adult development issues (see Kolb and Wolfe, 1981, for details). This latter group participated in an intensive series of self-assessment workshops over a three-year period, thus affording an in-depth assessment of their personalities and life situations.

Ego Development   One widely used measure of integrative development is Loevinger's Sentence Completion Instrument (Loevinger, 1976). In developing her model of the stages of adult ego development, Loevinger drew heavily on the work of Piaget, Kohlberg, and Perry, as well as the psychoanalytic school of ego psychology, most notably Erik Erikson. Scores on the Sentence Completion Test give an indication of a person's level of ego development as defined by her hierarchy of six ego-development stages—impulsive, self-protective, conformist, conscientious, autonomous, and integrated. As can be seen from Table 8.1, these stages are related to the six levels of adaptation defined in the experiential learning theory of development (see Table 6.1). In addition, Loevinger sees adaptive flexibility as a hallmark of development in her framework:

> Flexibility in the exchanges with the environment is no less an important property for survival. Because organisms are dependent on environments and open to them, and because environments can change, organisms need to adjust and accommodate, to substitute a new response for a once successful one. . . . The degree of flexibility . . . may be an indication of the organism's development. [Loevinger, 1976, p. 34]

For these reasons, we predicted a relationship between adaptive flexibility as measured by the ASI and a person's level of ego development. As a test for this relationship, the three samples of midlife adults were given the ASI and the Sentence Completion Instrument, which was scored according to instructions in the Loevinger test manual (Loevinger and Wessler, 1970). Most respondents

Table 8.1 Loevinger's Stages of Ego Development

Ego Level	Impulse Control/ Character Development	Interpersonal Style	Conscious Preoccupation	Cognitive Style
I. Impulsive	Does not recognize rules Sees action as bad only if punished Impulsive Afraid of retaliation	Dependent and exploitative; dependence unconscious Treats people as sources of supply	Sex and aggression Bodily functions	Thinks in dichotomous way Has simple, global ideas Conceptually confused Thinks concretely Egocentric
II. Self-protective	Recognizes rules but obeys for immediate advantage Has expedient morality: action is bad if person is caught Blames others; does not see self as responsible for failure or trouble	Manipulative and exploitative Wary and distrusting of others' intentions Opportunistic Zero-sum: I win, you lose Shameless; shows little remorse	Self-protection Gaining control and advantage, dominating Getting the better of others, deceiving them Fear of being dominated, controlled, or deceived by others	As above
III. Conformist	Partially internalizes rules; obeys without question Feels shame for consequences Concerned with "shoulds" Morally condemns others' views Denies sexual and aggressive feelings	Wants to belong to group, to gain social acceptance Feels mutual trust within in-group, prejudice against out-groups Has pleasing social personality: superficial niceness, helpfulness	Appearances Social acceptance and adjustment to group norms Status symbols, material possessions, reputation, and prestige	Thinks stereotypically Uses clichés Sees in terms of superlatives Has sentimental mentality Has little introspection: references to inner feelings are banal and stereotyped

Stage	Impulse Control, Character Development	Interpersonal Style	Conscious Preoccupations	Cognitive Style
IV. Conscientious	Standards self-evaluated: morality internalized; Self-critical, tendency to be hypercritical; Feels guilt for consequences	Has sense of responsibility, obligation; Has mutual, intensive relationships; Concerned with communication, expression of differentiated feelings	Achievement of long-term goals, as measured by inner standards; Attaining ideals; Motivation, reasons for behavior; Self: feelings, traits	Conceptually complex; Has sense of consequences, priorities; Aware of contingencies, perceives alternatives; Sees self in context of community, society
V. Autonomous	Add: [a] Behavior an expression of moral principle; Tolerates multiplicity of viewpoints; Concerned with conflicting duties, roles, principles	Add: [a] Wants autonomy in relations; Sees relations as involving inevitable mutual interdependence; Tolerates others' solutions of conflict; Respects others' autonomy; Open	Individuality and self-fulfillment; Conflicting inner needs	Has greater conceptual complexity; Tolerates ambiguity; Has capacity to see paradox, contradictions; Has broad scope of thought (time frame, social context); Perceives human interdependence
VI. Integrated	Add: [a] Reconciles inner conflicts and conflicting external demands; Renounces the unattainable; Concerned with justice; Spontaneous, creative	Add: [a] Cherishes individuality	Add: [a] Integrated sense of unique identity; "Precious life's work" as inevitable simultaneous expression of self, principle, and one's humanity	Add: [a] Has sense of self as part of flow of human condition

[a] "Add" means add to the description applying to the previous level. [Source: Adapted from Jane Loevinger, Ego Development (San Francisco: Jossey Bass, 1976).]

scored in the middle range of Loevinger's scheme. There were no "impulsive" (level 1) or "self-protective" (level 2) people and no "integrated" (level 6) people in the sample. There was one "autonomous" person. Even with this restricted range of ego development, however, there was a significant positive relationship between total adaptive flexibility and ego-development level ($r = .26$, $p < .003$). Most of this covariation in adaptive flexibility occured in reflective observation and abstract conceptualization (for instance ego level with ROAF, $r = .20$, $p < .02$; with ACAF, $r = .22$, $p < .01$). To the extent that the ego-development measure is an indication of integrative development, we can conclude that the ASI measures of adaptive flexibility are also indicative of integrative development. More detailed analysis of the data suggest, however, that the Loevinger instrument is perhaps more attuned to development of adaptive flexibility in the reflective and abstract adaptive modes than in the concrete and active orientation.

Self-direction   Perhaps a more active indicator of integrative development is people's ability to direct their own lives, to be an "origin" rather than a "pawn" (deCharms, 1968) in their life activities. The self-assessment workshops conducted for the group of midlife adults allowed researchers to rate participants on how self-directed they were in their current life situations (see Crary, 1981, for details). The criterion used for these ratings was the extent to which a person's set of life contexts determined that person's behavior as opposed to the behavior's being controlled by the person.

The relationship between total adaptive flexibility and the person's degree of self-directedness was significantly positive ($r = .26$, $p < .05$) and, as might be predicted, determined primarily by adaptive flexibility in active experimentation (self-directedness with AEAF, $r = .28$, $p < .05$). This suggests that those at higher levels of integrative development as measured by the ASI are more self-directed and display that self-directedness through choiceful variation of their active behavior in different situations.

Cognitive Complexity in Relationships   The experiential learning theory of development describes affective development in concrete experience as a process of increasing complexity in one's conception of personal relationships (see Table 6.1), resulting from integration of the four learning modes. Thus we would predict that increasing adaptive flexibility, particularly in the realm of concrete experience, would be associated with increased richness in construing one's interpersonal world. A major component of internal structural complexity is the constructions, as expressed in the words one uses, that can be called upon to describe and manipulate one's thoughts and interactions with the interpersonal environment. This notion was operationalized in the context of the self-assessment workshops. In the workshops, the midlife adults engaged in a number of exercises in which they portrayed the configuration of their life structures graphically and by analogy. During these exercises, the facilitating researchers noted the words each respondent used to describe his or her life structures. A list of each person's words was later presented to the respondent for verification as the person's own terminology. Each respondent had the opportunity to eliminate or add words in order to make the list truly representative of his or her set of constructs. The final list of constructs became the variable we are using here called "number of constructs."

As predicted, total adaptive flexibility was positively correlated with the total number of constructs a person used to describe his or her interpersonal world ($r = .25$; $p < .06$). This relationship was most significantly evidenced in the area of concrete experience (CEAF with number of constructs, $r = .28$, $p < .04$).

Taken together, the results above suggest that overall adaptive flexibility and adaptive flexibility in the four adaptive modes are meaningful indicators of integrative development. Total adaptive flexibility as measured by the ASI is significantly related to the level of ego development, to self-direction, and to the complexity of one's interpersonal constructs. Ego development, at least as it is measured in the Loevinger model, is most strongly associated with adaptive flexibility in reflection and conceptualization, reflecting the development and manipulation of internalized hierarchical structures for construing the world that characterizes higher levels of cognitive and ego development. Increased self-direction is more associated with flexibility in behavioral actions, and richness in one's constructs about the interpersonal world is associated most strongly with flexibility in concrete experiencing. These results, although limited to one sample, are promising, for they offer a measure of integrative development via the ASI that is sensitive both to development as a unitary process and to specialized development in different adaptive modes.

The Integrated Life Style

What can be said of the nature of the integrated life? How do people cope with the integrative challenges of adult life, and what can we learn from their example? Further results from our ASI study of adaptive flexibility, along with the case-by-case examination of the individual lives in our study of midlife adults, suggest some important characteristics of the integrated life style.

Proactive Adaptation   First, integrated people both adapt to and create their life structures. Their relationship with the world and others around them is transactional, in that they are proactive in the creation of their life tasks and situations and are shaped and molded by these situations as well. Paulo Freire describes this integrative stance toward one's life context as follows:

> Integration with one's context, as *distinguished from* adaptation, *is a distinctively human activity. Integration results from the capacity to adapt oneself to reality* plus *the critical capacity to make choices and to transform that reality. To the extent that man loses his ability to make choices and is subjected to the choices of others, to the extent that his decisions are no longer his own because they result from external prescriptions, he is no longer integrated. Rather, he has adapted. He has "adjusted." Unpliant men, with a revolutionary spirit, are often termed "maladjusted."*

The integrated person is person as subject. *In contrast, the adaptive person is person as* object, *adaptation representing at most a weak form of self-defense. If man is incapable of changing reality, he adjusts himself instead. Adaptation is behavior characteristic of the animal sphere; exhibited by man, it is symptomatic of his dehumanization. Throughout history men have attempted to overcome the factors which make them accommodate or adjust, in a struggle—constantly threatened by oppression—to attain their full humanity.*

As men related to the world by responding to the challenges of the environment, they began to dynamize, to master, and to humanize reality. They add to it something of their own making, by giving temporal meaning to geographic space, by creating culture. This interplay of men's relations with the world and with their fellows does not (except in cases of repressive power) permit societal or cultural immobility. As men create, re-create, and decide, historical epochs begin to take shape. And it is by creating, re-creating, and deciding that men should participate in these epochs. [Freire, 1973, pp. 3-4]

We found tantalizing suggestions of this proactive stance among integrated people when we examined the ASI adaptive flexibility scores of low- and high-ego-development people in our samples of adult professionals and midlife persons. Low-ego-development people, as we have already seen, showed less flexibility and variation from situation to situation. In addition, a case-by-case examination suggests that most of this variation was toward the press of the situation, such as becoming more active and concrete in accommodative situations or more abstract and reflective in assimilative situations. This pattern is suggestive of adjustment, or what Freire calls adaptation. High-ego-development people, on the other hand, showed greater variation, and much of this variation was counter to the press of the situation, such as responding reflectively in active situations or concretely in abstract situations. Here it appears that integrated people respond more creatively to situations supplying perspectives that from a holistic-learning point of view are missing. Thus, high-ego-development persons may respond to the abstract task of understanding the basic principles of something by seeking and exploring concrete examples, or they may deal with an active task such as completing a task on time by reflectively creating a plan.

This integrated response produces a creative tension between the person and his or her life situations, a tension that may in fact be essential for the creative response that integrative development engenders. Howard Gruber describes the importance of being one's own person in the creative process:

This obligation to move back and forth between radically different perspectives produces a deep tension in every creative life. In the course of ordinary development similar tensions begin to appear. What we mean by such terms as adaptation *and* adjustment *is the resolution of these tensions. But that is not the path of the creative person. He or she must safeguard the distance and the specialness, live with the tension. [Feldman, 1980, p. 180]*

Rich Life Structures   A second characteristic of the integrated life style is seen in the life structures of integrated people. The life structures of integrated persons mirror the integrative complexity of their personalities. It was Kurt Lewin (1951) who first noted the isomorphism between the person's development level and the level of complexity of his or her life space. When we examine the life structures of those who score high on the ASI measures of adaptive flexibility, we see complex, flexible, and highly differentiated life structures. These people experience their lives in ways that bring variety and richness to them and the environment. They engage with their environments by flexibly moving within those environments, by creating highly differentiated life spaces and relationships, and by building networks of relationships and contexts. Marcy Crary (1979) has defined these dimensions thus:

> Some people lead lives with a great deal of freedom of movement and variation in involvement within their different contexts. Either through their own person and/or the nature of the contexts they engage within, there is an appearance of a great deal of flexibility in their life structures. The contrasting life-style is one in which there is much routine, pre-arranged structuring of day-to-day events, likely leading to much repetition of events, activities, relationships within each of the person's contexts. Low rating on this scale would likely imply a higher degree of role-bounded situations and involvements. A high rating implies a relatively greater amount of "spontaneous" living. [Crary, 1979, p. 20]

A related dimension is that of differentiation within a person's life space. Crary states:

> This dimension relates to the degree of heterogeneity of contexts within a person's life-space. A life-space which is differentiated is multifaceted, containing a variety of components or regions within its boundaries. . . . Applied to the life-space as a whole (within and across contexts) the low end of the scale denotes a life space in which not one of the contexts seem to stand apart from the others in terms of the person's experience of them. The high rating refers to a life style in which the person clearly experiences variation and contrasts within and across their different contexts. [Crary, 1979, p. 10]

When Crary's ratings on these dimensions of life structure were correlated with adaptive-flexibility scores, significant relationships emerged. Flexible life structures were significantly associated with the integrated adaptively flexible people (TAF with flexibility in life structure, $r = .36, p < .01$; for AEAF, $r = .41, p < .005$; for ACAF, $r = .37, p < .01$; N.S. for ROAF and CEAF). Differentiation in life structure was also associated with adaptive flexibility (TAF with differentiation in life structure, $r = .35, p < .01$; for AEAF, $r = .34, p < .02$; for ACAF, $r = .40, p < .005$; for ROAF, $r = .30$, $p < .03$; N.S. for CEAF). The integrated person seems capable of constructing a rich, complex, and flexible life space that sustains him or her and provides new opportunities for growth.

Conflict   A key to the ability to manage complexity lies in a final characteristic of the integrated life style identified in our research—harmony, the constructive management of conflict. We found in our sample of midlife adults no significant difference overall between high-adaptive-flexibility and low-adaptive-flexibility people in the amount of stress and change they had to cope with in their lives. Yet when we measured the amount of conflict these people experienced in their lives, the adaptively flexible, integrated persons experienced much less conflict than those with low adaptive flexibility. A panel of researchers evaluated each respondent on a number of dimensions, including the degree of conflict. Conflict was defined as the extent of "incompatibilities, force and counter-force" (Crary, 1979) a person experiences among the various settings in his or her life, without regard to the number or complexity of the relationships among these settings. This rating was based on various exercises that respondents completed in the self-assessment workshops. These exercises served to portray the respondents' life space, their relationships with others, and a longitudinal view of their past and possible future.

When this rating was correlated with ASI adaptive-flexibility scores, high adaptive flexibility was associated with low conflict. (TAF with degree of conflict, $r = -.34$, $p < .02$; for AEAF, $r = -.30$, $p < .03$; for ACAF, $r = -.24$, $p < .06$; for CEAF, $r = -.27$, $p < .05$; N.S. for ROAF.) Further analysis, controlling for the amount of conflict in each individual life structure, showed that adaptively flexible people experienced the least stress in their lives in spite of the fact that their life structures, as we have seen, are the most complex. This harmony in life structure occurred in the context of the more balanced life structure that characterized most of those in our midlife sample (Kolb and Wolfe, 1981). Early in their lives, people have life structures that are heavily oriented around work (mainly for men) or family (for women). At midlife comes more balance in life investment, a balance that may be the foundation for the harmony and lower conflict in the lives of integrated people.

ON INTEGRITY AND INTEGRATIVE KNOWLEDGE

The pinnacle of development is integrity. It is that highest level of human functioning that we strive consciously and even unconsciously, perhaps automatically, to reach. The motivation to achieve integrity is a profound gift of humanity—a desire to reach out, understand, become, and grow, a pervasive motivation for mastery that Robert White has called motivation for competence. The *Random House Dictionary of the English Language* (1966) offers three definitions of integrity: "1. soundness of and adherence to moral principle and character . . . ; 2. the state of being whole, entire, or undiminished . . . ; 3. sound, unimpaired, or perfect condition" (p. 738). All these usages of the term are essential to define the concept as it is used here, but Warren Bennis's definition of integrity is perhaps more instructive of its meaning for the theory of experiential learning:

> *Integrity. Integration. The integral personality. Such permutations are permissible plays on the word, which shares roots with integer, the untouchable (in and tanger) whole number which links the most abstract of endeavors, mathematics, to the human condition. I am talking about the kind of unity—of purpose, goals, ideas, and communication—that makes three musketeers, Three Musketeers. It's a merging of identities and resolves into a coherent and effective whole. [Bennis, 1981-82, p.4]*

In the theory of experiential learning, integrity is a sophisticated, integrated process of learning, of knowing. It is not primarily a set of character traits such as honesty, consistency, or morality. These traits are only probable behavioral derivations of the integrated judgments that flow from integrated learning. Honesty, consistency, and morality are usually, but not always, the result of integrated learning. One need only reflect on the "immoral" behavior of men like Copernicus and Galileo to realize that integrity is the learning process by which intellectual, moral, and ethical standards are *created*, not some evaluation based on current moral standards and world views.

It is misleading to confuse these products of integrity, absolute and reasonable as they appear, with the process that creates them, for creators precede their creations in time and must create with no fixed absolutes to guide them. Integrity as a way of knowing embraces the future and the unknown as well as the codified conventions of social knowledge that are, by their nature, historical record. The prime function of integrity and integrative knowledge is to stand at the interface between social knowledge and the ever-novel predicaments and dilemmas we find ourselves in; its goal is to guide us through these straits in such a way that we not only survive, but perhaps can make some new contribution to the data bank of social knowledge for generations to come.

The knowledge structure of integrity does not comform to any one of the four knowledge structures identified in Chapter 5; it is usually some integrative synthesis of these in the emergent historical moment. As such, integrative knowing is essentially eclectic, if by the term is meant, "not consistent with current forms." It stands with one foot on the shore of the conventions of social knowledge and one foot in the canoe of an emergent future—a most uncomfortable and taxing position, one that positively demands commitment to either forging ahead or jumping back to safety. Stephen Pepper proposes the following guidelines for a reasonable eclecticism:

> *In practice, therefore, we shall want to be not rational but reasonable, and to seek, on the matter in question, the judgment supplied from each of these relatively adequate world theories. If there is some difference of judgment, we shall wish to make our decision with all these modes of evidence in mind, just as we should make any other decision where the evidence is conflicting. In this way*

> we should be judging in the most reasonable way possible—not dogmatically
> following only one line of evidence, not perversely ignoring evidence, but sensibly
> acting on all the evidence available. [Pepper, 1942, pp. 330-31]

Thus, in integrative learning, knowledge is refined by viewing predicaments through the dialectically opposed lenses of the four basic knowledge structures and then "acting sensibly."

The way in which this process is carried out is in many ways the topic of Pepper's last book, *Concept and Quality*. Here, Pepper proposes a fifth world hypothesis for integrative learning—selectivism—with the root metaphor purposive act. For it is in a single act of purpose that the psychological world of feeling, thought, and desire ("I want that goal") and the physical world (myself and the world as physical/chemical substances) are integrated, that value and fact, quality and concept, are fused. It is here that goal meets reality, "ought" meets "is." Selectivism as a world hypothesis turns out to be very much like contextualism or modern-day pragmatism in its emphasis on novelty and uncertainty as the basic adaptive problem facing the human species. The basic paradigm of selectivism is one where, seeking goals as judgments of value, we pursue realities based on judgments of fact. Reality in this paradigm is "what pushes back," to use E.A. Singer's (1959) apt phrase. Reality allows our conceptions of it, it does not cause them. Von Glasersfeld describes the selectivist paradigm thus:

> Roughly speaking, concepts, theories, and cognitive structures in general
> are viable and survive as long as they serve the purposes to which we put
> them. . . .
> If we accept this concept of viability, it becomes clear that it would be
> absurd to maintain that our knowledge is in any sense a replica or picture of
> reality. . . . [W]hile we can know when a theory or model knocks against the
> constraints of our experiential world, the fact that it does not knock against them
> but "gets by" and is still viable, does in no way justify the belief that the theory or
> model therefore depicts a "real" world. . . .
> [W]e must never say that our knowledge is "pure" in the sense that it
> reflects an ontologically real world. Knowledge neither should nor could have
> such a function. The fact that some construct has for some time survived
> experience—or experiments for that matter—means that up to that point it was
> viable in that it bypassed the constraints that are inherent in the range of
> experience within which we were operating. But viability does not imply
> uniqueness, because there may be innumerable other constructs that would have
> been as viable as the one we created. [von Glasersfeld, 1977, pp. 7-14]

An important implication of this constructionist view of reality is that theories are always combinations of value and fact, since it is value judgments that determine which aspects of reality are selected to be explored and how that exploration will take place. As a result, a primary dialectic that must be resolved in integrative knowledge is that of value and fact. Integrity requires the thoughtful articulation of value judgments as well as the scientific judgment of fact. The essential character of this dialectic integration is one of valuing via apprehension and creating facts via comprehension. The sense in which civilization is a race between such integrated learning and chaos is captured beautifully in Hegel's image of the owl of Minerva, the symbol of wisdom, beginning its flight just as darkness threatens.

> To say one more word about preaching what the world ought to be like, philosophy always arrives too late for that. As thought of the world it appears at a time when actuality has completed its developmental process and is finished. What the conception teaches history also shows as necessary, namely, that only in a maturing actuality the ideal appears and confronts the real. It is then that the ideal rebuilds for itself this same world in the shape of an intellectual realm, comprehending this world in its substance. When philosophy paints its gray in gray, a form of life has become old, and this gray in gray cannot rejuvenate it, only understand it. The owl of Minerva begins its flight when dusk is falling. [George W. F. Hegel, 1820]

Integrity requires that we learn to speak unselfconsciously about values in matters of fact. We need to develop, in the arena of values, inquiry methods that are as sophisticated and powerful as the methods of science have been in matters of fact.

No less significant for the attainment of integrative knowledge is the resolution of the dialectic between relevance and meaning. Western industrial societies have nearly run amok in their embrace of the extroverted materialism of relevance, ignoring and even actively denying the meaning of religious, humanistic, and spiritual ideals. Cast adrift from any meaningful connection with relevant work in the material world, internal lives can become wastelands of existential *angst* or sensual hedonism. The challenge of integrative knowledge, here, is to reimbue the pragmatic short-term choices and judgments that have given us polluted air and water, the threat of instant nuclear annihilation, the creation of a permanent underclass, and other such harmful side effects of our particular form of technological civilization, with the long-range perspective of meaning that arises from reflection on the human condition and the history of civilization. What we need is a theory of intentional action to guide us through these choices, to lay bare the plan whereby humanity has made these judgments in the past, and to suggest new "rules" for current circumstances.

In resolving the dialectic conflicts between value and fact, meaning and relevance, integrity is the master virtue. In a way that is similar to the identification of learning styles we can see in typical resolutions of these two dialectics, more specialized virtues (see Figure 8.2) whose primary function is to preserve and protect one pole of each dialectic: wisdom the protector of fact and meaning, justice the protector of fact and relevance, courage the protector of relevance and value, and love the protector of value and meaning. These

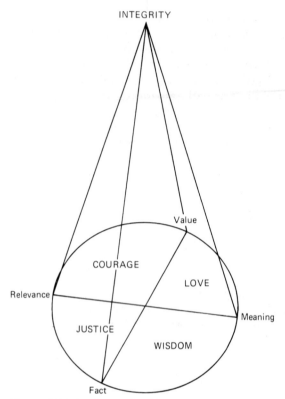

Figure 8.2 Integrity as the Master Virtue Integrating
Value and Fact, Meaning and Relevance, and the Specialized Virtues of Courage, Love, Wisdom, and Justice

specialized virtues are counterpress behavioral injunctions: They instruct us to
act against the demand characteristic of life situations, to *create*, not adjust.
Wisdom dictates that we do not blindly follow the implications of knowledge but
that we be choicefully responsible in the use of knowledge. Courage tells us to
push forward when circumstance signals danger and retreat. Love requires that
we hold our selfish acts in check until we have viewed the situation from the
perspective of the other—the Golden Rule. And justice demands fair and
equitable treatment for all against the expedience of the special situation.

The late Niels Bohr once remarked that his interest in complementarity in
physics had been stimulated by the thought that one cannot know another
human being at the same time in the light of love and in the light of justice. Thus,
the specialized virtues have a bias in favor of the dialectic poles they protect. It
remains for integrity and integrated knowing to rise above these biases for the
truly integrated judgment.

The Experience of Integrity—The Mandala Symbol

The experience of integrity and the characteristics of integrated knowing can be illustrated by the structure of the symbol that has represented them throughout the history of humanity. The mandala symbol is the most important symbol in the Jungian panopoly of the symbols and archetypes that populate the human psyche. This symbol of wholeness, unity, and integrity is to be found in most of the world's religions—the Christian cross, the star of David, and the intertwined fishes of *yin* and *yang*. Its value as a tool for meditation is renowned, producing a timeless centering of consciousness in which "you unify the world, you are the world itself, and you are unified by the world." Jung (1931) collected examples of the mandala symbol from paleolithic to modern times, from Eastern religions to Western art and literature. He saw in these symbols the characteristics of individuation, of integrity.

Mandala means a circle, especially a magic circle, signifying the integrity of experience, an external process where endings become beginnings again and again. "The mandala form is that of a flower, cross or wheel with a distinct tendency towards quadripartite structures" (Jung, 1931, p. 100). The typical four-part structure of the mandala often represents dual polarities, as in the Tibetian Buddhist Tantric mandala shown here (Figure 8.3). Here, double *dorjes* (*dorje* = "thunderbolt" of knowledge that cuts through confusion with penetrating wisdom) form a cross representing the interconnection of the earth realm (matter) and the realm of heaven (spirit).

It is the integration of these polarities that fuels the endless circular process of knowing. "Psychologically this circulation would be the 'turning in a circle around oneself'; whereby, obviously, all sides of the personality become involved. They cause the poles of light and darkness to rotate. . . ." (p. 104).

The product of this dialectic circulation process is a centering of one's experience. "The mandala symbol is not only a means of expression but works an effect. It reacts upon its maker. . . . [By meditating on it] the attention or, better said, the interest, is brought back to an inner sacred domain, which is the source and goal of the soul. . . . " [pp. 102-3]. Warren Bennis, in his recent study of effective leaders in all walks of life, has noted that this "centeredness" is a common trait among many of them (1980, p. 20). With centering comes the experience of transcendence, the conscious experience of hierarchic integration where what was before our whole world is transformed into but one of a multidimensional array of worlds to experience. In interviewing the associates of people who are perceived to "have integrity," I have been struck by the awe in which their integrative judgments are held; judgments that, like Solomon's decision to cut the baby in half, appear to rise above the confines of justice to include love; judgments that are seen as not only wise but courageous. The capacity for such integrated judgment seems to be borne out of transcendence, wherein the conflicts that those of us at lower levels of insight perceive as

Figure 8.3 Tibetan Buddhist Tantric Symbol

win-lose are recast into a higher form that can make everyone a winner, or can make winning and losing irrelevant. And finally, with centering comes commitment in the integration of abstract ideals in the concrete here-and-now of one's life. When we act from our center, the place of truth within us, action is based on the fusion of value and fact, meaning and relevance, and hence is totally committed. Only by personal commitment to the here-and-now of one's life situation, fully accepting one's past and taking choiceful responsibility for one's future, is the dialectic conflict necessary for learning experienced. The dawn of integrity comes with the acceptance of responsibility for the course of one's own life. For in taking responsibility for the world, we are given back the power to change it.

Bibliography

Allen, Frank, "Bosses List Main Strengths, Flaws Determining Potential of Managers," *The Wall Street Journal,* November 14, 1980.

Allport, Gordon, *Pattern and Growth in Personality.* New York: Holt, Rinehart & Winston, 1961.

Altmeyer, Robert, "Education in the Arts and Sciences: Divergent Paths," Ph.D. dissertation, Carnegie Institute of Technology, 1966.

American College Testing Program, "Survey of Prior Learning Assessment Programs at American Colleges and Universities," a report to the Council for the Advancement of Experiential Learning, 1982.

Arbeiter, S., C.B. Aslanian, F.A. Schnerbaur, and H.M. Brickell, *40 Million Americans in Career Transition: The Need for Information.* New York: College Entrance Exam Board, 1978.

Argyris, Chris, *Interpersonal Competence and Organizational Effectiveness.* Homewood, Ill.: Dorsey, 1962.

———, "On the Future of Laboratory Education," in G. Golembiewski and P. Blumberg, eds., *Sensitivity Training and the Laboratory Approach: Readings about Concepts and Applications.* Itasca, Ill.: Peacock, 1970.

———, **and Donald Schon,** *Organizational Learning: A Theory of Action Perspective.* Reading, Mass.: Addison-Wesley, 1978.

———, *Theory in Practice: Increasing Professional Effectiveness.* San Francisco: Jossey-Bass, 1974.

Arlin, P.K., "Cognitive Development in Adulthood: A Fifth Stage," *Developmental Psychology,* XI (1975), 602-6.

Bandura, Albert, "The Self System in Reciprocal Determinism," *American Psychologist,* 1978, pp. 344-57.

Barron, F., "Threshold for the Perception of Human Movement in Ink-Blots," *Journal of Consulting Psychology,* 19 (1955), 3-3.38.

Bash, K.W., "Einstellungstypus and Erlebnistypus: C.G. Jung and Hermann Rorschach," *Journal of Projective Techniques,* 19 (1955), 236-42.

Bates, W. Jackson, "The Crisis in English Studies," *Harvard Magazine,* September-October 1982.

Benne, Kenneth, "History of the T Group in the Laboratory Setting," in Leland Bradford et al., eds., *T Group Theory and Laboratory Method.* New York: John Wiley, 1964.

Bennet, Nancy, "Learning Styles of Health Professionals Compared to Preference for Continuing Education Program Format," unpublished Ph.D. dissertation, University of Illinois College of Medicine, 1978.

Bennis, Warren G., "A Goal for the Eighties: Organizational Integrity," *New Jersey Bell Journal,* 4, 4 (Winter 1981-82), 1-8.

———, "Interview," *Group and Organization Studies,* 5 (1980), 18-34.

Benton, Arthur L., "The Neuropsychology of Facial Recognition," *American Psychologist,* 35 (1980), 176-86.

Bereiter C., and M. Friedman, "Fields of Study and the People in Them," in N. Sanford, ed., *The American College,* pp. 593-96. New York: John Wiley, 1962.

Bieri, J., and Susan Messerley, "Differences in Perceptual and Cognitive Behavior as a Function of Experience Type," *Journal of Consulting Psychology,* 21 (1957), 217-21.

Biglan, A., "The Characteristics of Subject Matter in Different Academic Areas," *Journal of Applied Psychology,* 57 (1973a), 195-203.

———, "Relationships between Subject Matter Characteristics and the Structure and Output of University Departments," *Journal of Applied Psychology,* 51 (1973b), 204-13.

"Bill Moyers Journal," "A Conversation with Clark Clifford," Show No. 712-713. New York: WNET/Thirteen, 1981.

Bogen, J.E., "Some Educational Aspects of Hemispheric Specialization," *UCLA Educator,* 17 (1975), 24-32.

Bohm, D., *Physics and Perception in the Special Theory of Relativity.* New York: Benjamin, 1965.

Bok, D., "The President's Report," *Harvard Magazine,* May-June 1978.

Bradford, Leland, "Membership and the Learning Process," in Bradford et al., eds., *T Group Theory and Laboratory Method.* New York: John Wiley, 1964.

Bridges, Katherine, "Emotional Development in Early Infancy," *Child Development,* 3 (1932), 340.

Brim, Orville, and Jerome Kagan, *Constancy and Change in Human Development.* Cambridge, Mass.: Harvard University Press, 1980.

Bronfenbrenner U., "Toward an Experimental Ecology of Human Development," *American Psychologist,* 1977.

Broverman, Donald, Edward Klaiber, Yutaka Kobayashi, and William Vogel, "Roles of Activation and Inhibition in Sex Differences in Cognitive Abilities," *Psychological Review,* 75 (1968), 23-50.

Bruner, Jerome S., "The Course of Cognitive Growth," *American Psychologist,* 19 (1964), 1-15.

———, *On Knowing: Essays for the Left Hand.* New York: Atheneum, 1966a.

———, *The Process of Education.* New York: Vintage Books, 1960.

———, *The Relevance of Education.* New York: W.W. Norton, 1971.

———, *Toward a Theory of Instruction.* New York: W.W. Norton, 1966b.

———, **R. Oliver, and P. Greenfield,** *Studies in Cognitive Growth.* New York: John Wiley, 1966.

Brunswick, Egon, "Organismic Achievement and Environment Probability," *Psychological Review,* 50, (1943), 255-72.

Buckley, W., *Sociology and Modern Systems Theory.* Englewood Cliffs, N.J.: Prentice-Hall, 1967.

Burtt E.A., "The Status of World Hypotheses," *Philosophical Review,* 6 (1943), 590-604.

Cadwallader, M., "The Cybernetic Analysis of Change in Complex Social Systems," in W. Buckley, ed., *Modern Systems Research for the Behavioral Scientist.* Chicago: Aldine, 1968.

Carrigan, Patricia, "Extraversion-Introversion as a Dimension of Personality: A Reappraisal," *Psychological Bulletin,* 57 (1960), 329-60.

Certo, S., and S. Lamb, "Identification and Measurement of Instrument Bias within the Learning Style Instrument through a Monte Carlo Technique," *Southern Management Proceedings,* 1979.

Chickering, Arthur, *Experience and Learning: An Introduction to Experiential Learning.* New Rochelle, N.Y.: Change Magazine Press, 1977.

Christensen, M., C. Lee, and P. Bugg, "Professional Development of Nurse Practitioners as a Function of Need Motivation Learning Styles and Locus of Control," *Nursing Research,* 28 (January–February 1979), 51-56.

Churchman, C. West, *The Design of Inquiring Systems.* New York: Basic Books, 1971.

Clarke, D., S. Oshiro, C. Wong, and M. Yeung, "A Study of the Adequacy of the Learning Environment for Business Students in Hawaii in the Fields of Accounting and Marketing," unpublished paper, University of Hawaii, 1977.

Clifford, Clark, *Bill Moyer's Journal,* 1981.

Cohen, Morris, and Ernest Nagel, *Introduction to Logic and Scientific Method.* New York: Harcourt Brace, 1934.

Cole, M., V. John-Steiner, S. Scribner, and E. Souberman, eds., *L.S. Vygotsky: Mind in Society.* Cambridge, Mass.: Harvard University Press, 1978.

———, **et al.,** *The Cultural Context of Learning and Thinking.* New York: Basic Books, 1971.

Corballis, Michael, "Laterality and Myth," *American Psychologist,* March 1980, pp. 284-95.

Crary, Laura M., "Assessment of Patterns of Life Structure," unpublished manuscript, Department of Organizational Behavior, Case Western Reserve University, 1979.

———, "Patterns of Life Structure: Person-Environment Designs and Their Impact on Adult Lives," unpublished Ph.D. dissertation, Case Western Reserve University, 1981.

Darwin, Charles, *The Autobiography of Charles Darwin: 1809-1882.* London: Collins, 1958.

Davis, J., *Undergraduate Career Decisions.* Chicago: Aldine, 1965.

deCharms, Richard, *Personal Causation.* New York: Academic Press, 1968.

de Groot, Adriaan, *Thought and Choice in Chess.* The Hague: Mouton, 1965.

Deutsch, K., *The Nerves of Government.* New York: Free Press, 1966.

Dewey, John, *Art as Experience.* New York: G.P. Putnam, Capricorn Books, 1934.

———, *Experience and Education.* Kappa Delta Pi, 1938.

———, *Experience and Nature.* New York: Dover Publications, 1958.

———, *How We Think.* New York: D.C. Heath, 1910.

DeWitt, Norman, "Organism and Humanism: An Empirical View," in D.B. Harris, ed., *The Concept of Development: An Issue in the Study of Human Behavior.* Minneapolis: University of Minnesota Press, 1957.

234   Bibliography

Diekman, Arthur, "Biomodal Consciousness," *Archives of General Psychiatry,* 25 (1971), 481-89.

Doherty, A., M. Mentkowski, and K. Conrad, "Toward a Theory of Undergraduate Experiential Learning," *New Directions for Experiential Learning,* 1 (1978), 23-35.

Eaves, Lindon, and Hans Eysenck, "The Nature of Extraversion: A Genetical Analysis," *Journal of Personality and Social Psychology,* 32 (1975), 102-12.

Edwards, Betty, *Drawing on the Right Side of the Brain.* Los Angeles: J.P. Tarcher, 1979.

Elkind, David, *Children and Adolescence: Interpretative Essays on Jean Piaget.* New York: Oxford University Press, 1970.

Elliot, T.S., "Little Gidding," Harcourt Brace Jovanovich, Inc. and Faber and Faber Ltd., London, England.

Elms, A., "Skinner's Dark Year and Walden Two," *American Psychologist,* 36, 5 (1981), 470-79.

Erikson, Eric, "Identity and the Life Cycle," *Psychological Issues,* 1 (1959).

———, "The Roots of Virtue," in Julian Huxley, ed., *The Humanist Frame.* New York: Harper & Row, 1961.

———, *Young Man Luther.* New York: W.W. Norton, 1958.

Fallows, J., "The Passionless Presidency: The Trouble with Jimmy Carter's Administration," *The Atlantic Monthly,* May and June 1979.

Feigl, Herbert, "The "Mental" and the "Physical," in Feigl et al., eds., *Concepts, Theories and the Mind-Body Problem,* pp. 370-497. Minneapolis: University of Minnesota Press, 1958.

Feldman, David, *Beyond Universals in Cognitive Development.* Norwood, N.J.: Ablex Publishing, 1980.

Feldman, Kenneth, and Theodore Newcomb, *The Impact of College on Students,* Vols. I and II. San Francisco, Jossey-Bass, 1969.

Feldman, S., *Escape from the Doll's House.* New York: McGraw-Hill, 1974.

Ferrary, Jeannette, "On First Looking into Heisenberg's Principle," *Harvard Magazine,* November-December 1979.

Flavell, John, *The Developmental Psychology of Jean Piaget.* New York: Van Nostrand Reinhold Co., 1963.

Forrester, Jay W., *World Dynamics.* Cambridge, Mass.: Wright-Allen Press, 1971.

Frankfurt, H., "Descartes on the Creation of the Eternal Truths," *Philosophical Review,* 86 (1977), 36-57.

Freire, Paulo, *Education for Critical Consciousness.* New York: Continuum, 1973.

———, *Pedagogy of the Oppressed.* New York: Continuum, (1974), pp. 58, 62, 75-76.

Fry, Ronald E., "Diagnosing Professional Learning Environments: An Observational Framework for Assessing Situational Complexity," unpublished Ph.D. thesis, Massachusetts Institute of Technology, 1978.

Gardner, R.G., and Beatrice Gardner, "Teaching Sign Language to a Chimpanzee," *Science,* 165 (1969), 644-72.

Gendlin, E.T., "A Theory of Personality Change," in P. Worschel and D. Byrne, eds., *Personality Change,* pp. 100-148. New York: John Wiley, 1964.

Goldstein, K., and M. Scheerer, "Abstract and Concrete Behavior: An Experimental Study with Special Tests," *Psychological Monographs,* 53, No. 239 (1941).

Grochow, J., "Cognitive Style as a Factor in the Design of Interactive Decision-Support Systems," Ph.D. dissertation, Massachusetts Institute of Technology, Sloan School of Management, 1973.

Gypen, Jan, "Learning Style Adaptation in Professional Careers: The Case of Engineers and Social Workers," unpublished doctoral dissertation, Case Western Reserve University, 1980.

Hall, D., "The Impact of Peer Interaction During an Academic Role Transition," *Sociology of Education,* 42 (Spring 1969), 118-40.

Harlow, Harry, "Learning Set and Error Factor Theory," in S. Koch, ed., *Psychology: A Study or a Science,* vol. 2. New York: McGraw Hill, 1959.

Harvey, O.J., "System Structure, Creativity and Flexibility," in O.J. Harvey, ed., *Experience, Structure and Adaptability,* pp. 39-65. New York: Springer, 1966.

———, **David Hunt, and Harold Schroder,** *Conceptual Systems and Personality Organization.* New York: John Wiley, 1961.

Hegel, George F., "Philosophy of Right and Law 1820," in Carl Friedrich, ed., *The Philosophy of Hegel.* New York: Modern Library, 1953.

Helson, R., "Commentary: Reality of Masculine and Feminine Traits in Personality and Behavior," in S. Messick, ed., *Individuality in Learning.* San Francisco: Jossey-Bass, 1976.

Hickey, Joseph, and Peter Scharf, *Democratic Justice and Prison Reform.* San Francisco: Jossey-Bass, 1980.

Hofstadter, Douglas, *Gödel, Escher, Bach: An External Golden Braid.* New York: Basic Books, 1979.

Hudson, Liam, "Commentary: Singularity of Talent," in S. Massick, ed., *Individuality in Learning.* San Francisco: Jossey-Bass, 1976.

———, *Contrary Imaginations.* Middlesex, England: Penguin Books, Ltd., 1966.

Hunt, David E., *Matching Models in Education.* Toronto: Ontario Institute for Studies in Education, 1974.

Hursh, B., and L. Borzak, "Toward Cognitive Development through Field Studies," *Journal of Higher Education,* 50 (January-February 1979), 63-78.

Husserl, E., *Ideas.* New York: Collier, 1962.

Hutchins, Robert M., *The University of Utopia.* Chicago: University of Chicago Press, 1953.

Illich, Ivan, *Deschooling Society.* New York: Harrow Books, 1972.

James, William, *Pragmatism: A New Name for Some Old Ways of Thinking.* New York: Longmans, Green and Company, 1907.

———, *The Principles of Psychology,* Vols. I and II. New York: Holt, Rinehart and Winston, 1890.

Jaques, Elliott, "Taking Time Seriously in Evaluating Jobs," *Harvard Business Review,* September-October 1979, pp. 124-32.

Jung, Carl, Foreword and Commentary in R. Wilhelm, trans., *The Secret of the Golden Flower.* New York: Harcourt, Brace & World, 1931.

———, *Letters.* Princeton, N.J.: Princeton University Press, 1973.

———, *Psychological Types.* R.F.C. Hull, trans., Collected Works of C.G. Jung, Vol. 6. Bollingen Series XX, Princeton University Press (1977), pp. 12-13, 28, 68.

———, *The Structure and Dynamics of the Psyche.* New York: Bollingen Foundation, 1960.

———, "The Symbolic Life," in H. Read, M. Fordham, G. Adler, and W. McGuire, eds., R.F.C. Hull, trans., *Collected Works of Carl Jung,* Vol. 18. Princeton, N.J.: Bollingen Series XX, Princeton University Press, 1977.

Kagan, Jerome, and Nathan Kogan, "Individual Variation in Cognitive Processes," in P.H. Musser, ed., *Carmichael's Manual of Child Psychology,* vol. 1. New York: Wiley, 1970.

————, **B. Rosman, D. Day, J. Alpert, and W. Phillips,** "Information Processing in the Child: Significance of Analytic and Reflective Attitudes," *Psychological Monographs,* 78, 1 (1964).

Keeton, Morris, and Pamela Tate, eds., *Learning by Experience—What, Why, How.* San Francisco: Jossey-Bass, 1978.

Kelly, George, *The Psychology of Personal Constructs,* Vols. I and II. New York: W.W. Norton, 1955.

Klemke, E.D., *The Epistemology of G.E. Moore.* Evanston, Ill.: Northwestern University Press, 1969.

Knowles, Malcolm S., *The Modern Practice of Adult Education: Andragogy vs. Pedagogy.* New York: Association Press, 1970.

Kohlberg, L., "Stage and Sequence: The Cognitive-Developmental Approach to Socialization," in D.A. Goslin, ed., *Handbook of Socialization Theory and Research.* Chicago: Rand McNally, 1969.

Kolb, David A., "Applications of Experiential Learning Theory to the Information Sciences," paper delivered at the National Science Foundation Conference on contributions of the behavioral sciences to research in information science, December 1978.

————, "Experiential Learning Theory and the Learning Style Inventory: A Reply to Freedman and Stumpf," *Academy of Management Review,* April 1981.

————, *The Learning Style Inventory: Technical Manual.* Boston: McBer and Company, 1976.

————, "On Management and the Learning Process," M.I.T. Sloan School Working Paper No. 652-73, 1973.

————, **and Ronald E. Fry,** "Toward an Applied Theory of Experiential Learning," in C. Cooper, ed., *Theories of Group Processes.* London: Wiley, 1975.

————, **and Marshall Goldman,** "Toward a Typology of Learning Styles and Learning Environments: An Investigation of the Impact of Learning Styles and Discipline Demands on the Academic Performance, Social Adaptation and Career Choices of M.I.T. Seniors," M.I.T. Sloan School Working Paper No. 688-73, 1973.

————, **I. Rubin, and E. Schein,** "The TECH Freshman Integration Research Project: A Summary Report," unpublished report, M.I.T., 1972.

————, **and Donald Wolfe,** with collaborators, "Professional Education and Career Development: A Cross-Sectional Study of Adaptive Competencies in Experiential Learning," final report NIE grant no. NIE-G-77-0053, 1981. ERIC no. ED 209 493 CE 030 519.

Koplowitz, Herbert, "Unitary Operations: A Projection beyond Piaget's Formal Operations Stage," unpublished manuscript, University of Massachusetts, 1978.

Kuhn, Thomas, *The Structure of Scientific Revolutions.* Chicago: University of Chicago Press, 1962.

Kurtines, W., and E.B. Greif, "The Development of Moral Thought: Review and Evaluation of Kohlberg's Approach," *Psychological Bulletin,* 81 (1974), 8.

Lehman, H.C., *Age and Achievement.* Princeton, N.J.: Princeton University Press, 1953.

Lessor, J., "Cultural Differences in Learning and Thinking," in S. Messick, ed., *Individuality in Learning.* San Francisco: Jossey-Bass, 1976.

Levi-Strauss, Claude, *The Savage Mind.* Chicago: University of Chicago Press, 1969.

Levy, Jerre, "Cerebral Asymmetry and the Psychology of Man," in M. Wittrock, ed., *The Brain and Psychology.* New York: Academic Press, 1980.

Lewin, Kurt, *Field Theory in Social Sciences.* New York: Harper & Row, 1951.

Lewis R., and C. Margerison, *Working and Learning—Identifying Your Preferred Ways of Doing Things.* Bedfordshire, England: Management and Organisation Development Research Centre, Cranfield School of Management, 1979.

Lippitt, Ronald, *Training in Community Relations.* New York: Harper & Row, 1949.

Loevinger, Jane, *Ego Development.* San Francisco: Jossey-Bass, 1976.

————, "The Meaning and Measurement of Ego Development," *American Psychologist,* 21 (1966), 195-206.

————, **and Ruth Wessler,** *Measuring Ego Development,* Vol. 1. San Francisco: Jossey-Bass, 1978.

McCloskey, H., and J. Schaar, "Psychological Dimensions of Anomie,"*American Psychological Review,* 30 (1) (1963), 14-40.

McNemar, W., *Psychological Statistics.* New York: John Wiley, 1957.

Mager, Robert F., *Preparing Instructional Objectives.* Palo Alto, Calif.: Fearon Publishers, 1962.

Mann, L., "The Relation of Rorschach Indices of Extratension and Introversion to a Measure of Responsiveness to the Immediate Environment," *Journal of Consulting Psychology,* 20 (1956), 114-18.

Margerison, C.J., and R.G. Lewis, *How Work Preferences Relate to Learning Styles.* Bedfordshire, England: Management and Organisation Development Research Centre, Cranfield School of Management, 1979.

Margulies, Newton, and Anthony P. Raia, "Scientists, Engineers, and Technological Obsolescence," *California Management Review,* Winter 1967, pp. 43-48.

Marrow, Alfred J., *The Practical Theorist: The Life and Work of Kurt Lewin.* New York: Basic Books, 1969.

Mentkowski, M., and N. Much, *Careering After College: Perspectives on Lifelong Learning and Career Development.* Milwaukee, Wisconsin: Alverno Productions, 1982.

————, **and M.J. Strait,** "A Longitudinal Study of Student Change in Cognitive Development and Generic Abilities in an Outcome-centered Liberal Arts Curriculum." Paper presented at the annual meeting of the American Educational Research Association, Montreal, Canada, April, 1983.

Miller, G., E. Galanter, and L. Pribram, *Plans and the Structure of Behavior.* New York: Holt, Rinehart & Winston, 1960.

Mills, T., *Sociology of Small Groups.* Englewood Cliffs, N.J.: Prentice-Hall, 1965.

Mintzberg, H., *The Nature of Managerial Work.* New York: Harper & Row, 1973.

Myers-Briggs, I., *The Myers-Briggs Type Indicator Manual.* Princeton, New Jersey: Educational Testing Service, 1962.

Neugarten and Associates, *Personality in Middle and Late Life.* New York: Atherton Press, 1964.

Olsen, M., "Political Alienation Scale," in J. Robinson and P. Shauer, *Measures of Social Psychological Attitudes,* pp. 181-83. Institute for Social Research, University of Michigan, August 1969.

Ornstein, Robert E., *The Psychology of Consciousness.* New York: W.H. Freeman & Company, 1972.

Orwell, G., "Politics and the English Language," in S. Orwell and I. Angus, eds., *In Front* *of Your Nose*, Vol. 4, The Collected Essays of George Orwell. New York: Harcourt Brace & World, 1968.

Osipow, Samuel H., *Theories of Career Development*, 2nd ed. New York: Appleton-Century-Crofts, 1973.

Palmer, J.O., "Attitudinal Correlates of Rorschach's Experience Balance," *Journal of Projective Techniques*, 20 (1956), 207-11.

Papaert, S., *Mindstorms: Children, Computers, and Powerful Ideas*. New York: Basic Books, 1980.

Pepper, S., *World Hypotheses*. Berkeley, Calif.: University of California Press, 1942.

Perkins, M., "Matter, Sensation and Understanding," *American Philosophical Quarterly*, 8, (1971), 1-12.

Perry, William, *Forms of Intellectual and Ethical Development in the College Years*. New York: Holt, Rinehart & Winston, 1970.

Pfaff, W., "Mr. Carter's Slide Rule," *New York Times*, op-ed page, June 6, 1979.

Piaget, Jean, *Genetic Epistemology*. New York: Columbia University Press (1970a), p. 77.

——, *The Place of the Sciences of Man in the System of Sciences*. New York: Harper Torchbooks (1970b), p. 14.

——, *Play, Dreams and Imitation in Childhood*. New York: W.W. Norton, 1951.

——, *Psychology and Epistemology*. Middlesex, England: Penguin Books, 1971.

——, *Structuralism*. New York: Harper Torchbooks, 1968.

——, "What Is Psychology?" *American Psychologist*, July 1978, pp. 648-52.

Pigg, K., L. Busch, and W. Lacy, "Individual Learning Styles and the Development of Extension Education Programs," unpublished paper, University of Kentucky, 1978.

Plovnick, Mark, "A Cognitive Ability Theory of Occupational Roles," Working Paper #524-71, M.I.T. School of Management, Spring 1971.

——, "Individual Learning Styles and the Process of Career Choice in Medical Students," doctoral dissertation, M.I.T. Sloan School of Management, 1974.

——, "Primary Care Career Choices and Medical Student Learning Styles," *Journal of Medical Education*, vol. 50, September 1975.

Polanyi, Michael, *Personal Knowledge*. Chicago: University of Chicago Press, 1958 and Routledge and Kegan Paul, London, England.

——, *The Tacit Dimension*. New York: Doubleday, 1966.

Pounds, William, "On Problem Finding," Sloan School Working Paper No. 145-65, 1965.

Read, H., M. Fordham, and G. Adler, eds., *The Collected Works of C.G. Jung*, Bollingen Foundation, 8, 1961-67.

Roe, Anne, "Early Determinants of Vocational Choice," *Journal of Counseling Psychology*, Vol. 4, 3, 212-17.

——, *The Psychology of Occupations*. New York: John Wiley, 1956.

Rogers, Carl, *On Becoming a Person.* Boston: Houghton Mifflin, 1961.

Rorschach, H., *Psychodiagnostics*, 5th ed., (trans. P. Lemkau and B. Kronenberg). Berne Switzerland: Verlag Hans Huber, 1951.

Rubin, Zick, "Does Personality Really Change after 20?" *Psychology Today*, May 1981, pp. 18-27.

Russell, B., *The Problems of Philosophy*. London: Butterworth, 1912.

Sagan, Carl, *The Dragons of Eden*. New York: Random House, 1977.

Samples, Bob, *The Metaphoric Mind*. Reading, Mass.: Addison-Wesley, 1976.

Samuelson, Judith, "Career Development and Cognitive Styles," unpublished paper, Ohio State University, 1982.

Schein, Edgar, *Professional Education: Some New Directions.* New York: McGraw-Hill, © The Carnegie Foundation for the Advancement of Teaching, 1972.

——, **and Warren Bennis,** *Personal and Organizational Change through Group Methods.* New York: John Wiley, 1965.

Schiller, Friedrich, *Uber Die Asthetischa Erziehung Das Menschen.* Hamburg: Cotta'sche Ausgabe, Bd. xviii, 1826.

Schilpp, Paul A., *Albert Einstein—Philosopher Scientist.* La Salle, Ill.: Library of Living Philosophers, Open Court Publishing, 1949.

Schroder, H.M., M.J. Driver, and S. Streufert, *Human Information Processing.* New York: Holt, Rinehart & Winston, 1967.

Scott, William A., "Flexibility, Rigidity, and Adaptation: Toward Clarification of Concepts," in O.J. Harvey, ed., *Experience, Structure and Adaptability,* pp. 369-400. New York: Springer, 1966.

Signell, K.A., "Cognitive Complexity in Person Perception and Nation Perception: A Developmental Approach," *Journal of Personality,* 34 (1966), 517-37.

Simon, H.A., *Administrative Behavior.* New York: Macmillan, 1947.

Sims, Ronald, "Assessing Competencies in Experiential Learning Theory: A Person-Job Congruence Model of Effectiveness in Professional Careers," unpublished Ph.D. dissertation, Case Western Reserve University, 1981.

——, "Preparation for Professional Careers and Changing Job Roles: An Assessment of Professional Education," qualifying paper, Department of Organizational Behavior, Case Western Reserve University, 1980.

Singer, E.A., *Experience and Reflection.* Philadelphia: University of Pennsylvania Press, 1959.

Singer, J.L., and H.E. Spohn, "Some Behavioral Correlates of Rorschach's Experience-type," *Journal of Consulting Psychology,* 18 (1954), 1-9.

——, **Harold Wilensky, and Vivian McCraven,** "Delay Capacity, Fantasy and Planning Ability: A Factorial Study of Some Basic Ego Functions," *Journal of Consulting Psychology,* 20 (1956), 375-83.

Skinner, B.F., *Walden II.* New York: Macmillan, 1948.

Snow, C., *The Two Cultures: On a Second Look.* Cambridge, England: Cambridge University Press, 1963.

Sperry, R.W., M.S. Gazzaniga, and J.E. Bogen, "Interhemispheric Relationships: The Neocortical Commissures; Syndromes of Hemispheric Disconnections," in P.J. Vinken and G.W. Bruyn, eds., *Handbook of Clinical Neurology.* Amsterdam: North Holland Publishing, 1969, pp. 273-89.

Stabell, C., "The Impact of a Conversational Computer System on Human Problem Solving Behavior," unpublished working paper, Massachusetts Institute of Technology, Sloan School of Management, 1973.

Super, D.E., R. Starishevsky, N. Matlin, and J.P. Jordaan, *Career Development: Self Concept Theory.* New York: CEEB Research Monograph, No. 4, 1963.

Taylor, F.C., "Relationship between Student Personality and Performance in an Experiential Theoretical Group Dynamics Course," Faculty Working Paper #132, Kent State University, 1973.

Terman, L., and M. Oden, *The Gifted Child Grows Up.* Stanford, Calif.: Stanford University Press, 1947.

Torbert, William, *Learning from Experience: Toward Consciousness.* New York: Columbia University Press, 1972.

————, "Organizing Experiential Learning," in Douglas E. Wolfe and Eugene Byrne, eds., *Developing Experiential Learning in Professional Education,* no. 8. San Francisco: Jossey-Bass, 1980.

Torrealba, D., "Convergent and Divergent Learning Styles," master's thesis, Massachusetts Institute of Technology, Sloan School of Management, 1972.

Tough, Allen, *Major Learning Efforts: Recent Research and Future Directions.* Toronto: Ontario Institute for Studies in Education, 1977.

Turner, Terence, "Piaget's Structuralism," *American Anthropologist,* 76 (1973), 351-73.

Tyler, Leona, *Individuality.* San Francisco: Jossey-Bass, 1978.

Vannoy, J., "Generality of Cognitive Complexity-Simplicity as a Personality Construct," *Journal of Personality and Social Psychology,* 1965, pp. 385-96.

Vickers, Geoffrey, *Value Systems and Social Process.* Middlesex, England: Penguin Books, 1968.

von Glasersfeld, E., "The Concepts of Adaptation and Viability in a Radical Constructionist Theory of Knowledge," paper presented at the Theodore Mischel Symposium on Constructivism at the 7th Annual Meeting of the Jean Piaget Society, Philadelphia, May 19-21, 1977.

Wallas, G., *The Art of Thought.* New York: Harcourt Brace, 1926.

Weathersby, Rita, "A Developmental Perspective on Adults' Formal Uses of Education," doctoral dissertation, Harvard University Graduate School of Education, June 1977.

————, "Life Stages and Learning Interests," in *The Adult Learner.* Washington, D.C.: American Association for Higher Education, 1978.

Weisner, Frank, "Learning Profiles and Managerial Styles of Managers," S.M. thesis, Sloan School of Management, M.I.T., 1971.

Werner, Heinz, *Comparative Psychology of Mental Development.* New York: International University Press, 1948.

————, "The Concept of Development from a Comparative and Organismic Point of View," in D.B. Harris, ed., *The Concept of Development: An Issue in the Study of Human Behavior,* pp. 125-48. Minneapolis: University of Minnesota Press, 1957.

Whitehead, A.N., *Adventures of Ideas.* New York: Macmillan, 1933.

————, *Science and the Modern World.* New York: Macmillan, 1926.

Willingham, Warren, John Valley, and Morris Keeton, *Assessing Experiential Learning: A Summary Report of the CAEL Project.* Columbia, Md.: CAEL, 1977.

Witkin, H., "Cognitive Styles in Academic Performance and in Teacher-Student Relations," in S. Messick, ed., *Individuality in Learning.* San Francisco: Jossey-Bass, 1976.

Wober, M., "Adapting Witkin's Field Independence Theory to Accommodate New Information from Africa," *British Journal of Psychology,* 58 (1967), 29-38.

Wolfe, D., *America's Resources of Specialized Talent.* New York: Harper Bros., 1954.

Wolfe, Donald, and David Kolb, "Beyond Specialization: The Quest for Integration in Midcareer," in Brooklyn Derr, ed., *Work, Family and the Career: New Frontiers in Theory and Research.* New York: Praeger Publishers, 1980.

————, *Learning Processes in Adult Development: A Study of Cognitive and Social Factors in Mid-Life Transition.* Final Report to the Spencer Foundation, 1982.

Wunderlich, R., and C. Gjerde, "Another Look at Learning Style Inventory and Medical Career Choice," *Journal of Medical Education,* 53 (1978), 45-54.

Wynne, B.E., Abstraction, Reflection and Insight—Situation Coping Style Measurement Dimensions," working paper, University of Wisconsin, Milwaukee School of Business Administration, Winter 1975.

Zajonc, R.B., "Feeling and Thinking: Preferences Need No Inferences," *American Psychologist,* 35 (February 1980), 151-75.

Zen Buddhism. Mount Vernon, N.Y.: Peter Pauper Press, 1959.

Index